AMERICAN HISTORIANS AND EUROPEAN IMMIGRANTS, 1875-1925

AMERICAN HISTORIANS
AND
EUROPEAN IMMIGRANTS
1875–1925

BY

EDWARD N. SAVETH, Ph.D.

NEW YORK
RUSSELL & RUSSELL · INC
1965

STUDIES IN HISTORY, ECONOMICS AND PUBLIC LAW

Edited by the

**FACULTY OF POLITICAL SCIENCE
OF COLUMBIA UNIVERSITY**

TO

My Mother and Father

EVA and ISIDOR SAVETH

CONTENTS

8   CONTENTS

CHAPTER VIII

INTRODUCTION

In the period with which we are here occupied—the years
from 1875 to 1925—historians had hardly more than oc-
casional insight into the role of immigration in our national
development. When they treated the subject of European immigration at all, they treated it as a sort of historiographic
hangnail—a side issue to which little attention need be paid.
Consequently, a large part of the present study is concerned
with the attitudes of the various American historians toward
immigrants and immigration, more so than with their constructive approaches or interpretations.

However, in the half century ending with 1925 certain constructive trends in the treatment of the immigrant in American
historical literature were already making themselves felt—
trends that were to influence later treatment of the subject both
by general American historians and by monographists. Since
continuity exists in historiography no less than in history,
these trends have been considered in relationship to their bearing upon developments in the historiography of immigration
in the years following 1925.

In writing of the reactions of American historians to
European immigrants, particularly immigrants of non-English
derivation and their descendants, it has been found necessary to
spread our net wide, considering operation not only of regional,
class, and ethnic factors but of ideological forces as well. The
approach is a broad one, relating treatment of immigrant
peoples to the historian's total orientation in so far as it can be
determined.

At the outset, there is some account of background factors
shaping historians' attitudes toward immigrants and of the
influence of the Teutonic germ theory of institutional development upon late nineteenth century American historians. This
theme is further developed in chapter two with reference to
John Fiske, John W. Burgess, Henry Cabot Lodge and their

reactions to non-Teutonic immigrants. In chapter three, Henry Adams' attitude toward immigrants and Jews is related to his rejection of the Teutonic hypothesis and his respect for the Romanic tradition.

Some historians who were not Social Darwinists accepted the Teutonic hypothesis, and, on the other hand, some who were Social Darwinists declined to accept that hypothesis. Nevertheless, in American historiography of the late nineteenth and early twentieth centuries, a relationship did exist between the Teutonic hypothesis and certain aspects of Social Darwinist thinking. The idea, exploited by the Teutonists, of a maturing institutional germ was one of several themes borrowed from biology which found their way into historical writings. Other biological conceptions, exploited by historians, were the Darwinist theories of natural selection and the survival of the fittest. The influence of these theories upon historians' attitudes toward immigrants is described at the outset of chapter four, the bulk of which is given over to a discussion of the views of Francis Parkman and Theodore Roosevelt concerning the influence of the American forest upon the Europeans who settled in it. Parkman and Roosevelt were both concerned in their narratives with phases of the American frontier. The relationship of the frontier theme in American historiography to the treatment of immigrant groups is discussed in the succeeding chapter, with particular reference to the attitudes of Frederick Jackson Turner and Woodrow Wilson toward European immigrants.

Chapter six takes up the theme of the European immigrant in American political history as reflected in the writings of the classical political historians: Von Holst, Schouler, and Rhodes. In the succeeding chapter, the immigrant's relationship to American social development is explored in the volumes of McMaster, Oberholtzer, Osgood and Channing. The first part of the final chapter is devoted to filiopietistic conceptions of the roles played by various non-English peoples in the nation's history, while the concluding section relates trends in the historiography of immigration before 1925 to developments after that date.

The first, third, and eighth chapters of this volume formed the basis of the following articles: " Race and Nationalism in American Historiography: The Late Nineteenth Century," *Political Science Quarterly,* LIV (September 1939), 421-41; " Henry Adams' Norman Ancestors," *Contemporary Jewish Record,* VIII (June 1945), 250-61; " The Immigrant In American History," *Commentary* II (August 1946), 180-5.

I am appreciative of the assistance given me by Professor Allan Nevins who guided the present study and by Professor Henry Steele Commager who read the manuscript carefully and offered numerous valuable suggestions. I am also indebted to Professor Michael Kraus who read the proofs with great care. I am deeply grateful to my wife, Betty Norr Saveth, for assisting with the manuscript and for encouraging its completion.

CHAPTER I

TRENDS IN LATE NINETEENTH CENTURY AMERICAN HISTORIOGRAPHY: THE THEORY OF TEUTONIC ORIGINS

THE BACKGROUND

THE attitudes of American historians toward European immigrants between 1875 and 1925 were the product of a number of factors. Of primary importance were the historians' Anglo-American Protestant heritage and their derivation, in the main, from middle and upper class backgrounds. They had, too, no small respect for English tradition; particularly in so far as it was enmeshed with the mores of the society into which they were born.

The mere presence of the immigrant served to strengthen the historian's group consciousness, which increased as the social distance between him and the immigrant widened; or as the source of European immigration moved eastward and the newcomer became increasingly strange in custom and appearance. Frequently, the immigrant was unmindful and even unappreciative of what had been before, and this made him seem all the more menacing.

Increased tempo of the tide of immigration coincided with growing industrialization, the concomitants of which were urbanization, slums, poverty, corruption in government, and class conflict. To the popular mind and even to some scholars, these evils appeared to be increasing as ethnic homogeneity declined. The immigrant was associated, therefore, not with the conserving forces in American society, but with some of the more unsavory innovations. Industrialism threatened to reduce the old families to a secondary position in the socio-economic hierarchy, and some historians, conscious of their ancestry, feared this tendency. At times, they fumbled in fixing responsibility for what was happening, and much of the resentment that should have been directed against the industrial system was harbored instead against the immigrant.

In the cities of the Atlantic seaboard, especially Boston and Philadelphia, historians watched the foreigners come by the boatload—first, almost entirely from central Europe and Ireland and, after the 1880's, mainly from the countries of southern and eastern Europe. But not all the adverse reaction took place in the New England village and the parlors of Boston's Beacon Hill and of Philadelphia's upper class. Much as the frontier historians insisted upon their emancipation from the prejudices of the seaboard, they also had a tradition to conserve. The frontier came to be, before very long, almost as jealously guarded a heritage as Plymouth Rock. Just as the frontiersmen and western settlers knew not the landmarks of Boston and Philadelphia, so the millions of immigrants who came after them and settled in cities did not share in that phase of American experience which derived from life in the wilderness. In the canons of American experience, the immigrant of the late nineteenth century was twice denied.

Supplementing the prejudices of birth and breeding were certain firmly-held concepts which influenced historians' judgments of immigrants. The belief that the United States was essentially an Anglo-Saxon country and the desire to preserve it as such; the assumption that labor disturbances and the class struggle were aspects of the European rather than the American scene and were introduced into the United States by the immigrant; the population theory of Francis A. Walker, which held that immigration served merely to curtail the native birthrate and did not constitute a gain in any sense to the nation; the belief that the immigrant influx tended to reduce living standards, and to increase criminality and political and social evils—all these ideas tended to prejudice historians against the immigrants.

On the other hand, ideas of a different nature were also widely current. There was the idea of the United States as a refuge for the oppressed of Europe; there was the realization of the value of immigrant labor in an undeveloped nation; there was the recognition that this was a land of opportunity for natives and immigrants alike; there was the belief in the assimilative power of free land, in the efficacy of the melting pot, in America's destiny as a composite nation. Many historians were imbued with these ideas, and the more they were so imbued the more favorably disposed they were towards newcomers.

These two sets of more or less indigenous concepts were not the only forces which determined the historian's attitude toward immigrants; that attitude was affected also by intellectual currents from abroad. Among the more important trends in European thought which influenced American historiography were the tenets of Social Darwinism. By use of the comparative method, a familial relationship among peoples of " Aryan ancestry " was supposedly demonstrated, and theories trading under the name of Darwin were called upon to justify the ascendancy of the Anglo-Saxon and prove the superiority of his institutions.

Relatively early in the period covered by this volume, the German-born historian, Hermann Eduard Von Holst, popularized in America the concept of the " Times-Spirit " which he asserted, could be fully comprehended only by the Germanic and the Anglo-Saxon mind. Somewhat later, a generation of American historians enrolled in German universities to hear extolled the glories of Germanism—but, with John W. Burgess as virtually sole exception, they took Germanism to mean Anglo-Saxonism, and went home to apply what they had learned to an analysis of American political evolution as a continuation of the experience of the Anglo-Saxon " race." Young Henry Adams, however, who had a liking for things Romanic, rejected both Teutonism and Anglo-Saxonism and would not have traded a single stained-glass window in a Norman Cathedral for all of Anglo-Saxondom.

A number of other currents of thought had their influence upon late nineteenth century American historiography. There was the rise of a school of scientific historians who, as Edward Channing said, based their accounts upon original sources rather than upon what they were able to copy from one another;[1] there was the realization of the importance of the frontier; there was the nascent theory of geographic determinism. There was also a growing interest in social and economic history. None of these trends was without effect upon historians' treatment of immigrant peoples. In the late nineteenth century, the most important of them was the Teutonic hypothesis.

THE TEUTONIC HYPOTHESIS AND THE COMPARATIVE METHOD

In the last quarter of the nineteenth century, the American historian was primarily concerned with vindicating the standing of his profession. In this period, achievements in the natural sciences were making a great impression upon the community and the historian felt bound to adopt the language of science.[2]

In American historical thinking there have been, generally, "two distinct and contradictory conceptions of scientific history." One is the belief that scientific history consists of "a search for facts alone, with no laws or generalizations and with a renunciation of all philosophy"; the other is the belief that there are historical laws or generalizations which may be formulated.[3] The historiography of the late nineteenth century

1 Remarks in communicating a paper on "The Genesis of the Massachusetts Town and the Origin of Town-Meeting Government," *Proceedings of the Massachusetts Historical Society*, second series, VII (January 1892), 242-4.

2 Social Science Research Council, *Theory and Practice in Historical Study: A Report of the Committee on Historiography* (New York, 1945), p. 25. Bulletin no. 54.

3 W. Stull Holt, "The Idea of Scientific History in America," *Journal of the History of Ideas*, I (June 1940), 356-7.

wavered between these two views. There was the relentless pursuit of facts and there was, at the same time, the tendency to interpret the facts in accordance with the theory that American institutions were Teutonic in origin.

In accepting the Teutonic theory of American institutional origins, American scholars were enlisting in one of the rival camps of a controversy that was of long standing in Europe.[4] In England, Romanists and Germanists had long been at odds over the sources of that country's greatness. Speaking for the Romanists who preferred France to Germany and leaned toward the acceptance of Roman Catholicism, Francis Palgrave insisted upon the continuity of the Romanic tradition in England. This, he maintained, antedated and survived the Anglo-Saxon invasions and was reenforced by the Normans after 1066. Only the Romanic peoples, said Palgrave, introduced significant and indestructible traits into English culture.[5]

The Romanists, however, hardly made themselves heard above the rumble of the Germanists—Edward Augustus Freeman, William Stubbs, and John Richard Green. Each of these three was widely read by American historians in the late nineteenth century, but it was Freeman who had the greatest influence upon them—Freeman, historian of the Norman Conquest, of whom it was said: "on his coat of arms were emblazoned the Anglo-Saxon militant, the Teuton rampant, and the Aryan eternally triumphant."[6]

In his study of English history, Freeman laid great stress upon the comparative method, which Sir Henry Maine had

4 For background of the controversy see Paul Vinogradoff, *Villainage in England; Essays in English Mediaeval History* (Oxford, 1892), pp. 13, 15, 23; George P. Gooch, *History and Historians in the Nineteenth Century* (New York, 1935), pp. 286-9, 346-52; W. S. Holdsworth, *The Historians of Anglo-American Law* (New York, 1928), p. 35.

5 James W. Thompson, *A History of Historical Writing* (2 vols., New York, 1942), II, 382.

6 W. A. Dunning, *Truth in History and Other Essays* (New York, 1937), p. 157.

used before him.[7] This method, he was convinced, opened up a new world to the historical investigator, "and that not an isolated world, a world shut up within itself, but a world in which times and tongues and nations which before seemed parted poles asunder, now find each one its own place, its own relation to every other, as members of one common primaeval brotherhood."[8]

Institutional and linguistic similarities which Freeman discovered as a consequence of his use of the comparative method confirmed him in his Germanist viewpoint and contributed to a theory of English institutional origins which was approximately as follows. He postulated an original pre-historic homeland of the Aryan peoples where they evolved a unique institutional pattern. The dispersal of the Aryans from this early cradle of civilization led to institutional recapitulation wherever they or their descendants settled in Greece, Rome, Germany, England and, finally, in America.[9] The Teutons, chronologically the last of the Aryan peoples and like their predecessors, the Greeks and the Romans, destined to be rulers and teachers of the world, were recipients of the finest fruits of the racial heritage. Just as among the Greeks and Romans the Aryan institutional heritage culminated in the city-state and empire, so the entrance of the mighty Teuton upon the historic scene marked the dawn of a new era in political organization—that of the nation state.[10]

In Freeman's view the Teutonic character was most highly developed not on the European continent, where the blood of the Germans had suffered a Romanic infusion, but in England where, despite Roman and Norman invaders, the institutions of the Anglo-Saxon prevailed. Widely as the contemporary British constitution differed from the practices of the followers

7 Thompson, *op. cit.*, II, 383.

8 E. A. Freeman, *Comparative Politics* (London, 1873), p. 302.

9 *Ibid.*, pp. 3, 17, 18.

10 *Ibid.*, pp. 120, 134.

of Cedric, who had carried the Teutonic heritage from the mainland to the island forests, there was no break between them. It was the distinctive trait of British nationality that, alone among the greater states of Europe, Great Britain possessed a Parliament whose descent could be traced from the Teutonic institutions of earliest times.[11]

Freeman also believed that the ties of race transcended national boundaries. The English people had not one, but three homes: originally on the European mainland, then in England and, finally, in the United States. Those who came to Britain with Hengest in the fifth century and those whom the Mayflower brought to a New World centuries later were alike carriers of the original Teutonic heritage.[12] The institutions of the early Massachusetts towns were part of the inheritance of the Teutonic race, and their establishment in New England was part of the history of the Aryan people.[13] Wrote Freeman,

> To me the English-speaking commonwealth on the American mainland is simply one part of the great English folk, as the English-speaking kingdom in the European island is another part. My whole line of thought and study leads me to think, more perhaps than most men, of the everlasting ties of blood and speech, and less of the accidental separation wrought by political and geographical causes.[14]

Trends in European historiography were bound to make themselves felt in America, since American historians in increasing numbers were pursuing graduate studies at European, especially German, universities. As early as 1870, astute Professor W. F. Allen, of the University of Wisconsin, had

11 *Ibid.*, pp. 46-7; "An Introduction to American Institutional History," *Johns Hopkins University Studies in Historical and Political Science* (Baltimore, 1883), first series, no. I, p. 15. Hereinafter cited as *Johns Hopkins Studies*.

12 *Comparative Politics*, pp. 65-7.

13 "An Introduction to American Institutional History," p. 13.

14 *Some Impressions of the United States* (New York, 1883), pp. 15-16.

suggested to Sir Henry Maine that the latter's study of the characteristics of the village community throughout the world should be extended to New England,[15] where, according to Allen, there had been reproduced a community not unlike the ancient Teutonic *tun*.[16] To trace, by means of the comparative method, the relationship between American and Germanic institutions was the essence of a scheme of historical research which Herbert Baxter Adams, newly returned from studies under Bluntschli and Erdmannsdorffer at Heidelberg, introduced at Johns Hopkins.

Adams' seminar combined the study of early European history, and especially the history of the Germanic peoples, with research into the history of the local institutions of the United States. Mindful of the emphasis placed by G. L. von Maurer [17] and Sir Henry Maine upon the mark or village community as a basic political unit, Adams sought to relate the New England village community to earlier Aryan forms.[18] " History," he explained, " should not be content with describing effects when it can explain causes. It is just as improbable that free local institutions should spring up without a

15 For earlier theories of the origin of New England towns see J. F. Sly, *Town Government in Massachusetts, 1620-1930* (Cambridge, 1930), pp. 52-5.

16 Professor Allen's communication was published in *The Nation*, September 22, 1870 as a note upon Maine's *Ancient Law*. Other articles by Professor Allen appeared in *The Nation*, January 10, 1878 and November 10, 1881. Henry Maine's *Village Communities in the East and West* (London, 1871), p. 201 identified the early New England village community with other village settlements in the history of the human race. Maine cites Palfrey's *History of New England* as proof of his contentions, pp. 13-14. See also, Henry Maine, *Dissertations on Early Law and Custom* (London, 1883), p. 331.

17 G. L. von Maurer, *Einleitung zur Geschichte der Mark-, Hof-, Dorf-und Stadtverfassung und der offentlichen Gewalt* (München, 1854) ; H. J. Peake, " Village Community," *Encyclopedia of the Social Sciences* (8 vols., New York, 1937), VIII, 253-9.

18 Herbert Baxter Adams, " The Germanic Origin of New England Towns. With Notes on Cooperation in University Work," *Johns Hopkins Studies*, first series, 1883, no. II.

germ along American shores as that English wheat should
have grown here without planting." [19]
The Teutonic theory of American institutional origins was
closely allied to certain Social Darwinist contentions: that
ontogeny recapitualtes philogeny; that there exists biological
analogies in history; that institutional evolution occurs from
a primitive "seed." Social Darwinism and the Teutonic
hypothesis were combined in the writings of Herbert Baxter
Adams. The ancient Teutons, wrote Adams, had evolved in
their councils and village moots "the seeds of self-government, of commons and congresses." In the German forest was
developed "the single head of the state, the smaller council
. . . and the general assembly of the whole people," nuclei of
the institutions of Holland, Germany, England, New England,
and the United States.[20] "These little communes," Adams
regarded as "the germs of our state and national life . . . the
primordial cells of the body politic." In Bagehot's *Physics and
Politics,* Adams had read that small things were but the
miniatures of greater. Accepting the theory that ontogeny
recapitulated philogeny, Adams held that the various branches
of the Aryan race had retained an identical basic inheritance
and had lived through much the same historical cycle.[21]

As the procedure of the scientist was from the specific to the
general—as the process of development was from the simple to
the complex—so Adams believed that historians should study
first local, then national, and finally international aspects of
history. This view was a tremendous stimulus to the investi-

19 *Ibid.,* p. 1.

20 *Ibid.,* 1, 23, 38. Adams maintained that the English Saxon agricultural
community was the historic survival of the Teutonic village. "Under the heel
of the Norman conqueror, the old communal spirit of the Saxons endured."
Ibid., p. 21. Adams revealed further Teutonic survivals in "Saxon Tithing-
Men in America," *ibid.,* no. IV, pp. 18-20 and in "Norman Constables in
America," *ibid.,* no. VIII, p. 13. See also his "Village Communities of Cape
Ann and Salem," *ibid.,* nos. IX-X, *passim.*

21 Editor's introduction to J. H. Johnson, Jr., "Rudimentary Society
Among Boys," *ibid.,* second series, no. XI, pp. 6-7.

gation of town, county, municipal, and state institutions in the United States with emphasis upon the relationship between American political institutions and earlier forms.[22] Under Adams' editorship, the *Johns Hopkins University Studies in Historical and Political Science* stressed publications of this sort. In 1881, Freeman visited Baltimore and later extended his blessing to the undertaking in the form of an introduction to the studies. A chance phrase of his, " History is past politics; politics present history," was inscribed on the title page of each of the separate studies.[23]

Adams' theory of American political evolution was consonant with his New England origin and Anglo-Saxon ancestry.[24] Regarding institutions as of slow, evolutionary development, Adams leaned toward conservatism and distrusted sudden social change. He advised that those who wished to improve the conditions of workingmen adopt the " individual " rather than the " collective " approach, and warned against substituting agitation for education and intelligent direction.[25] Although Adams made no attempt to justify such practices as farming out the labor of the town's poor, the whipping post, the southern chain gang, and the poll tax, his reverence for " Saxon " servitude to law prevented him from condemning those who upheld such institutions.[26]

22 H. B. Adams, " Methods of Historical Study," *ibid.*, second series, nos. I-II, p. 103; " Cooperation in University Work," pp. 49, 52.

23 "An Introduction to American Institutional History," *passim.*

24 Adams was sufficiently curious concerning his ancestry to publish his genealogy, *History of the Thomas Adams and Thomas Hastings Families of Amherst Massachusetts* (Amherst, 1880).

25 " Work Among Workingmen in Baltimore," Notes supplementary to the *Johns Hopkins Studies*, sixth series, 1889, pp. 1, 8; " The Church and Popular Education," *ibid.*, eighteenth series, nos. VIII, IX, *passim*; " Notes on the Literature of Charities," *ibid.*, fifth series, 1887, no. VIII, p. 44.

26 " Saxon Tithing-Men," p. 11; W. Stull Holt, ed., *Historical Scholarship in the United States, 1876-1901: As Revealed in the Correspondence of Herbert B. Adams* (Baltimore, 1938), p. 42. Adams was well aware that this entire methodology contributed to the reenforcement of nationalism and

The pattern of conservatism that is apparent in Adams' work is duplicated in the writings of John Fiske, John W. Burgess, and Henry Cabot Lodge, all of whom made the Teutonic hypothesis the basis of their approach to history. It is also evident in the volumes of James K. Hosmer, contributor to the *John Hopkins Studies,* who went much further than Adams in drawing parallels between ancient Saxon institutions and those of the New England village community.[27]

Hosmer, like Adams, was of New England birth, and pride in that birth was even stronger in him than it was in Adams. He was ever mindful both of his descent from eleventh century Saxondom and of the fact that his " stock had been fixed in America since 1635." [28] Hosmer lamented the passing of the New England community with its agrarian economy, which, he claimed, was the embodiment of economic egalitarianism, homogeneity, and primitive democracy, and the transformations wrought by industrialization and immigration. Stressing the Teutonic origin of the New England " folk-mote " or town meeting, and the essentially Teutonic character of the American institutional structure which he believed grew out of it, he identified the preservation of the nation with the numerical preponderance of the Anglo-Saxon stock. He would not deny that the French Canadians and Irish who were entering New England in great numbers possessed many desirable qualities; however, he considered them " unprogressive " and uncongenial

---

conservatism in Germany. " The conservatives were perhaps wiser than the radicals. . . . " " Leopold Von Ranke," *American Academy of Arts and Sciences,* XXII, pt. 2, p. 550. This article also describes the importance of heredity as a factor in national evolution, p. 542.

27 Hosmer compared the Teutonic *laet* to the American Indian or indentured servant, the *theow* to the slave in colonial America, and the free colonist to the *ceorl. A Short History of Anglo-Saxon Freedom. The Polity of the English Speaking Race. Outlined in Its Inception, Development, Diffusion and Present Condition* (New York, 1890), pp. 8-9.

28 James K. Hosmer, *The Last Leaf; Observations, During Seventy-five Years, of Men and Events in America and Europe* (New York, 1912), pp. 188, 321.

by virtue of their inheritance to the institutions of the "folk-mote" and consequently to the derivative New England and American institutional pattern. Only as new generations came forward could it be hoped that "they take on the characteristics of the people among whom they have come to cast their lot." [29]

Hosmer's complaint against the immigrant element in the New England population was merely an aspect of a more general indictment of the entire pattern of civilization that confronted him in the late nineteenth century and a desire to return to the somewhat idealized circumstances of a half century earlier. He summed up the situation:

> The influx of alien tides to whom our precious heirlooms are as nothing, the growth of cities and the inextricable perplexities of their government, the vast inequality of condition between man and man—what room is there for the little primary council of freemen, homogeneous in stock, holding the same faith, on the same level as to wealth and station . . . [30]

That Hosmer attributed a Germanic source to American institutions, did not imply on his part a correspondingly high opinion of the German immigrant to the United States. Hosmer cited as representative of "the best English opinion" as to why the Confederates fought as well as they did during the American Civil War, a letter of Sir Charles Lyell: "Englishmen may feel proud of the prowess of the southern army, in which was not that large mixture of Celtic and German blood found on the Northern side." [31]

29 "Samuel Adams: The Man of the Town Meeting," *Johns Hopkins Studies*, second series, 1884, no. IV, p. 218. *Samuel Adams* (New York, 1885), p. 420.

30 *Ibid.*, pp. 429-30.

31 *Outcome of the Civil War 1863-1865* (New York, 1907), p. 252. Hosmer regarded the Jews as a people apart from the "Aryans"—"Semitic flotsam and jetsam thrown upon the Aryan current." Evaluating Jewish characteristics as consequences of their Asiatic blood and Oriental origin, in Hosmer's opinion, the gap between Jew and Aryan could be bridged about

Although Hosmer buttressed his conclusions with citations from the *Johns Hopkins Studies,* his was an extremist interpretation of the evidence therein. So, too, was Alexander Johnston's contention that the federal constitution was directly descendant from the institutions of three Connecticut towns —Watertown, Newton, and Dorchester. In these towns, according to Johnston, the Teutonic institutional " primordial-germs " were purest and it was due to its emergence from this source that the federal government owed its superiority. [32] More moderate conceptions of the Teutonic hypothesis found widespread acceptance not only at Johns Hopkins but among the general run of late nineteenth century American historians. That American institutions were *"Teutonic in origin"* was a fundamental principle which Albert Bushnell Hart insisted should be " sharply defined in the minds of the students at Harvard." [33] Hart believed that the " Teutonic race " combined the greatest love for personal freedom with the greatest respect for law.[34] At Cornell, Andrew D. White and Moses Coit Tyler stressed Teutonic history,[35] and John W. Burgess expounded a similar viewpoint at Columbia. Herbert Levi Osgood observed that Adams' monograph on " The Germanic Origin of New Eng-

---

as easily as that between native New Englander and Irish immigrant. *The Story of the Jews Ancient, Mediaeval, and Modern* (New York, 1893), pp. 5, 365, 368.

32 *Connecticut: A Study of a Commonwealth-Democracy* (New York, 1887), pp. 62, 322. This study appeared originally as " The Genesis of a New England State," *Johns Hopkins Studies,* first series, no. XI.

33 " Methods of Teaching American History," G. S. Hall, editor, *Methods of Teaching History* (Boston, 1883), p. 3.

34 *Introduction to the Study of Federal Government* (Boston, 1891), p. 23.

35 A. D. White, " Historical Instruction in the Course of History and Political Science at Cornell University," Hall, *op. cit.,* p. 76. So impressed was Moses Coit Tyler with the international implications of the Teutonic hypothesis that he found in the period between 1763 and 1783 elements of " pathos and tragedy " which marked the birth of a needless race feud. *The Literary History of the American Revolution, 1763-1783* (2 vols., New York, 1897), I, viii-ix.

land Towns," was "intended as an incitement to the comparative study of early American and European local institutions,"[36] and so effectively had it accomplished its purpose that Charles McLean Andrews, writing of the status of "Theory of the Village Community" in 1891, observed that "so wide has been its acceptance, and so strongly installed is it in the minds both of students and readers that it may seem more bold than discreet to raise the question regarding the soundness of the theory."[37]

Nevertheless, the thesis had a number of challengers. Edward Channing[38] traced colonial town and county government no further back into history than the English common-law parish as it existed about 1600. Insisting that the theory of the derivation of American institutions from Teutonic sources had no real evidence to support it, Channing deplored the tendency of the Teutonists to argue from analogies which, he said, were not the equivalents of "identities." Nor did institutional similarity, in his opinion, indicate heredity.

> The argument that because a New England town and a German village were each surrounded by a defensive wall, the one is descended from the other, proves too much. A similar line of argument would prove the origin of New England towns to be the Massai enclosure of Central Africa.[39]

But Channing failed to see that this criticism of the methodology of Adams and his disciples was applicable as well to his own use of the comparative method in the attempt to prove that

36 J. N. Larned, ed., *The Literature of American History* (Boston, 1902), p. 295.

37 *Papers of the American Historical Association*, V (New York, 1891), p. 47.

38 Channing's attitude toward the Teutonic hypothesis was influenced by his having translated B. Delbrück's *Introduction to the Study of Language: A Critical Survey of the History and Methods of Comparative Philology of the Indo-European Languages* (Leipzig, 1882).

39 Remarks on "The Genesis of the Massachusetts Town and the Origin of Town-Meeting Government," pp. 244, 250.

American institutions were derived from the seventeenth century English parish.[40] Moreover, despite his effective critique of the Teutonic hypothesis, Channing, in his major work, vested responsibility for American political evolution in the nature of the "English race" whose "most marked political characteristic . . .has always been its conservatism in adhering to that which is old for no other reason than because it is that which exists." [41]

Between the institutions of ancient Germany and those of seventeenth century America, Charles McLean Andrews thought "there is more that is unidentical than there is that is identical." Yet he favored the Teutonic hypothesis to the extent of asserting that the township system was exclusively English; "that the Celts and Slavs never developed local government by themselves, and the Romance peoples were governed, so to speak from above, not from within"; that in the institutional pattern that the Angles and Saxons carried to England "were embraced many of the foundation principles according to which the German *tun* is supposed to have been built; and that many of these customs, political, legal, social, agrarian, and philological, were brought by the settlers to America." All of this, concluded Andrews, "no reasonable scholar will pretend to deny." [42]

Two years later, Andrews' attitude toward the Teutonic hypothesis was more critical. He at this time denied that knowledge of the character of the Germanic village community, which was transplanted to England in the sixth century, was sufficient to warrant the conclusion that identical forms were reproduced in seventeenth century New England. Andrews did

40 "Town and County Government in the English Colonies of North America," *Johns Hopkins Studies*, second series, no. X, pp. 487-9. Channing also stressed the role of environmental factors in determining the character of local political organization. *Ibid.*, p. 5.

41 *A History of the United States* (6 vols., New York, 1925), I, 512.

42 "The River Towns of Connecticut A Study of Wethersfield, Hartford, and Windsor," *Johns Hopkins Studies*, seventh series, 1889, nos. VII-VIII-IX, pp. 30-1 fn.

not hesitate to point to the inconclusive character of the evidence upon which Kemble, Freeman, Maine, von Maurer, and others to whom H. B. Adams looked for direction, erected their theories. " I know of no better panacea for superficial comparisons than greater thoroughness of study. Before we talk about Germanic *tuns* and Saxon manors, it would seem to be more scholarly to understand accurately the agrarian condition of England . . . ." [43] Such an undertaking was Andrews' own careful study of the manor.[44]

Having studied in Berlin and taken his doctorate under John W. Burgess at Columbia University, Herbert Levi Osgood, with much the same training as many of the adherents of the Teutonic hypothesis, denied the validity of this theory.[45] Moreover, in his early studies of the philosophies of socialism and anarchism, Osgood rejected what so many adherents of the Teutonic hypothesis affirmed: existence of a relationship between race and politics. He wrote:

It is useless to claim that it [anarchy] is wholly a foreign product, and for that reason to clamor for restrictions upon immigration. Newspaper utterances on this phase of the subject have consisted too largely of appeals to ignorance and prejudice. There probably are good reasons why immigration should be restricted, but this should weigh very lightly among them. . . . Anarchism, so far as it has a scientific basis, is, like socialism, a natural product of our economic and political conditions. It is to be treated as such, both theoretically and practically. . . . It is as much at home on American soil as on European.[46]

43 " Theory of the Village Community," pp. 48, 50, 53, 56, 60.

44 *The Old English Manor A Study in English History* (Baltimore, 1892), *Johns Hopkins Studies*, extra vol. XII.

45 Larned, *op. cit.*, pp. 81, 102, 295-6. A. C. McLaughlin was also critical of the Teutonic explanation of American institutional origins in a review of Freeman's " Introduction to American Institutional History," *ibid.*, p. 295.

46 " Scientific Anarchism," *Political Science Quarterly*, IV (March 1889), 30-1.

Osgood's major work on "the nature and growth of government in the American colonies" did not stress Teutonic origins. Moreover, whereas the adherents of the Teutonic hypothesis made a point of emphasizing the dominant Anglo-Saxon strain in the English people, Osgood conceived of England as a country "whose population is so mixed in origin as to constitute a standing puzzle for ethnologists." Osgood did not regard English immigration into the American colonies as part of the history of the Anglo-Saxon "race" but rather as continuing the original mixture of stocks.[47]

Charles Francis Adams was skeptical both of the theory that townships institutions stemmed from ancient Germanic sources and of Channing's contention that they were derived from the early English parish.[48] Not only did Adams regard town government rather as a genuine New England product than as derived from remote and alien sources,[49] but he also dispelled the aura of idealism with which Hosmer and others surrounded it. "The ideal town-meeting," wrote Adams,

> is one thing; the actual town-meeting is apt to be a very different thing. To the theorist in history who should attend one, it would, not improbably, be the rude dispelling of a fanciful delusion. He would come away from it rather amazed that civilized government was possible through such a system than understanding how New England had been built up on it.[50]

Part of the reason for Adams' critical attitude toward the town meeting was that his service as moderator in Quincy had acquainted him with its shortcomings.[51] With a dispassionate

47 *The American Colonies in the Eighteenth Century* (4 vols., New York, 1924), II, 486-7.

48 *Three Episodes of Massachusetts History* (2 vols., Boston, 1892), II, 646-53, 980-1.

49 *Ibid.*, p. 815.

50 *Ibid.*, p. 967.

51 W. C. Ford, "C. F. Adams," Allen Johnson and Dumas Malone, eds., *Dictionary of American Biography* (20 vols., New York, 1928), I, 51.

attitude typical of the later generations of Adamses in considering social and institutional patterns that their ancestors had a
role in making, Charles Francis Adams noted the inadequacies
of the town meeting in coping with the increase in population,
with industrialization, with social problems, with rising group
antagonism, and with the influx of alien stocks. Adams regarded the influx of foreigners as being " too rapid " and " un-
settling," producing

> change also for the worse. The older order of things was
> doubtless slow, conservative, traditional; but it was economi-
> cal, simple and business-like. The new order of things was in
> all respects the reverse. The leaders in it prided themselves on
> their enterprise, their lack of reverence for tradition, their con-
> fidence in themselves; but they were noisy, unmethodical, in
> reality incompetent, and much too often intemperate.[52]

This evaluation could scarcely be interpreted as favorable to
the foreign element, but it was not far from being a true
description of what had happened. It was, moreover, un-
accompanied by lamentation over the passing of the Anglo-
Saxon and that maudlin sentimentality about institutions that
had outlived their usefulness which entered into contemporary
treatments of a comparable theme. Adams, having concluded
his account of the rise and decline of town government, made
this very natural observation: " The past was secure;—would
the future better it?" But there was no turning back for the
town of Quincy, and Adams was too much the social evolutionist to think or hope that history could be reversed. He
merely wanted " the ancient system—so endeared . . . by
custom and time—laid away as a parent that was gone,—
silently, tenderly, reverently." [53]

The early historical writings of Charles Francis Adams
were milestones in New England historiography. The tradition
of filiopietism, of which Palfrey's work was typical, had been

52 *Three Episodes of Massachusetts History*, II, 949.

53 *Ibid.*, p. 1009.

shattered by a native of natives. The appointment of Edward
Channing to Harvard also boded ill for New England history
written in the filiopietistic tradition, and it was to Channing's
class in American history that Adams in 1892 communicated
the substance of an iconoclastic volume which was later published under the title *Massachusetts: Its Historians and Its
History*.[54]

Despite the not inconsiderable light which the search for
confirmation of the Teutonic hypothesis cast upon local and institutional history, the belief that American institutions were
Teutonic in origin represented retrogression in American historiography. It granted a new lease on life to ancestor worship
as an aspect of the historiography of New England. Now one
could be both proud of one's ancestors and " scientific " about
them at the same time. The Teutonic hypothesis strengthened
the conviction that the Germanic peoples and particularly the
Anglo-Saxons were of a superior type, and increased distrust
of non-Teutons—the Irish, the French Canadians and the
nationalities of the new immigration. The hypothesis also served
to reenforce patterns of conservatism, because " those who
think of new problems exclusively in terms of historical
analogies get tangled in their own traces and think that what
has been must remain forever." [55] But perhaps more than anything else, adherence to the Teutonic hypothesis was an
affirmation of faith in heredity and in the kind of surroundings
into which the historians were born. The proponents of the
hypothesis and those who rejected it had much of the same
background—New England, Anglo-Saxon, Protestant—but,
while the critics were able to take a dispassionate view of the
matter, the proponents embraced the theory with warmth because it confirmed them in the belief that the old ways were,
after all, the best; it assured them that what they already felt
in their hearts to be true, was true by scientific demonstration.

54 (Boston, 1894).

55 Morris R. Cohen, *Reason and Nature, An Essay on the Meaning of
Scientific Method* (New York, 1931), p. 375.

CHAPTER II

TEUTON AND IMMIGRANT

JOHN FISKE

THE barrage of criticism levelled against the Teutonic hypothesis was successful in the long run in undermining it.[1] However, largely through the writings and lectures of the prolific John Fiske, the theory of the Teutonic origin of American nationality was presented to an audience many times as wide as that which was reached by Andrews, Channing, and Osgood, or, by the contributors to the *Johns Hopkins Studies.*

Fiske's training and early publications were philosophical rather than historical in character. He had not inconsiderable intellectual capacities,[2] and the transition from popularizing Spencer and Darwin to writing a number of volumes on American history was, for him, not as difficult as it might seem. He managed to incorporate into his histories some of the charm of style that gave his articles on evolution such wide popular appeal. Fiske made no real contribution to scholarly historical writing, but he should be recognized as a force in American intellectual life; while many historians exceeded him in originality of contribution, very few have been more widely read.

Fiske was born in 1842 and grew up in his grandparents' home in Middletown, Connecticut. Twenty years before the Civil War, the inherited wealth of the town—a town inhabited by the descendants of colonial merchants, traders, and ship-owners—was but a reminder of former commercial activity; and the factory with its concomitants of class conflict and an immigrant working class had not yet appeared. Pre-Civil War

1 As late as 1918, however, James Truslow Adams fully accepted the Teutonic hypothesis. *History of the Town of Southampton (East of Canoe Place)*, (Bridgehampton, Long Island, 1918), pp. 94-6.

2 J. S. Clark, *The Life and Letters of John Fiske* (2 vols., New York, 1917), I, 254.

Middletown offered the kind of surroundings Fiske liked best and served as a model for his description of the New England township, descriptions which he incorporated in the lectures that he gave before audiences here and abroad.[3] Petersham, Massachusetts, where Fiske courted Abby Morgan Brooks and where in later life he made his home, was, as he described it in 1862, even less of a city than Middletown, being "but two streets and two stores" within the limits of which "neither Irishman nor negro ever sets foot."[4]

In "The Town Meeting"—a lecture the title and substance of which he was fond of repeating—Fiske described what, in his view, was happening to the New England township through the impact of industrialism. He would begin by telling his audience about the New England town that was part of his earliest recollection. He would speak of the homogeneity of the community, the absence of class strife, the universality of manual labor, and the almost complete absence of poverty. "A state of society so completely democratic," he commented, "had not been found in connection with a very high and complex civilization."

Sadly, Fiske noted the latter-day tendency for farms to pass into the hands of "proprietors of an inferior type to that of the former owners," for "ugly factories to disfigure the beautiful ravines, and to introduce into the community a class of people very different from the landholding descendants of the Puritans." "When once a factory is established near a village," he said, "one no longer feels free to sleep with doors unbolted."[5] When they wrote on the theme of the passing of the old township, Fiske, Hosmer, and even H. B. Adams were all alike overcome by nostalgia.

---

3 *Ibid.*, pp. 20-1. Fiske's father, Edmund Green, was of New Jersey Quaker descent, but his mother was of Puritan ancestry. Fiske maintained a lively interest in his antecedents, particularly his mother's family, whose name he adopted. Ethel Fisk, ed., *The Letters of John Fiske* (New York, 1940), pp. 374, 554.

4 *Ibid.*, pp. 88, 89.

5 *American Political Ideas Viewed from the Standpoint of Universal History* (New York, 1911), pp. 17, 18.

Fiske's interests were broader and less academic than those of the editor of the *Johns Hopkins Studies*. The two men had very similar theories as to the role played by the township in the introduction of Teutonic political institutions into the United States, but Fiske was better able to contribute depth and background to an approximately similar theory of institutional origins. Fiske's acquaintance with the findings of late nineteenth century ethnology, geology, and philology enabled him to arrive at what he believed was " a tolerably correct idea of what is meant by the word Aryan." In 1883, Fiske was wiser than some of his contemporaries in insisting that the term was a linguistic one only. " It is never safe to use language as a direct criterion of race," he wrote, " for speech and blood depend on different sets of circumstances which do not always vary together." He maintained " that all races which have long wandered and fought have become composite to a degree past deciphering." [6]

Though he acknowledged that the peoples who speak Aryan languages are of mixed blood, Fiske nevertheless spoke of the " Aryan race " just as " we speak without error of the English race, though we know that many race elements have combined their energies in the great work of English civilization." He considered that the heritage of the " Aryan race " consisted in common habits of thought and a common culture pattern.[7] He was very skeptical in regard to theories which held that the early Aryans were physiologically similar; even the opinion of " such a cautious ethnologist " as Professor Huxley failed to carry such weight as to convince him on this point.[8]

6 *Excursions of an Evolutionist* (Boston, 1893), pp. 101, 103.

7 *Ibid.*, p. 103.

8 *Ibid.*, p. 107. Fiske is here referring to Huxley's *On Some Fixed Points in British Ethnology Critiques and Addresses* (London, 1873), pp. 167-80. Fiske at this time considered it within the realm of probability that differences of complexion between the blond and brunette types of Europe are " apt to be correlated with deep-seated physiological differences of temperament." *Excursions of an Evolutionist*, p. 104. Fiske conceived of European man as mainly resultant from the fusion of dark complexioned " Iberians " and fair skinned "Aryans." *Ibid.*, p. 56.

As a Spencerian, Fiske was well aware that historical evolution is determined at each stage by many factors, but he did lay great stress upon the " English race " and the " Aryan " political heritage as factors in world development and particularly in the development of America.[9] In his opinion, the " English race " was largely responsible for some of the great steps of human advance—for industrialism, for Protestantism, for individualism, and for the idea of the federal state. The principle of Federalism was, according to Fiske, the chief mark of the English idea of the state as distinguished from that of imperial Rome, and this principle was intimately associated with the rise of the middle class.[10]

From Freeman, Fiske derived the idea of an Anglo-Saxon golden age preceding the Norman invasion of England. Fiske maintained that after the Norman Conquest the Anglo-Saxons were reduced to the status of a middle-class yeomanry; that as such, despite their Romanized rulers, they kept alive the traditions of Saxon freedom; and that, in the seventeenth century, they carried these traditions with them to New England.[11]

The English middle class, continued Fiske, was the making not only of New England but of Virginia as well. This Fiske attributed to the eventual intermingling of the Saxon middle class and the Norman nobility in the course of English history

9 *Ibid.*, pp. 175-202.

10 *Ibid.*, pp. 240-1, 286-8; *A Century of Science and other Essays* (Boston, 1899), p. 135; *The Unseen World and other Essays* (Boston, 1876), pp. 139-45, 147-68.

11 *American Political Ideas*, pp. 20, 42, 44; *The Beginnings of New England; or, The Puritan Theocracy in Its Relations to Civil and Religious Liberty* (Boston, 1889), p. 25. Although Fiske at this time was insistent on the purity of the Anglo-Saxon strain in England and that it did not assimilate with the sixth-century Romanic inhabitants, in 1869 he believed that " we—the English—are at least three-quarters Celtic, and the term 'Anglo-Saxon' when closely scrutinized is delightfully vague, and not much more ... I believe that in blood, we are quite as near to the French as to the German—probably more so." Fisk, *Letters of John Fiske*, p. 182.

—in the manner reminiscent of the happy outcome of the Norman Conquest as described in Freeman's fifth volume. In the veins of Virginia Cavalier and New England Puritan, Fiske maintained, flowed both middle-class and aristocratic blood,[12] a factor which he deemed of transcendent importance in the success of the English settlements. In the business of state-making, Fiske insisted, the matter of genealogy was not to be taken lightly.

> A hundred years ago, the most illustrious of Americans felt little interest in his ancestry; but with the keener historic sense and broader scientific outlook of the present day, the importance of such matters is better appreciated. The pedigrees of horses, dogs, and fancy pigeons have a value that is quotable in terms of hard cash. Far more important, for the student of human affairs, are the pedigrees of men. By no possible ingenuity of constitution-making or of legislation can a society made up of ruffians and boors be raised to the intellectual and moral level of a society made up of well-bred merchants and yeomen, parsons and lawyers. . . . It is, moreover, only when we habitually bear in mind the threads of individual relationship that connect one country with another, that we get a really firm and concrete grasp of history. Without genealogy the study of history is comparatively lifeless.[13]

Mindful of the historic role played by the middle-class Anglo-Saxon, Fiske did not look with favor upon social tendencies

12 *Old Virginia and Her Neighbours* (2 vols., Boston, 1897), II, 13, 14, 28, 30. " Families with titles have intermarried with families that have none, the younger branches of a peer's family become untitled gentry, ancient peerages lapse while new ones are created, so that there is a ' circulation of gentle blood ' that has thus far proved eminently wholesome." *Ibid.*, p. 14. Admitting the middle class origin of the majority of Virginia settlers (*Ibid.*, II, 187) Fiske nevertheless exaggerated the importance of the Cavalier immigration between 1649-60 (*Ibid.*, II, 16). This is the opinion of T. J. Wertenbaker, *Patrician and Plebian in Virginia or the Origin and Development of the Social Classes of the Old Dominion* (Charlottesville, Virginia, 1910), p. 28. For Wertenbaker's estimate of Fiske's treatment of Virginia history, *ibid.*, p. 223.

13 *Old Virginia and Her Neighbours*, II, 26.

which appeared to threaten the dominant position of this element within the American community. He opposed as antagonistic to middle-class interests the high tariff and excessive urbanization; the former because it fostered plutocracy and the latter for drawing upon the population of farming communities.[14] Fiske was also opposed to free silver; he considered that the tariff demands of the iron masters of Pennsylvania and the currency program of the Nevada silver mine owners constituted greater threats to the welfare of the American people than " all the ignorant foreigners that have flocked to us from Europe." [15] He was very unsympathetic toward the strike wave which swept the country during the nineties and emphatically denied that it had anything in common with the action of the colonists in the American Revolution.[16] Particularly in *The Critical Period of American History* is Fiske insistent that the American revolutionary tradition is the monopoly of the middle-class Anglo-Saxon and does not have the faintest tinge of proletarianism about it.[17]

As a Spencerian, Fiske could be expected to endorse the principle that a heterogeneous population is, within limits, a good thing. Maintaining that the " English race " had " a rare capacity for absorbing slightly foreign elements and moulding them into conformity with a political type that was first wrought out with centuries of effort on British soil," in 1880 he told an English audience that " the American has absorbed considerable quantities of closely kindred European blood, but . . . is rapidly assimilating it all, and in his political habits and

14 *A Century of Science*, p. 70; *The Unseen World*, p. 327.

15 *Essays, Historical and Literary* (2 vols., New York, 1902), I, 130, 174, 179, 310-11, 324; II, 158-9. Fiske opposed plutocracy and protectionism but he was equally against "the paternal, socialistic or nationalistic theory of government—it is the same old cloven hoof under whatever specious name you introduce it." *A Century of Science*, p. 219.

16 *Essays Historical and Literary*, II, 164, 173, 195.

17 *The Critical Period of American History, 1783-1789* (New York, 1916), pp. 101, 106.

aptitudes he remains as thoroughly English as his forefathers
. . . ." [18] Fiske seemingly had in mind the non-English elements
in the colonial population; particularly the Dutch, Huguenot,
Jewish, German, and Scotch-Irish groups whose role in the
early settlement of the country he was to describe later. Without challenging the political primacy of the Anglo-Saxon,[19] he
regarded these other elements as valuable additions. All but the
Jews were Protestants, and the Jews, too, had a long heritage
of suffering from persecution; there was a strong bond, therefore, between the Anglo-Saxon elements and these others—
Dutch, German, Huguenot, Scotch-Irish, and Jewish. Fugi-
tives from religious persecution were, in Fiske's opinion, more
desirable as immigrants than those who, like the redemptioners
and indented servants, came seeking economic gain.[20]

Spencer never defined precisely the degree of ethnic heterogeneity that, in his opinion, contributed to national well-being.
He merely stated on one occasion that in the United States the
eventual mixture of the various branches of the Aryan race
would produce "a finer type of man than has hitherto
existed." [21] Fiske not only believed that there was a point
beyond which the principle of heterogeneity when applied to
population produced undesirable results, but thought he knew
just where that point was.

In 1894, Fiske was elected President of the Immigration
Restriction League, an organization with headquarters in
Boston. The avowed aim of this organization was to curtail
the immigration from southern and eastern Europe, which,
after 1881, exceeded that from northern and western
Europe.[22] Fiske, in a defense of the League, did not deny that

18 *American Political Ideas*, p. 97.

19 Established in the first chapter of *The Beginning of New England*.

20 *The Dutch and Quaker Colonies in America* (2 vols., Boston, 1900), II,
330-56; *Old Virginia and Her Neighbours*, II, 186-8.

21 Cited in Richard Hofstadter, *Social Darwinism in American Thought,
1860-1915* (New York, 1943) p. 44.

22 Fisk, *Letters of John Fiske*, p. 635.

the United States had profited as a result of immigration, but he insisted that there was a point in national development when variety as a source of strength was counterbalanced by depreciation in the character of the individual immigrant. In language reminiscent of *Old Virginia and Her Neighbours,* Fiske asserted that " no ingenuity of constitution making can evolve good political results out of base human material." [23]

Fiske went on to say that the exclusion of undesirable immigrants was as much in the American tradition as the maintenance of a liberal immigration policy. He also contended that in the first half of the nineteenth century the effort required to cross the ocean was a selective factor which brought to this country only those who " were likely to surpass the average in strength and energy of character," whereas under contemporary conditions transportation no longer constituted this selective hazard.

Even the pre-Civil War immigration was not, according to Fiske, an unmixed blessing. He cited the opinion of Francis A. Walker [24] that the arrival of German and Irish immigrants

---

23 *Supra,* p. 36.

24 Francis Walker (1840-97) was of New England birth and ancestry. As chief of the Bureau of Statistics and as Superintendent of the tenth census Walker established a not inconsiderable reputation as an economist and statistician. He was professor of political economy and history in the Sheffield Scientific School of Yale (1873-81) and president of the Massachusetts Institute of Technology (1881-97).

Walker attributed mounting class antagonisms in the United States neither to the fuller settlement of the country nor to the large accumulation of capital. The introduction of vast numbers of persons "not born on our soil nor bred under our laws " was, in his opinion, entirely responsible for this development.

Labor unions, Walker said, were supported mainly by workers of foreign extraction who lacked the " desultory genius " of the native population, and the latter's impatience of restraint, and their progressiveness. " If," he went on, " the children and grandchildren of our population of thirty years ago were alone concerned, it would still be true that the working classes of this country had no occasion to ask favors in production and trade, or to ask to escape the utmost pressure of industrial competition." Davis Dewey, ed., *Discussions in Economics and Statistics by Francis A. Walker* (2 vols., New York, 1899), II, 307-9, 311, 326.

in the United States reduced the rate of increase of the native population and instead of bringing about a net gain in the population simply resulted in a replacement of native by foreign stocks.[25] Concerning the recent immigrants from southern and eastern Europe, the main target of the Immigration Restriction League, Fiske quoted Walker:

> They are beaten men from beaten races; representing the worst failures in the struggle for existence. Centuries are against them, as centuries were on the side of those who formerly came to us. They have none of the ideas and aptitudes which fit men to take up readily and easily the problem of self-care and self-government.

Fiske denied that the nation, because of humanitarian considerations, was obliged to take immigrants of this sort.[26]

Fiske's attitude toward the immigrants from southern and eastern Europe was determined largely by his Social Darwinist views and his pro-English feeling.[27] At ease in England, and to a lesser degree in Germany and Switzerland, he felt to judge from his letters, a sense of disquietude amid French and Italian scenes.[28] Although he included the Russians as members of the Aryan institutional family, holding that they maintained "an element of sound political life" in the village community or *mir,* he held that the way in which they were taxed was a feature which—even more than their imperfect system of property and their low grade of mental culture—separates them

25 While visiting Ireland in 1873, Fiske had observed that "the Paddy at home, if he is in a decent station in life, appears far better than his degenerate brother who comes to America. The Paddy at home has never learned to be democratic and sassy, i. e. he shows a reverence in his manners which greatly becomes him." Fisk, *Letters of John Fiske,* p. 228. On the other hand, commenting upon a group of German and Scandinavian immigrants whom he had met en route to Oregon, he found them "a very nice, cosy, well-behaved, respectable crowd." *Ibid.,* p. 537.

26 *Ibid.,* p. 670.

27 *Ibid.,* p. 310.

28 *Ibid.,* pp. 313, 320, 324.

by a world-wide interval from the New England township. . . ." [29]

Although Fiske, on occasion, wrote favorably of German achievement, when it came to a choice between that country and England there could be no doubt as to which he preferred. Fiske credited England and not Germany with the preservation of the local independence that was characteristic of the ancient Germans.[30] Moreover, he had many friends in English intellectual circles. It was Freeman who hailed Fiske's *Critical Period* as expressing fully the unity of the English race on both sides of the Atlantic,[31] and Fiske described Freeman as " our greatest master in history, almost the greatest that ever lived." [32] " We New Englanders," he wrote in 1900, a year before his death, " are the offsprings of Alfred's England." [33] Should there ever be a clash between England and Germany, Fiske felt that the United States would be drawn into the conflict on the side of England.[34]

It is difficult to determine the extent to which Fiske's attitudes towards peoples and nations were the result of intellectual conviction and in what measure they were the outgrowth of deep-seated feelings and preferences. Undoubtedly, one complemented the other. The intellectual process alone need not have led Fiske to the conclusion that American institutions

---

29 *American Political Ideas*, p. 44. That the Teutons in Gaul adopted the language and religion of their Romanized subjects, was, Fiske believed, largely responsible for the lack of success of the French in the colonization of the New World. *Ibid.*, p. 46.

30 *Beginnings of New England*, pp. 25-30.

31 Fisk, *op. cit.*, p. 568.

32 *Ibid.*, p. 592.

33 *Ibid.*, p. 689.

34 *Ibid.*, p. 706. John Fiske is seemingly regarded by Federal Union, I'nc. as a forerunner of the idea of unity within the scope of a federal system between the United States and England. A pamphlet publication of the organization entitled *It Must Be Done Again The Case for a World Federal Union* (New York, 1940), consists of verbatim excerpts from John Fiske's *Critical Period of American History*.

were English in origin. Indeed, the comparative method and even the Teutonic hypothesis served many masters; they were exploited on various occasions to prove that American institutions were derived from English, German, Dutch,[35] Scotch-Irish,[36] Hebrew [37] and Bohemian [38] sources, depending upon the author's feelings about the matter. Were Fiske's personal preferences different from what they were, by using the same methodology he could have justified his predilection for any one of a variety of peoples and nations. This is clearly demonstrated in the case of John W. Burgess who, although utilizing the comparative method and the Teutonic hypothesis, arrived at conclusions which were at variance with those advanced by Fiske.

JOHN W. BURGESS

Logically, the idea of the resemblance between American and Teutonic institutions could be expected to support the view that the ties between Germany and the United States should be strengthened. Actually, however, the theory of the Teutonic origin of American institutions reenforced, in the main, the essentially English orientation of those American historians who were its proponents.[39] The unity of Teutonic peoples was recognized to a lesser extent than that of the Anglo-Saxons; in much the same way as the basic resemblances among the

35 Irving Elting, "Dutch Village Communities on the Hudson River," *Johns Hopkins Studies*, fourth series, no. I; Douglas Campbell, *The Puritan in Holland, England and America* (2 vols., New York, 1892).

36 Charles Hanna, *The Scotch-Irish, or The Scot in North Britain, North Ireland, and North America* (2 vols., New York, 1902), Henry Ford, *The Scotch-Irish in America* (Princeton, 1915).

37 Oscar Straus, *The Origin of Republican Form of Government in the United States of America* (New York, 1885), pp. 109-111.

38 Robert Vickers, *History of Bohemia* (Chicago, 1894), mdcccxciv.

39 For a discussion of the rapprochement between England and the United States during the nineties, toward which the Teutonic hypothesis incidentally contributed, see B. A. Reuter, *Anglo-American Relations During the Spanish-American War* (New York, 1924), pp. 150-90.

Aryans were made secondary to those which existed among the Teutons. An important exception to the trend was the Germanist viewpoint of John W. Burgess.

Whereas Fiske stressed the ameliorative influence of centuries of English historical development upon the original Teutonic stock, particularly upon the section which was transplanted to America, Burgess was little impressed by these modifications. On the contrary, he considered the Teutonic character of English nationality as relatively imperfect, since it had suffered the French infusion that was the result of the Norman Conquest. It remained for the American wilderness to strip the " Norman-French " veneer from the seventeenth century English immigrant and bring " the German element in the English character again to the front." There was, said Burgess, more German than English blood in the American population at the beginning of the twentieth century, which in his opinion provided a basis for an understanding between Germany and the United States. " The German Nation," wrote Burgess, " stands closer, ethnically, than any other European Nation, to the American people." [40]

In 1908, Burgess urged a tripartite alliance among England, Germany, and the United States, with the eventual inclusion of the peoples of northern Europe, all of whom were destined to be allied with the Teutonic powers against the Romanic and Slavic " races." He pleaded that

> If Great Britain is our motherland, Germany . . . is the motherland of our motherland; and when the Americans consent to dwell under the same diplomatic roof with the mother

[40] " Germany, Great Britain and the United States," *Political Science Quarterly*, XIX (March 1904), 2; *Germany and the United States*; *An Address Delivered before the Germanistic Society of America, January 24, 1908* (New York, 1909), p. 8. Burgess insisted the immigrants from Norway, Sweden, and Holland were of German blood. On the other hand, having a low opinion of the political capacities of the Irish, he did not include them among the English. Consequently, his conclusion followed that the German element was numerically predominant in the United States.

who has chastised them, they are not going to allow the grandmother, who has always taken their part to be left out in the
cold.[41]

The inception of Burgess' pro-Germanic point of view can be
traced, in part, to his student days in Germany. An old man
writing his memoirs, Burgess remembered a sunny day in 1870
when the German armies, fresh from victory over France,
paraded their might in Berlin. At that time, Burgess and Elihu
Root were taking graduate work at Göttingen, but they ab-
sented themselves from classes to see the great show. Burgess
was fond of recalling the spectacle—the prancing horses,
polished helmets gleaming in the sun, row upon row of
Prussian soldiers. He once told the Kaiser how proud he had
been to witness the coming of age of the German nation.[42]

At the university, Burgess became acquainted with phases
of the ideology behind the bayonets which had prostrated
France. He discovered that this military achievement was to
some extent the fulfillment of the teachings of Kant, Humboldt,
Hegel, Treitschke, and Gneist. In the classroom of Professor
Droysen, he learned more specifically about the ideology of the
New Germany. The lesson was brought home to him in a
curious way. One day he made a casual remark to the effect
that it was a pity for the academic career of Droysen's son to
be interrupted by compulsory military service. The remark was
overheard by Droysen père, who made it the occasion for an
impromptu lecture concerning the nature and purpose of the
German army.

Droysen said that the German state, guardian of Teutonic
civilization, was constantly menaced by the Slavs in the East
and by the Latin races in the West and South, and was therefore compelled to remain in a state of defensive preparedness.
He denied emphatically that the army was designed for aggres-

---

41 "Germany, Great Britain and the United States," p. 14.

42 John Burgess, *Reminiscences of an American Scholar; the Beginnings of Columbia University* (New York, 1934), pp. 26-9, 96.

sion and declared that compulsory military training developed in the individual the salutary characteristics of courage, patriotism, and obedience. "Covered with confusion," Burgess neither resented nor forgot Droysen's words. He after recited the incident when explaining to American audiences the aims and character of the German army.[43]

While Droysen impressed him with the sanctity of Teutonic civilization and the importance of the incessant struggle that had to be waged for its preservation, it was Theodor Mommsen to whom Burgess looked for a plan for the furtherance of world peace. The racial factor was again in the foreground, since Mommsen's scheme rested on the assumption that the Teutonic character of the populations of Germany, England, and the United States made these nations essentially alike. Once the race consciousness of the German, English, and American peoples was stirred, predicted Mommsen, it would be a simple matter for these nations to unite for the preservation of peace and the advancement of civilization. He urged his young American student to "preach this doctrine far and near, wherever and whenever occasion will permit," that the ties of blood and race which bound England to the United States might be expanded to include the Teutonic motherland, Germany.[44]

Burgess returned to the United States in 1873—a firm believer in the mission of the Teutonic people. Although he later referred to himself as "an Anglo-American of the earliest stock and the most pronounced type," his educational experience made him far more conscious of the values of German than of English civilization.[45]

Burgess' progress in academic life was rapid; in 1880 he was asked by the trustees of Columbia University to formulate a

43 *Ibid.*, pp. 128-9.

44 *Ibid.*, p. 125; "Germany, Great Britain and the United States," p. 1.

45 Letter in the *Springfield Republican*, August 17, 1914.

plan for a separate faculty and school of political science. This he conceived of as a place for the training of the future rulers of the Republic. The study of political science would not only acquaint students with what he considered the finest flower of civilization, but would also instruct them in the domain of practical statecraft.[46] At Columbia, Theodore Roosevelt was one of Burgess' students.

In his classes, Burgess maintained that political forms were conditioned by ethnic factors. Borrowing heavily from his notes on the lectures of the German ethnological statistician, Johann Edward Wappäus,[47] he spoke of the nations of Europe as being derived from the Greek, Latin, Celtic, Teutonic, and Slavic races. The political psychology of the Greeks and Slavs, he said, caused them to conceive of the ideal state as something no greater than the smallest circle of political life, the community. A people so lacking in political genius could expect no better fate than to have their political institutions organized for them by a foreign power. The Czar, the church, the heartless tryranny of the Imperial regime were not unnatural to the Russian masses. Caesarism, concluded Burgess, must be the general system of Russian political organization so long as the political psychology of the Slav is what it is.

The Celts were relegated by Burgess to an even lower political plane. Personal attachment in small bodies to a chosen chieftain was the dominant Celtic political trait and, Burgess observed, the characteristic form of Celtic political organization was the petty military state constantly in the turmoil of civil

46 " Political Science and History," *Annual Report of the American Historical Association*, I (1896), 203-11. Burgess believed that what he described as the trend toward state socialism in the United States was induced by the " reduction in number of the lawyer class in our legislatures and administration." *Reminiscences*, p. 72.

47 *Ibid.*, pp. 101-3. Wappäus was the author of numerous statistical studies including, *Allgemeine Bevölkerungsstatistik* (2 vols., Leipzig, 1859-61).

war. Violence and corruption, springing from want of political genius, were to Celtic politics what law, order, and honesty were to the Anglo-Saxon.[48]

Burgess believed that every European state owed its organization to the Teutonic element in its population.

> The Visigoths in Spain, the Suevi in Portugal, the Lombards in Italy, the Franks in France and Belgium, the Anglo-Saxons and Normans in England, the Scandinavian Teutons in Denmark, Norway and Sweden, and the Germans in Germany, Holland, Switzerland and Austria have been the dominant elements in the creation of these modern states. . . . The United States also must be regarded as a Teutonic national state. In the light of history and of present fact, our proposition cannot be successfully disputed, that the significant production of the Teutonic political genius is the national state. . . . [49]

In the United States, " Teutonic individualism " and the " Aryan " principle of nationhood, Burgess insisted, demanded the preservation of the widest realm of activity for private enterprise. " American genius," derived from Teutonic sources, would not sanction a policy of government ownership of public utilities. On the contrary,

> the freedom of association, incorporate and unincorporate, must continue to exist under full constitutional guaranty, protected by the courts, of all those rights and immunities which are of a purely private character.[50]

Burgess feared that " the masses " might capture control of the government and utilize political power thus acquired for the distribution of the wealth of " the classes." Socialism he regarded as a greater menace to the Aryan tradition than the theory of states' rights. To forestall inroads made by this

48 *Political Science and Comparative Constitutional Law* (2 vols., Boston, 1891), I, 33.

49 *Ibid.*, p. 38.

50 " The Ideal of the American Commonwealth," *Political Science Quarterly*, X (September 1895), 413.

ideology, he urged admittance to membership in the American nation of only " such non-Aryan race-elements as shall have become Aryanized in spirit and in genius. . . ." The Teuton, said Burgess, could never regard the exercise of political power as a natural right of man; on the contrary, it was a right which must be based on political capacity, and of this capacity the Teutons themselves were the only qualified judges. " Aryan nationalities alone," wrote Burgess, " have created democratic states "; and again " no other peoples or population have ever given the slightest evidence of the ability to create democratic states."[51]

Although Burgess regarded the defense of liberty against the encroachments of government as the essence of constitutional law, he was no subscriber to the doctrine of the natural rights of man. In his view, the privileges and immunities guaranteed the individual under constitutional government were legal and historical rather than natural. Their preservation depended upon the maintenance of upper class and Teutonic dominance within the national state.[52]

In 1906-7, Burgess served as Roosevelt Professor of American History and Institutions at Friedrich-Wilhelm University in Berlin, the first exchange professor under a plan that envisioned closer intellectual relations between Germany and the United States. In his inaugural address, delivered before the royal family and a distinguished audience in the aula of Berlin University on October 27, 1906, Burgess congratulated the Hohenzollern dynasty for fulfilling the teachings of Kant, Humboldt, Hegel, Treitschke, and Gneist concerning the unification of Germany. He further asserted that " the best interests of the United States and of the world might be promoted by a

51 *Ibid.*, p. 407.

52 *Reminiscences*, pp. 250-1. Burgess realized that he was under attack by the adherents of the natural rights philosophy. His defense was that the basis of the state was the nation composed of like-minded people within a specific geographic area. The state, he said, created the government to carry out its ends, but the government was limited in its acts by the constitution, which defined a sphere of individual liberty.

large Teutonic immigration into South America, so that the
colonization of that gigantic continent through people capable
of a high culture would be assured . . . ." [53]

Burgess told his German audiences of the ethnic changes
taking place in the American population. Earlier immigrants,
representatives of the " Teutonic races "—Germans, Swedes,
Norwegians, Danes, Dutch, and English—Burgess described as
possessing both conscience and self-control and therefore prepared for the enjoyment of civil and political liberty.

> But now we are getting people of a very different sort—Slavs,
> Czechs, Hungarians. . . . They are inclined to anarchy and
> crime. . . . They are, in everything which goes to make up folk
> character, the exact opposite of genuine Americans. It remains
> to be seen whether Uncle Sam can digest and assimilate such
> a morsel.[54]

Immigrants from southern and eastern Europe, in Burgess'
opinion, had caused a strengthening of the police power of the
state " in order to protect our society against them." The police
had been used mainly to suppress strikes " carried on and supported chiefly by the new immigrants and those sympathizing
with them "; but, because the constitution guaranteed equal
protection of the laws to all persons, the yoke of police power
was now heavy upon the neck of Teuton and non-Teuton as
well.

Burgess was opposed to the Spanish-American War and regarded our entry into it as brought about by profiteers. Stories
of atrocities committed under Spanish rule in Cuba, Burgess

---

53 *Reminiscences*, p. 376.

54 *Uncle Sam! Address at Cologne, March 3, 1907.* Besides the altered
character of immigration, Burgess regarded the increased wealth and power
of corporations, the labor movement, and the government's new colonial
interests acquired as a result of the Spanish-American War as all contributing to an increase in the power of the government at the expense of
individual liberty. Though he viewed the expansion of corporate power as
an evil, Burgess made no concrete proposal for its control. *Reminiscences*,
p. 397.

insisted, were manufactured by the British for the express purpose of involving the United States in war with Spain. Germany, according to Burgess, was the only power interested in
keeping the peace in 1898, and her plans were frustrated by
British machinations.[55]

Burgess seems to have been reluctant to have the United
States become a world power, but once dependencies had been
acquired he was in favor of keeping them. The Teuton must ful-
fill his civilizing mission not only in the Philippines but in
China, where German and American influence was destined to
replace Russian and English.[56] Burgess, moreover, was not
content merely to theorize about colonial administration but
advised Sanford Dole, leader of the provisional government in
Hawaii after the deposition of Queen Liliuokalani, concerning
the political situation on the island. All political power,
counseled Burgess, should be concentrated in the hands of
Hawaii's 5,000 " Teutons," and " Teutons " alone should be
appointed to military office.[57]

In 1914, Burgess boasted of a ten-year acquaintance with the
Kaiser, for whom he had surpassing admiration. In 1908, he
referred to Theodore Roosevelt and the Kaiser as " the two
greatest men and statesmen among the rulers of the world." [58]
" I have never," he wrote, " acquired as much knowledge, in
the same time, from any man whom I have ever met, as from
the German Emperor." [59] He denied that the Kaiser wanted
war. In a letter to the *Springfield Republican,* he contended that
Germany was fighting for the protection of Teutonic civilization on continental Europe against " the oriental Slavic
quasi-civilization on the one side, and the decaying Latin

55 *Ibid.*, pp. 313-17 ; " Germany, Great Britain and the United States," p. 8.

56 " Germany and the United States," p. 24.

57 " Letters of Sanford B. Dole and John W. Burgess," *Pacific Historical
Review,* V (1936), 74.

58 " Germany and the United States," p. 5.

59 *New York Times,* October 17, 1914.

civilization on the other." [60] The British Empire, argued Burgess, had outlived its usefulness and historical necessity demanded its destruction.[61]

Thus the comparative method and the Teutonic hypothesis served as well to strengthen the pro-German bias of John W. Burgess as it did to strengthen the pro-English bias of John Fiske. In the case of Henry Cabot Lodge, however, adherence to the Teutonic hypothesis had a different result.

HENRY CABOT LODGE

Although the disciples of the Teutonic hypothesis differed among themselves as to how the institutional similarities revealed by the comparative method should be interpreted, they were generally agreed that the Germanic strain in English and American character was far superior to the Norman. That in 1066 the Norman French defeated the Saxon yeomen of England was something the Germanists would have liked to forget or, being unable to do so, to minimize. This was a curious reversal of an earlier tendency in New England thought, for it had once been the fashion to say that it was the Norse, or Norman, element that had made great nations of England and the United States, and to refer to the Anglo-Saxons as " a slow, sluggish and stupid race." [62]

Henry Cabot Lodge gave full credence to the Teutonic hypothesis, but his pride in his own antecedents, and his firm belief that ancestry determines character,[63] caused his evaluation

60 August 17, 1914.

61 *America's Relations to the Great War* (Chicago, 1916), pp. 164-5.

62 Oscar Falnes, " New England Interest in Scandinavian Culture and the Norsemen," *New England Quarterly*, X (June 1937), 216.

63 " The waves of democracy have submerged the old and narrow lines within which the few sat apart, and definition of a man's birth and ancestry has become more necessary. Moreover, Darwin and Galton have lived and written, Mendel has been discovered and revived, and the modern biologists have supervened, so that a man's origin has become a recognized part of his biographer's task." *Early Memories* (New York, 1913), p. 3. See also Lodge's memorial address in *Charles Francis Adams, 1835-1915, An Autobiography* (New York, 1916), xiii.

of the Norman's role in English and American development to differ from that of most Teutonists.

Lodge was born in Boston in 1850, the son of John Ellerton and Anna Sophia Cabot Lodge. His great grandfather, Giles Lodge, was, on one side, of Huguenot descent and, on the other, a member of the Ellerton family which had resided in England from the time of the Norman Conquest. Anna Sophia Cabot Lodge was a descendant of George Cabot, the ancestor Lodge himself most admired and whose biographer he became.[64] Lodge described the Cabots as being of " pure Norman extraction " and as accompanying William the Conqueror to England.[65] They were, he said, " of that Norman race which did so much for the making of England, and sprang from the Channel Islands which have been a part of the kingdom of Great Britain ever since William the Conqueror seized the English crown." [66] Influenced partly by loyalty to his Norman ancestors, partly by the ideas of Henry Adams, Lodge endeavored to rehabilitate the reputation of the Normans. On the authority of Carlyle, he denied that the Normans who invaded England were Frenchmen. They were, instead,

> Saxons who spoke French . . . the most remarkable of all people who poured out of the Germanic forests. . . . To them we owe the marvels of Gothic architecture, for it was they who were the great builders and architects of mediaeval Europe. They were great military engineers as well and revived the art of fortified defense. . . . They were great statesmen and great generals, and they had only been in Normandy about a hundred years when they crossed the English Channel, conquered

64 Karl Schriftgiesser, *The Gentleman from Massachusetts: Henry Cabot Lodge* (Boston, 1944), pp. 4, 12.

65 *Early Memories*, p. 8; *Life and Letters of George Cabot* (Boston, 1887), pp. 1, 2.

66 " Certain Accepted Heroes and Other Essays " in *Essays in Literature and Politics* (New York, 1897), p. 200.

the country, and gave to England for many generations to come her kings and nobles.[67]

Lodge's interpretation of English history differed from that which Fiske derived from Freeman in that it ascribed Germanic origin to the Norman invaders and gave them much of the credit for English achievement. While Fiske and Freeman viewed the Normans as a somewhat foreign element which was eventually assimilated to the Anglo-Saxon pattern, Lodge regarded the Saxon invasion as a continuing process, the eleventh century aspect of which was as important as the sixth. In an early essay which he wrote on Anglo-Saxon law, he accepted Freeman's theory that the Norman invasion introduced no revolutionary change in the existing legal pattern;[68] but whereas Freeman urged this theory in support of his belief in the vitality of Anglo-Saxon institutions before a foreign invader, Lodge welcomed it as proof of the racial similarity of Saxon and Norman.

Like Fiske and Herbert Baxter Adams, Lodge was convinced that the Puritan immigrants reproduced in the New World, " unconsciously, of course, but in all essential features the village community which the Saxons, Angles and Jutes had brought to England, more than a thousand years before from the forests of Germany." [69] He made a great point of the innate conservatism of the " English race." For example, he argued against the adoption of the initiative, referendum, and recall because they were, he said, opposed to the representative principle and therefore contrary to English racial experience.[70] The shades of his ancestors were ever present with Lodge the his-

67 *The Restriction of Immigration*, Speech of Hon. Henry Cabot Lodge of Massachusetts in the Senate of the United States, March 6, 1896, p. 8.

68 " The Anglo-Saxon Land Law," Henry Adams, ed., *Essays on Anglo-Saxon Law* (Boston, 1876), p. 119.

69 *A Short History of the English Colonies in America* (New York, 1881), p. 414; *A Frontier Town and Other Essays* (New York, 1906), pp. 23, 43.

70 *Ibid.*, pp. 44, 111.

torian, and his political sympathies were, in the Federalist tradition of his most illustrious forbear, George Cabot.

Prominent in the recollections of New Englanders of the generation of Henry Adams and Henry Cabot Lodge were such things as the snowball fights between Boston's north-enders and south-enders. Lodge wrote of how the tide of battle gradually began to turn against the Latin School boys, who were overwhelmed by their more numerous Irish opponents. The victories of the Irish in these street fights were signs of their growing numbers and increasing influence. In 1885, the commonwealth census figures showed that the children of Irish parentage in Boston far outnumbered the children of the natives; in that year, too, Boston had an Irish mayor and Massachusetts an Irish Republican governor.[71]

Alteration in the ethnic structure of the community was paralleled by the rapid progress of industrialism. A new industrial elite arose to challenge the position of the aristocratic New England families whose fortunes were merchant capitalist in origin. The price of a political career for Henry Cabot Lodge was, therefore, a two-fold compromise: with the industrial capitalists and with the rapidly growing Irish element. Henry Adams, who was Lodge's instructor at Harvard and who hoped to win him over to scholarship warned him that as a politician he would find it difficult to reconcile the various New England standards with each other:

> State Street and the banks exacted one stamp; the old Congregational clergy another; Harvard College, poor in votes, but rich in social influence, a third; the foreign element, especially the Irish, held aloof, and seldom consented to approve any one; the new socialist class, rapidly growing, promised to become more exclusive than the Irish.[72]

71 Wallace Stegner, "Who Persecutes Boston?" *Atlantic Monthly*, CLXXIV (July 1944), 47-8. The consolidation of the Irish community in Boston is described by Oscar Handlin, *Boston's Immigrants, 1790-1865* (Cambridge, 1941).

72 *The Education of Henry Adams, An Autobiography* (Boston, 1918), p. 419.

The transformation of New England had made of Henry Adams a pariah in his homeland; a relic of a bygone era who would not conform to the tempo of industrial America and for his stubbornness was doomed to wander the face of the globe. Journeys to the South Seas, Japan, Egypt, Russia, and Turkey; daydreams of the twelfth century and the never-ending pursuit of bric-a-brac; residence now in Washington, now in Paris, —these things seem to have served Henry Adams as a more or less satisfactory escape from the problem of adjustment to life in the twentieth century. They were apparently insufficient for Lodge. The Lodge family had a somewhat closer connection than had the Adams family with New England industrial development, and Lodge could make a better adjustment to counting room politics than his early mentor. Moreover, unlike Adams, Lodge did not have the handicap of feeling that he must carry on a family tradition of distinguished public service. Lodge could and did compromise; Adams merely stood abashed in the shadow of his ancestors.

Lodge's adjustment to these recent but dominant elements on the Massachusetts scene, was a compromise and nothing more. Despite legislative service rendered the New England industrialists, socially Lodge stood aloof from them.[73] He liked best the " essentially English " society into which he was born, the traditions of which extended " to the first white settlement and the days of Elizabeth and James." [74] It was with fondness

---

[73] It was with no little bitterness that he observed the "nouveau riche" replacing the old families as the dominant element in society. "To the modern and recent plutocrat," Lodge said, "the old American family meant nothing." He knew no history, had bad manners and cared little for the traditions of state and country. Lodge regarded the rapid expansion of fortunes as provoking "in some degree" the socialist movement. Yet, despite his denunciation of the "tyranny of money . . . [as] the coarsest and most vulgar tyranny "—his voting record did not reflect the misgivings that were confided to his memoirs. *Early Memories*, pp. 209, 211-2, 216-7; *A Frontier Town*, p. 26.

[74] *Early Memories*, p. 208.

that he recalled the Boston of his boyhood that " still had personality, lineaments which could be recognized, and had not yet lost its identity in the featureless, characterless masses inseparable from a great city." [75] Lodge, to his credit, was appreciative of the humanistic quality of Puritan tradition and critical of its more repressive aspects.[76]

Before the heterogeneous Massachusetts electorate, Lodge, said Adams, was never really at ease,

> whatever leg he stood on, but shifted, sometimes with painful strain of temper, from one sensitive muscle to another, uncertain whether to pose as an uncompromising Yankee; or a pure American; or a patriot in the still purer atmosphere of Irish, Germans, or Jews; or a scholar and historian of Harvard College. English to the last fibre of his thought—saturated with English literature, English tradition, English taste—revolted by every vice and most virtues of Frenchmen and Germans . . . Lodge's plumage was varied, and, like his flight, harked back to race. He betrayed the consciousness that he and his people had a past, if they dared but avow it, and might have a future if they could but divine it.[77]

The opinion of the Irish which Lodge expressed in his professional writings was markedly different from that expressed in his public speeches. In a *Short History of the English Colonies,* he wrote of them as

> a very undesirable addition at that period. Scarcely more than a third of the latter succeeded as farmers; and they were a hard-drinking, idle, quarrelsome, and disorderly class, always at odds with the government, and did much to give to govern-

75 *Ibid.,* p. 18.

76 The New Englander's pride of race, according to Lodge, served to retard the assimilation of immigrants in that area; the race prejudice and race pride of the Puritan were modified rather than lost in the stress of circumstances. In this " pride of race," Lodge thought, the good outweighed the evil. *Boston* (New York, 1891), pp. 203-5, 218.

77 *Education,* p. 420.

ment and to politics the character for weakness and turbulence, which, beginning before the Revolution, has broken out at intervals down to the present day.[78]

Statements of this sort evoked a stinging rebuke from the American Irish Historical Society, one of whose leading spirits assailed Lodge for his defective mental vision and amazing credulity. " He is so enwebbed in tradition and so steeped in myth and legend that this role of historian is a decided misfit." Lodge, apparently, was surpassed only by John W. Burgess in the ability to distort the Irish contribution to American nationality.[79]

Such criticism could not have meant much to Lodge in an academic sense. It could, however, easily have influenced the political attitude of a sensitive minority. At any rate, Lodge in his speeches on immigration restriction was careful not to offend that section of his constituency which was Irish. Addressing the House of Representatives, he maintained that the European nationalities which contributed most to the upbuilding of the thirteen colonies were the English, Scotch-Irish, Dutch, Germans, and Huguenot French and that was consistent with what he had written of these people in *The English Colonies*;[80] but he acknowledged the role of the Irish and Scandinavians in furnishing " the chief component parts of the immigration which has helped to populate so rapidly the territory of the United States." [81]

Speaking before the Senate approximately five years later, Lodge described the Irish as of different race stock than the

78 *English Colonies*, p. 228.

79 Joseph Smith, "American History as it is Falsified," *Journal of the American-Irish Historical Society*, I (1898), 86-88. Burgess was referred to as a " mental invalid " and " an hysterical Celtophobe." *Ibid.*, p. 86.

80 *English Colonies*, pp. 161, 220, 332, 407-9. *The Democracy of the Constitution and other Addresses and Essays* (New York, 1915), p. 168.

81 *Immigration*, Speech of Hon. Henry Cabot Lodge of Massachusetts in the House of Representatives, February 19, 1891 (Washington, 1891), p. 8.

English but as " closely associated with the English-speaking people " for nearly a thousand years. They speak the same language, and during that long period the two races have lived side by side, and to some extent intermarried." [82] On home territory, before the Boston City Club, Lodge was even more explicit in stating that his constant agitation for immigration restriction was in no way a reflection upon the Irish. Lodge now declared that the Irish immigration " presented no difficulties of assimilation, and they adopted and sustained our system of government as easily as the people of the earlier settlement." [83] But Lodge had previously asserted in his history of Boston that the Irish and German immigrants of the fifties did not readily assimilate because of unfamiliarity with American habits and ways of thought; that the presence of Irish and German immigrants was a factor contributory to the rise of professional politicians, ignorant and vicious voting, and the nexus of evils arising out of the taxation of the rich by the poor.[84] Lodge the politician must have made Lodge the historian squirm.

Lodge praised the French Canadians as " a strong and most valuable element," while the Italians were extolled as heirs of the civilization of ancient Rome and therefore akin to the peoples of western Europe. His German and Scandinavian constituency, Lodge could placate with less intellectual inconsistency. They and the English were of the same " race stock," and their common ancestors had roamed the forests of Germany and the Scandinavian peninsula.[85] As for the Dutch, the Swedes, and the Germans—here in the United States they blended again with the English-speaking people, who like them were

82 *The Restriction of Immigration,* March 16, 1896, p. 11.

83 *Speech on the Subject of Immigration* ... by Hon. Henry Cabot Lodge, before the Boston City Club, March 20, 1908, p. 3. Senate Doc. No. 423, 60th Congress, 1st Session.

84 *Boston,* pp. 198-9.

85 Speech before the Boston City Club, March 20, 1908, p. 4.

descended from the Germanic tribes whom Caesar fought and Tacitus described.[86]

Still, Lodge apparently did not believe that these related peoples were the equals of the " English race." This was the conclusion drawn in a study he made in 1891 of " The Distribution of Ability in the United States." In this study he analyzed the derivations of those persons who had been thought worthy of being included in *Appletons' Cyclopaedia of American Biography*. He found that the overwhelming majority of those selected were of English extraction.[87]

Lodge's study attracted wide attention and provoked much comment. Its message was simple and clear: the English had predominance in the upbuilding of the United States, and " if we add to the English the people who came from other parts of Great Britain and Ireland that predominance becomes overwhelming." [88] But the study contained errors which were soon detected.[89] In assigning each person listed in the *Cyclopedia* to one or another " race," Lodge sometimes took " the paternal line as the one to fix race origin." At other times, he accepted name and place of birth as determinants of " race," which they are not. Moreover, although Lodge claimed that the study would " throw a good deal of light on what we owe in the way of ability to each of the various races which settled in the

86 *The Restriction of Immigration*, March 16, 1896, p. 11.

87 *Historical and Political Essays* (Boston, 1892), pp. 138-68. This first appeared, in part, in the *Century Magazine*, new series, XX (September 1891), 687-94.

88 *Century Magazine*, p. 694.

89 One of the more important critiques was made some years later by Frederick Jackson Turner who challenged Lodge's conclusions concerning the West. " New England had been a going concern since 1620 or 1630, according to whether you are a Cape Codder or a Hub man, while the North Central States were chiefly a land of buffalo, deer, moose and Indians, who could hardly hope to be embalmed in Mr. Fiske's biographical dictionary for the whole period of colonial and revolutionary history, during which the Old Thirteen were furnishing names to the encyclopedia." " The Children of the Pioneers," *The Significance of Sections in American History* (New York, 1932), p. 256.

United States," his conclusions could hardly have been other
than what they were, considering the preponderance of the
English element in the total population. At the time *Appletons'
Cyclopaedia* was in preparation,[90] the mid-nineteenth century
immigration from northern and western Europe had not had
time to consolidate itself in the United States, while the " new
immigration " from the south and east of Europe had hardly
more than begun. Lodge probably realized the limitations inherent in his analysis, for in stating the results of the inquiry
he refrained from direct criticism of those nationalities whose
contribution was slight.

As the source of immigration shifted steadily eastward,
Lodge pressed more and more his contention that barriers
must be erected against the influx of what he described as
utterly alien " races." Arguing in favor of the restriction of
immigration before the United States Senate,[91] Lodge stated
that according to ethnical science there were no pure races.
Even the English were an artificial entity which, like the French
and Germans, had been developed into a " race " as a consequence of the " operation during a long period of time of
climatic influences, wars, migrations, conquests, and industrial
development." To the historian and statesman, argued Lodge,
the primary divisions of mankind were of relatively little importance,

> but the sharply marked race divisions which have been gradu-
> ally developed by the conditions and events of the last thousand
> years are absolutely vital. It is by these conditions and events
> that the races or nations which today govern the world have
> been produced, and it is their characteristics which it is im-
> portant for us to understand.[92]

90 The seven volumes were published between 1887 and 1900 and edited
by James Grant Wilson and John Fiske.

91 March 16, 1896.

92 *Ibid.*, p. 7.

Race, therefore, was a nexus of "the moral and intellectual characters, which in their association make the soul of a race, and which represent the product of all its past, the inheritance of all its ancestors, and the motive of all its conduct." Each "race," Lodge insisted, possessed an "indestructible, unconscious inheritance upon which argument has no effect." These factors were innate, irrational; were to be believed rather than argued; and remained to "guide us in our short-lived generation as they have guided the race itself across the centuries." [93]

On the authority of the French sociologist, Le Bon, Lodge asserted that the English, as a consequence of the mingling of ancient Briton, Saxon, and Norman, constituted a fixed, homogeneous "racial type." Should this superior race mingle with an inferior one, he said, the lower type would prevail. This thesis, derived from Le Bon, carried with it the implication that the civilization of the superior race would decline as the race itself lost ground.

And now Lodge ceased speaking in generalities and called upon the American people to assert its "race instinct" by curbing immigration, particularly that of the peoples from the South and East of Europe. "More precious even than form of government," Lodge warned the Senators, "are the mental and moral qualities which make what we call our race." And to drive the point home, Lodge told them that socialism in the United States was not so much a war of classes as it was a conflict of races.[94]

Travel in eastern Europe confirmed Lodge in the opinion that the people of that area were not the equals of, or were at least inherently different from, northern and western Europeans. He was willing to grant the economic capacity of the Poles and Jews, but these peoples lacked "the nobler abilities

93 *Ibid.*, p. 13.

94 *Ibid.*, p. 15. Lodge did not condone lynch law, but he believed that the existence of this evil was aggravated by unrestricted immigration. "Lynch Law and Unrestricted Immigration," *North American Review*, CDII (May 1891), 602-12.

which enable a people to rule and administer and to display that social efficiency in war, peace, and government without which all else is vain." The Russians, according to Lodge, shared with the people of the United States "no common ground, no common starting-place, no common premise of thought and action." [95] The immobility of the *moujik* when compared with the progressive spirit of the modern American, Lodge declared, had " its roots deep down in the nature of the race." [96]

Although he accepted the Teutonic hypothesis, Lodge did not, as did Fiske and Burgess, urge closer relations between the United States and either England or Germany. His " inborn Yankee disinclination towards Great Britain " was strengthened by British policy during the American Civil War.[97] In the nineties, when many American expansionists were upholding blood ties among the Teutonic powers as basis for an alliance, Lodge, although the exponent of an aggressive foreign policy, favored independence in its pursuit.[98] In this respect, as in a number of others, his viewpoint differed from those of Fiske and Burgess although all three employed identical methodology in so far as they made use of the comparative method and the Teutonic hypothesis.

It was not the comparative method and the Teutonic hypothesis alone, therefore, which was responsible for the attitudes of those who accepted it. Rather was that hypothesis a vehicle for the expression of a preconceived attitudinal pattern; a contributory rather than the total cause of each historian's bias. This conclusion is affirmed by an analysis of the attitudes toward peoples and nations of other historians, some of whom accepted and others who did not accept the Teutonic hypothesis.

95 " Some Impressions of Russia," *A Fighting Frigate and Other Essays and Addresses* (New York, 1907), pp. 261, 269.

96 *Ibid.*, p. 275.

97 Schriftgiesser, *op. cit.*, p. 23.

98 *Ibid.*, pp. 144-8; " Our Blundering Foreign Policy," *Forum*, XIX (March 1895), 817; *Early Memories*, pp. 148-50.

Albert Shaw, for example, traced the institutions of Illinois to a Teutonic original,[99] but nevertheless weighed the pros and cons of immigration restriction without reference to this theory of American historical evolution.[100] Sydney George Fisher, on the other hand, rejected the Teutonic hypothesis and the comparative method as specious arguments designed to sustain the predilection of a writer for some particular nation.[101] Concerning the composition of the American population, however, Fisher was more insistent upon the importance of homogeneity than was almost any of the Teutonists. It was his contention that "the most splendid achievements of the race in its New World environment" took place in the period preceding the American Civil War and in those communities where the population was most uniformly English. After that time, he said, degradation induced by immigration manifested itself in political and cultural decline.[102]

While acceptance of the comparative method and the Teutonic hypothesis has some bearing upon historians' attitudes towards peoples and nations, it is also clear that such attitudes are emergent from the conditioning of the individual. Fiske's New England background, Burgess' student days in Germany, Lodge's excessive pride in birth and ancestry were far more important in determining their attitudes toward immigrants

99 "Local Government in Illinois," *Johns Hopkins Studies*, first series, no. III, *passim*.

100 *Political Problems of American Development* (New York, 1907), pp. 62-86.

101 S. G. Fisher, *The Evolution of the Constitution of the United States* (Philadelphia, 1897), p. 340.

102 "Alien Degradation of American Character," *Forum*, XIV (January 1893), p. 614; "Has Immigration Increased Population?" *Popular Science Monthly*, XLVIII (December 1895), 244. Despite admiration of the homogeneous English stock, Fisher was distrustful of England, particularly her imperialist ambitions. Like Lodge, Fisher could not forget the American Revolution. *The American Revolution and the Boer War* (Philadelphia, 1902); *The True History of the American Revolution* (Philadelphia, 1902), p. 358.

than was their acceptance of the Teutonic hypothesis. The latter, after all, was but the rationalization of attitudes emergent from historians' backgrounds. It is the subjective experience of the individual historian which is of key significance and which is more difficult to trace. In the absence of intimate biographical data, it is almost impossible to describe the evolution of an attitudinal pattern in accordance with which Fiske, Burgess, and Lodge reacted to immigrants and of which the Teutonic hypothesis was merely an aspect.

Attitudes are sometimes more fully revealed in private letters than they are in articles, speeches, and histories. This is true of Fiske, if not of Lodge—the latter having been careful to edit his correspondence before its publication. In the case of Henry Adams, there exists a plenitude of letters. The extent to which they reveal the motivation of his attitudes, remains to be seen.

CHAPTER III

HENRY ADAMS' NORMAN ANCESTORS

REVIEWING Freeman's *Historial Essays* in 1872, Henry Adams complained that despite the author's labors, " the history of the Norman Conquest and an accurate statement of Anglo-Saxon institutions still remain as far from realization as ever . . . . " [1] Adams did not accept entirely Sir Francis Palgrave's Romanist view of English history, but he was sufficiently influenced by it to deplore Freeman's exclusively Germanic emphasis.[2] As Professor of Medieval History at Harvard, Henry Adams, unlike Herbert Baxter Adams, was not interested exclusively in Germanic origins but rather in " fixing the share " of Germanic influences in forming the Common Law.[3] The *Essays in Anglo-Saxon Law* that he and his students prepared,[4] considered Norman as well as Anglo-Saxon contributions to the English legal and political systems.

As a student, Adams had flung himself " obediently into the arms of the Anglo-Saxons in history." But the embrace was not lasting. Spending the summer of 1895 in Normandy with the Lodges visiting Caen, Coutances, and Mont-Saint-Michel, he came into first-hand contact with Norman civilization and in so doing arrived at " a new sense of history." [5] The Normandy experience served to crystallize feelings that he had long had, for " he had preached the Norse doctrine all his life against the stupid and beer-swilling Saxon boors whom Freeman loved, and who, to the despair of science, produced Shakespeare." [6]

1 *North American Review*, CXIV (January 1872), 195.

2 Worthington Ford, ed., *Letters of Henry Adams, 1858-1918* (2 vols., Boston, 1930-8), II, 134.

3 *Ibid.*, I, 265.

4 Besides an introductory essay by Adams this volume contained the doctoral dissertations of Lodge, Ernest Young, and James Laurence Laughlin.

5 *Education of Henry Adams*, p. 355.

6 *Ibid.*, 412.

Apart from the technicalities of the controversy with Freeman—technicalities that can best be followed by reading the
articles in the *North American Review,* in which Adams and
Lodge reviewed the volumes of the Germanists, Adams seemed
to take the matter rather personally.[7] Not only did Freeman's
company annoy him (as well it might),[8] but he took a bit of
malicious delight in the observation that Freeman's major
work was "far from attaining its aim so completely" as the
author's *Early English History for Children;*[9] that Freeman,
unlike most historians, was seemingly unappalled "at the difficulties of inspiring enthusiasm for the English of the eleventh

7 Stubb's *Constitutional History of England,* was reviewed in the *North
American Review,* CXIX (July 1874), 235-8; Henry Maine, *Lecture on the
Early History of Institutions, ibid.,* CXXI (April 1875), 435-7; Kenelm
Digby, *An Introduction to the History of Real Property, ibid.,* CXX
(October 1875), 430-3.

8 For Adams' personal reaction to Freeman, *Letters,* I, 220, 236, 257, 261,
288, 334. Mrs. Henry Adams tells an amusing anecdote of a dinner party at
which she, Henry Adams, and Mr. and Mrs. Freeman were present. "Ye
Gods, what a feast it was! No stylographic could narrate it. Let us draw
a veil over nine-tenths of it... On we went. The canvasbacks entered.
Three of them—fresh and fair, done to a turn; and weltering in their gore.
Says Mrs. Bancroft, with a growing hauteur of manner as of a turning
worm, 'Do you appreciate our canvasbacks, Mr. Freeman?' 'I cannot eat
raw meat,' he said angrily, while a convulsive shudder shook his frame.
Then the *picador,* which is latent in me when nature is outraged, rose in me,
and I said to him, all unconscious of his theories and the scheme of all
his writing, 'I wonder that you do not like rare meat. Your *ancestors,* the
Pict and Scots, ate their meat raw, and tore it with their fingers." At which
he roared out, 'O-o-o-o! Whur did yer git that?' Unheeding, careless
of consequences, I said, 'Well, your Anglo-Saxon ancestors, if you prefer.'
He thereupon pawed the air and frothed at the mouth.
"... Never having read one line of Freeman, I did not know until the next
day the exquisite point of my historical allusions. As I casually repeated
them, Henry became purple in the face and rolled off his chair, and he,
the husband of my bosom, who is wont to yawn affectionately at my yarns,
he at intervals of two hours says, 'Tell me again what you said to Freeman
about the Picts and Scots and Anglo-Saxons.'"
Ward Thoron, ed., *The Letters of Mrs. Henry Adams, 1865-1883* (Boston,
1936), pp. 331-2.

9 *North American Review,* CXVIII (January 1874), 176.

century, probably the only pure German race which was ever conquered twice in half a century and held permanently in subjection by races inferior to itself in wealth and power." [10]

But there was more to the controversy with Freeman than a mere academic dispute or a clash of personalities. Adams could justifiably assail Freeman for his Anglo-Saxon bias; but his own admiration for the Norman was no less extreme and of all the more importance because it constituted an important aspect of his social adjustment.

Adams felt that in large measure his estrangement from twentieth century civilization was due to his being at heart an eleventh century Norman whose "retarded development" rendered him incapable of finding a place in the world.[11] Yet, though mindful of the handicap imposed by ancestry upon career making, Adams would scarcely have traded his Norman ancestors for success in the world in which he lived. Norman ancestry, Adams maintained, enabled one to appreciate Norman architecture far more than the average tourist. But beyond this, he was happy in the thought that in the eleventh and twelfth centuries, the Normans " stood more fully in the centre of the world's movement than our English descendants ever did; " that the Normans of that day were " a serious race " which was " everywhere in the lead of their age." [12]

In a letter to his brother, Brooks, Adams penned what amounts to an epitaph upon Norman achievement. The contemporary Norman, Henry explained, could never equal the artistic accomplishment of his eleventh century predecessors. Since then,

> our ancestors have steadily declined and run down until we have reached pretty near the bottom. They have played their little part according to the schedule. They have lost their religion, their art and their military tastes. They cannot now

10 *Ibid.*, p. 177; CXIV (January 1872), 193.

11 *Letters*, II, 79.

12 *Mont-Saint-Michel and Chartres* (Boston, 1905), p. 4.

comprehend the meaning of what they did at Mont. St. Michel. They have kept only the qualities which were most useful, with a dull instinct recalling dead associations. So we get Boston.[13]

Neither Boston nor any other phase of the mechanical and commercial civilization of the late nineteenth century was to Henry Adams' liking. Consequently, it is not surprising to discover him turning from the chaos and turmoil about him, and seeking solace in the medieval world of his Norman ancestors. The eleventh and twelfth century Normans were declared by Adams to be "imaginative" and "artistic" types par excellence. Among them he sought the understanding denied him by the "economic" type of his own day. The Virgin, symbol of the unity and endeavor of the twelfth century, had no more ardent admirer than Adams.

The concept of the medieval synthesis that is the essence of *Mont-Saint-Michel and Chartres* betrayed this element of incongruity. Adams is aware that Jews formed no part of the unified whole that was Christian and Norman civilization in the eleventh and twelfth century; they are referred to throughout the volume as elements of unbelonging and discord.[14] Norman architecture seemed to Adams to deny Jewish influence and thereby gain in dignity. The "quiet strength of these curved lines, the solid support of these heavy columns, the moderate proportions, even the modified lights, the absence of display, of effort, of self consciousness" contrasted with the Gothic arch which Adams deemed an unhappy illusion: restless, grasping, speculative, exploiting the world, "the legitimate child of the Jews." [15]

The Virgin, according to Adams, shared in the general feeling of antipathy toward the Jew. The Heavenly Queen of the twelfth century like other queens, "had many of the failings

13 *Letters*, II, 80.

14 *Mont-Saint-Michel*, pp. 99, 173, 253.

15 *Letters*, II, 80.

and prejudices of her humanity. In spite of her own origin, she disliked Jews, and rarely neglected a chance to maltreat them." The Virgin, in this view, was beloved of the common people; her enemies were the bankers and money lenders who, Adams sadly related, eventually dethroned her.[16]

No one with Adams' power and desire to merge himself with this age long dead—he wrote of the twelfth century as if he were a sentient stone in a Romanesque cathedral—could possibly manage the transition to the twentieth century without a deep longing to preserve intact his conception of the earlier period. Again, as an external, disturbing element, the Jew interfered with the preservation of the medieval image. Adams rejoiced that the world had not discovered the beauty of the windows of the Cathedral at Chartres; that in the twentieth century one had the "legendary chaos" of the stained glass windows of the twelfth "to one's self without much fear of being trampled upon by the critics or Jew dealers in works of art." [17] Adams would have the dramatic character of the Virgin's miracles remain unexploited—"one does not care to see one's Virgin put to money-making for Jew theatre-managers. One's . . . ancestors shrink." [18]

Adams believed that the human mind had reached its peak development in the artistic and imaginative creations of the twelfth century. He was, in consequence, no admirer of the economic type which, in accordance with his scheme of historical evolution, was destined to and actually did replace the far more agreeable types of the twelfth century.[19] Adams thought of the Jew as the embodiment of the economic type—as, therefore, not only external to the medieval synthesis but also antagonistic to it. For this reason, Adams scorned Jewish taste

16 *Mont-Saint-Michel*, pp. 263, 275.

17 *Ibid.*, p. 179.

18 *Ibid.*, p. 279.

19 Henry Adams, *The Degradation of the Democratic Dogma* (New York, 1919), pp. 229, 231.

in art and literature as defiling the artistic achievement of a people whose mind-set was entirely different.

The Jew, in Adams' opinion, was an exploiter and not a creator of art. He cornered the bric-a-brac market and forced prices up. " Anything these Jews touch," wrote Adams, the outraged collector, " is in some strange way vulgarized. One does not want it any more. It has become a trade—the equivalent of a certificate for South American stock—and one buys to sell again." [20] Bad taste in furniture, painting, and interior decoration Adams branded as " typically Jew." [21] Adams evaluated Valois art as a " Jewish kind of gold-bug style, fit to express Francis I and Henry VIII, with their Field of Cloth of Gold and their sensual appetites." [22] In 1875 Adams told Lodge of his fear that the *North American Review* would " die on my hands or go to some Jew." [23]

The panic of 1893 affected several members of the Adams family, although Henry Adams himself suffered no severe losses. In Quincy, site of the Adams ancestral home, where Henry had come to console Brooks Adams for the economic reverses the latter had experienced, on many garden walks the two brothers discussed at length the panic and its causes.[24] Brooks later recalled the hot August evenings of 1893 and the endless talk

> of the panic and of our hopes and fears, and of my historical and economic theories, and so the season wore away amidst an excitement verging on revolution. Henry, of course, was much less keenly personally interested than I but as he very frankly says in his " Education," his instincts led toward silver. My historical studies led the same way, as well as my private situation, as one of the debtor class.[25]

20 *Letters*, II, 233.

21 *Ibid.*, pp. 480-1, 568.

22 *Ibid.*, p. 81.

23 *Letters*, I, 267.

24 *Degradation of the Democratic Dogma*, p. 90.

25 *Ibid.*, p. 94.

Finally, Brooks had Henry read the incomplete manuscript of *The Law of Civilization and Decay* which was, in part, a dissertation on the influence of currency upon history, and in which it was maintained that the course of events since the Crusades and long before led in direct sequence to the present crisis. Henry loved the book, called it his "Bible of Anarchy"[26] and took comfort in its prophecy of civilization's chaos and decline and in the explanation it offered of Brooks' and his own maladjustment to society.[27]

From Brooks' manuscript, Henry learned of the role of money as an instrument of exploitation and domination under the Roman Empire; of its agency in the overthrow of the imaginative types of the Middle Ages and its effect upon the modern world; of the rise of London as the financial center of the world with the bank of England and the gold standard as instruments of subjugation and oppression. He discovered, too, how " productive " industrial capitalism had been superseded by " parasitic " finance capitalism. The latter represented for Henry that height of centralization which he associated with the last days of the Roman Empire when the imperial and bureaucratic centralization of ancient times collapsed and paved the way for an era of diffusion and localism that culminated in the civilization of Henry's beloved twelfth century.

Henry Adams prophesied that in his lifetime, or not long after it, there would be a collapse of civilization comparable to that which occurred when the people of Rome became the slaves of the usurers, when the sterile ruling class rotted and the barbarians tore the Empire asunder. A devout reader of the

26 *Letters*, II, 83.

27 *Degradation of the Democratic Dogma*, p. 93. Brooks said to Henry: " Here have I for years, been preparing a book to show how strong hereditary personal characteristics are, while the world changes fast, and that a type must rise or fall according as it is adjusted to its environment. It is seldom that a single family can stay adjusted through three generations. That is a demonstrable fact. It is now full four generations since John Adams wrote the constitution of Massachusetts. It is time that we perished. The world is tired of us."

" Bible of Anarchy" could come to no other conclusion than that the course of society was an immutable cycle beginning with barbarism and diffusion, terminating in civilization and concentration, and then reverting to its original state. This was the law of civilization and decay.

In " A Letter to American Teachers of History " written in 1910, Henry Adams endeavored to prove that the theory of the sociological degradation of energies was a reflection of physics' immutable laws. The universe, in his opinion, had entered upon a downward cycle. By the second decade of the twentieth century when, Adams predicted, thought would reach the limit of its possibilities,[28] the planet would be well on its way to becoming a place in which all nature's energies would vanish in space after being converted to heat—" until, at the last, nothing would be left except a dead ocean of energy at its lowest possible level." [29] In such an ocean, Brooks observed, "tempests are generated by the operations of usurers . . . . " [30]

The crisis Brooks Adams predicted in *The Law of Civilization and Decay,* Henry Adams thought to be at hand during the gold-silver controversy in 1896. He likened the situation in the United States to that in ancient Rome at the time of the Gracchi, when a money-lending and a money-borrowing class were pitted against each other.[31] He was further struck by the "astonishing parity" between the Elder Pliny and Brooks Adams as prophets of a faltering civilization.[32] Pullman, Carnegie, and Cleveland he likened to Crassus, Pompey, and Caesar; he called them the American triumvirate.[33] Yet Henry Adams was unwilling to join the populist and labor forces in opposition to McKinley.

28 *Ibid.,* p. 114.
29 *Ibid.,* p. 145.
30 *Ibid.,* p. 116.
31 *Letters,* II, 67.
32 *Ibid.,* p. 83.
33 *Ibid.,* p. 53.

Rather was he conscious of the position of his class as a holdover from the Victorian era, about to be crushed between the rival juggernauts of capital and labor. Opposed to McKinley, he was by no means sympathetic toward Debs and organized labor.[34] Partial to neither of the major contending elements, his contribution to the fray was a twisted, nihilistic thing sent down from Olympian Heights above the grand mêlée. He actually hoped that the triumph of the gold standard in 1896 would speed the collapse of civilization he so eagerly anticipated.[35] " I'm for Morgan, McKinley and the Trusts," he wrote. " They will bring us to ruin quicker than we could do it ourselves." [36] Such were the fruits of Adams' idea of politics, the intention of which was " to hasten rather than retard results." Silver, he said, was in the interests of the finance

34 *Ibid.*, pp. 53, 402, 586. Between rule by the capitalist and rule by the trade unionists, Adams definitely preferred the former. (*Ibid.*, p. 402) " Much as I loathe the regime of Manchester and Lombard Street in the nineteenth century," Henry Adams wrote Brooks, " I am glad to think I shall be dead before I am ruled by the Trades Unions of the twentieth." (*Ibid.*, II, 184, note 3).

35 *Ibid.*, pp. 95, 107, 114.

36 *Ibid.*, p. 97. There is a contradiction in Adams' attitude toward silver. He once confessed to Brooks that " as a man of sense I am a gold bug and support a gold bug government, and a gold bug society. As a man of the world, I like confusion, anarchy and war." (*Ibid.*, p. 69) While his personal economic interests were linked to a triumph of gold, he was convinced that silver alone could save the world from serious financial crisis. (*Ibid.*, p. 88). His position was that of a gold bug by economic interest, a silverite by conviction, while as a consequence of a predisposition toward anarchy he longed for a cataclysm and nourished the hope that the politicians would reject silver. (*Ibid.*, p. 88.) The result was that in July 1896 he hoped for the election of McKinley but did everything he possibly could to aid Bryan. (*Ibid.*, p. 109.)

At the start of his career, Adams was not a soft money man. He favored the resumption of specie payment during the seventies, and attributed the manipulation of Fisk and Gould in the gold market to the unsound monetary policies that grew out of greenback financing during the American Civil War. " The Legal-Tender Act," in collaboration with Francis A. Walker, Henry Adams, *Historical Essays* (New York, 1891), pp. 279, 306-9; *ibid.*, " The New York Gold Conspiracy," p. 364. In this last essay he refers to the Jewish ancestry of Jay Gould, p. 324.

capitalists " and would prolong indefinitely the money-lender's reign, whereas gold is fatal to it." [37]

Adams was far more favorably disposed toward industrial than toward finance capitalism; the latter he closely identified with the Jews. McKinley he regarded as the servant of " industrial capital rather than the Jews," and he thought the distinction did McKinley credit. Granting that McKinley could have been brought to the point of serving capital in any form, " consciously or unconsciously, if the times with us reached that stage; to murder him was a gross absurdity that makes me despair of anarchy. The true person to kill was Hanna,—the senator. . . ." [38]

According to Adams, the long arm of Jewish finance, so potent in the affairs of Europe,[39] was not without influence in America. In 1896, he charged that Jewish bankers had conspired to prevent the free coinage of silver by threatening to withdraw 600 to 1,000 million pounds lent to America on call. " We are in the hands of the Jews," Adams lamented. " They can do what they please with our values." He advised against investment except in the form of gold locked in a safe deposit box. " There you have no risk but the burglar. In any other form you have the burglar, the Jew, the Czar, the socialist, and, above all, the total irremediable, radical rottenness of our whole social, industrial, financial and political system." [40]

While Lombard Street Jewry ruled England and extended its influence to America, the Jews, Adams insisted, were equally in control of affairs in Berlin and Paris.[41] Particularly in the field of foreign policy did he find their influence baneful. Adams, who feared the latent possibilities of the huge mass that was Russia, insisted in 1895 that the " Jew business " of money-

37 *Letters*, II, 53.

38 *Ibid.*, p. 356.

39 *Ibid.*, pp. 422, 425, 587.

40 *Ibid.*, p. 111.

41 *Ibid.*, pp. 72, 253.

lending was not conducive to a vigorous British and American foreign policy against the Russian menace.[42]

The same fear of Russia is reflected in his proposed "Atlantic system" of nations. Adams, in 1903, hoped for a combination among nations that would result in an equilibrium based on an "intelligent allotment of activities."[43] This combination was to consist of the nations included in the area extending from the Rocky Mountains in the West to the Elbe on the East.[44] Sweden, Norway, and Great Britain belonged to the Atlantic system and not to eastern Europe—on the ground that the Baltic separates while the Atlantic unites, and also on the ground that in the very beginning of history Europe was cut in half at the Vistula. Sentimental reasons, too, impelled Adams to include the Scandinavian peoples within the Atlantic system; on a visit to Norway he recalled that " our respective ancestors came from hereabouts."[45] Moreover, he admired the Scandinavians, regarding them as among the most energetic of peoples.

Because of Russia's sheer bulk, Adams believed that Germany was irresistibly attracted to it; and the two together must have constituted in his mind a threat to the "Atlantic system." He was also uneasy lest France, lured by the bait of a *rapproachement* with Germany, fall within the magnetic attraction of the Russian mass.

The more Adams thought about Russia, the more the problem of the tremendous inertia of the Russian people perplexed him. Europe, he finally concluded, had never changed.

> The imaginary line that crossed the level continent from the Baltic to the Black Sea, merely extended the northern barrier-line. The Hungarians and Poles on one side still struggled

42 *Ibid.*, p. 72.

43 *Education*, p. 503.

44 *Letters*, II, 448.

45 *Ibid.*, p. 352. Adams included the Russians among the least energetic peoples of the world. *Ibid.*, p. 358.

against the Russian inertia of race, and retained their own
energies under the same conditions that caused inertia across
the frontier. Race ruled the conditions; conditions hardly
affected race; and yet no one could tell the patient tourist
what race was, or how it should be known.

Adams was wisely unwilling to add his guess as to the nature of
the racial factor.[46]

Wishing to detach France from eastern Europe, Adams
considered himself thwarted in this endeavour by Jews and
bankers. He complained of a conspiracy in the *haute banque,*
to excite and maintain enmity between England and France so
that the latter might be diverted from the desire for revenge
upon Germany. "At one time I thought Russia was doing it.
Now I am inclined to think it is Berlin, and that the Jew bankers
are helping the Kaiser to bring it about." [47]

Adams cherished the thought that, in his losing fight against
the Jewish influence, he held one trump card. He was convinced
that civilization hovered upon the brink of disaster—that the
victories of the Jews were Pyrrhic, destined to impel the world
toward its fated end. Still, the tenacity of the Jews in defiance
of his calculations amazed him. That the catastrophe did not
occur in 1896, he ascribed to the Jews having kept up the stock
market and having carried the bankrupt governments rather
than face a general panic.[48] In August of that year he again
predicted a general collapse, stating that it was bound to occur
within five years.[49] In 1898 he declared that France was in the

46 " History offered a feeble and delusive smile at the sound of the word
[race] ; evolutionists and ethnologists disputed its very existence; no one
knew what to make of it; yet, without the clue, history was a fairy tale."
Education, pp. 411-12. Adams avoided a racial interpretation of American
character in his analysis of American nationality. *History of the United
States of America* (9 vols., New York, 1889), I, p. 42.

47 *Letters,* II, 297-8.

48 *Ibid.,* p. 107.

49 *Ibid.,* p. 111.

grip of the Jews and debt, and was on its way to ruin along with the rest of Europe.[50]

In November, 1899, however, Adams was in a more optimistic mood. He had read a book by the Marxist revisionist, Edouard Bernstein, "a Jew like the rest, and a German Jew at that." Adams noted with some satisfaction Bernstein's conclusion that the socialists would become integrated into the structure of capitalism. Now he believed "anarchy" to be a long way off. Nevertheless, he noted the "frightening conditions" under which the markets of Europe maintained their steadiness.[51] Two months later, with British defeats in the Boer War reported in the press, Adams again viewed Europe as trembling on the verge of disaster. "For seven years," he wrote, "I have been preaching, like John the Baptist, the downfall of the Jews, and have figured it up in parallel columns...."[52] But certain as he was of collapse at this time, the course of events again eluded his calculations.

Though he repeatedly declared that the breakdown of civilization was imminent, Adams rarely paused to speculate as to the type of society that would succeed the civilization he loathed. At times he predicted "anarchy"; at other times "communism."[53] But the question interested him little. It was the chaotic and destructive aspects of a disintegrating society that fascinated him. In 1870 young Henry Adams had written a powerful indictment of the machinations of the financiers, Fisk and Gould, and had warned the country that those who wielded vast economic power were bound to seize political control. He had urged that the democratic sinews be strengthened so that

50 *Ibid.*, p. 200.

51 *Ibid.*, p. 248.

52 *Ibid.*, p. 258.

53 "With communism I would exist tolerably well, for the commune is rather favorable to social consideration apart from wealth; but in a society of Jews and brokers, a world made up of maniacs wild for gold, I have no place." *Ibid.*, p. 33. At this time he confessed the wish to see all of society destroyed.

the people could curb the menace represented by the concentration of wealth.[54] In later life, Adams was less prone to appeal to constructive action by democratic means against the usurpers.[55] Now he called upon the god of chaos to smash the entirety of civilization. Never a great democrat, he was, perhaps, by this time convinced that democracy was a failure; but it may well have been that the standards he originally established for its success were too high.[56]

For all that he professed not to care what was happening in the world, that he branded himself and his class as " extinct " and " not worth saving," [57] that he referred to himself as a " dead man " indulging in a few narrow prejudices [58]—for all this, Adams was greatly aroused by the Dreyfus case. Until Dreyfus was proved innocent beyond the shadow of a doubt, Adams stood by his Norman ancestors as a staunch defender of traditional France. He complained that the " beastly Reformation," besides taking all the fun out of society,[59] had replaced the military by the industrial impulse.[60] The Dreyfus case he interpreted as being another challenge to the position of the military. Consequently, Adams was pleased with " how emphatically the army, through the court-martial, set its foot on the Jews and smashed the Dreyfus intrigue into a pancake.[61]

54 *Historical Essays*, p. 365.

55 Adams thought little of Roosevelt's attack upon the trusts. *Education*, p. 501; *Letters*, II, 590.

56 " Could it transmute its social power into the higher forms of thought? . . . Could it give new life to religion and art? Could it create and maintain in the mass of mankind those habits of mind which hitherto belonged to men of science alone? Could it physically develop the convolutions of the human brain? Could it produce, or was it compatible with the differentiation of a higher variety of the human race? Nothing less than this was necessary for its complete success." *History of the United States*, I, 184.

57 *Letters*, II, 402.

58 *Education*, p. 330.

59 *Letters*, II, 130.

60 *Ibid.*, p. 136.

61 *Ibid.*, p. 144.

Adams had strong personal feelings about the prestige of the military and explained his position as an anti-Dreyfusard by saying that he had " but one rule, which is to back the Army and Navy against everything everywhere on every occasion. . . . When the army makes a mistake and shoots the wrong man, I am sorry, and would do all I could to redress the injustice; but the Army and the Navy have saved me and mine so many times that I'm not going back on it whatever it does. . . . . "[62] When at last convinced of the innocence of Dreyfus, Adams was very eager to exonerate the army from the charge of having conspired to imprison an innocent man. A " reasonable error " rather than a " conspiracy " on the part of the general staff was, in Adams' opinion, the root of the trouble.[63]

The question of Dreyfus' guilt or innocence, however, was subordinate, in Adams' mind, to the larger issue involved, the destiny of France.[64] It was not Dreyfus who was on trial but France, its army and people.[65] The Dreyfus case was to Adams symptomatic of collapsing western civilization;—Dreyfus could not be acquitted without France being condemned, and this would bring about a debacle worse than Sedan. Adams feared that France would be reduced to a dependency of central Europe and as an ally of Germany and Russia would oppose the aims of the United States, particularly in Asia and the Pacific.[66] The Dreyfus affair was

> a blow at the Republic and at France and at society itself that seems to me fatal. I can see now nothing ahead but sooner or later the socialist experiment. Sedan was merely a military defeat like many; but the Dreyfus affair is a moral collapse

62 *Ibid.*, p. 240. Although Adams evinced considerable admiration for the military spirit, *ibid.*, p. 92, he nevertheless admitted that " no one really likes being potted by machine-guns a mile off and invisible." *Ibid.*, p. 255.

63 *Ibid.*, p. 241.

64 *Ibid.*, pp. 144-5.

65 *Ibid.*, pp. 239.

66 *Ibid.*, p. 234.

that involves soldiers and civilians alike, and the capacity of
the French to maintain a character of any sort in a world like
Europe. The socialists alone profit by it, and what a socialist
France would be, is a grave question for America.[67]

Adams was of the opinion that " the campaign which the
Jews have made for him [Dreyfus] " served to stimulate anti-
Semitism, the current of which was particularly strong

> now that the whole extent of the Jew scandal is realised. For
> no one doubts that the whole campaign has been one of money
> and intrigue; and that the French are very furious. Of course,
> all the English and Americans are with the Jews, which makes
> it worse . . .

How strongly Adams felt about this matter is indicated more
than once. He writes of a stroll he took down the Boulevard
after dark: " There was an ominous hum in the air that made
me look about me; for, if anybody was going to visit Alphonse
Rothschild, I've a sort of notion I'd like to go too." [68] In
September, 1893 he wrote, " in the coming rows, you will
know where to find me. Probably I shall be helping the London
mob to pull up Harcourt and Rothschild on a lamppost in
Piccadilly.[69]

Zola's *J'Accuse* was published in *L'Aurore* on January 13,
1898 and Adams was delighted with the furor it aroused. " But
Zola howled; and the Bourse actually fought—Jews and Gen-
tiles—till the police came in. A good day's work! and rioting
too in Havana! and a new outbreak in India! *Tiens! ca marche.*
One can't imagine larks like this every day, to be sure; . . " [70]

A month after Zola's letter appeared, Adams said that the
writer deserved being jailed if not for a specific offense then
certainly for the character of his novels. " And," Adams added,

67 *Ibid.*, p. 235.

68 *Ibid.*, p. 145.

69 *Ibid.*, p. 33.

70 *Ibid.*, pp. 144-5.

" on the whole I think he had better have joined his friend Dreyfus on the Devil's Island some time ago, with as much more French rot as the island would hold, including most of the press and the greater part of the theatre, with all the stock-brokers and a Rothschild or two for example." Once again he could not understand the sympathy expressed for Dreyfus by the British and the Americans.[71]

Meanwhile the Boer War was in the offing and Adams was inclined to connect it with the Dreyfus case, declaring that both were " Jew wars " with the former far worse than the Dreyfus commotion. " But," he observed bitterly,

> our interests require that the Boers should be brought into our system, and so we must kill them till they come; because all England and all America and all the Transvaal are a Jew interest,—that is, a great capitalist machine, and we must run it, no matter whom it hurts. So we try to run the French army, in Jew interests, and we shall ultimately break it down, no doubt, as well as we shall break down the Boers.[72]

Adams needed no earth-shaking episode comparable to the Dreyfus case to stir his anti-Jewish feeling. The mere sight of of a Jew was enough to set him off. Aboard ship,[73] on a Chicago elevated train,[74] in Madrid,[75] London,[76] Paris,[77] Washington,[78] Vienna,[79] their presence was obnoxious to him. Finally, in Warsaw, he came upon the Polish Jew who proved " a startling revelation even to me, who has seen *pas mal de Jew*." " The Jews and I," he wrote, " are the only curious

71 *Ibid.*, pp. 150-1.

72 *Ibid.*, p. 241.

73 *Ibid.*, p. 557 ; *Letters*, I, 255.

74 *Ibid.*, p. 388.

75 *Ibid.*, p. 315.

76 *Letters*, II, 74, 288.

77 *Ibid.*, p. 289.

78 *Ibid.*, p. 620.

79 *Ibid.*, p. 178 note.

antiquities in it [Warsaw]. My only merit as a curio is antiquity, but the Jew is also a curiosity. He makes me creep." [80]

In 1914, four years before his death, Adams, a lonely old man, seemed to feel that he had lost in his battle with the Jew. His circle of friends was narrowing. " The atmosphere really has become a Jew atmosphere. It is curious and evidently good for some people, but it isolates me. I do not know the language, and my friends are as ignorant as I. We are still in power, after a fashion. Our sway over what we call society is undisputed. We keep Jews far away, and the anti-Jew feeling is quite rabid . . . yet we somehow seem to be more Jewish every day." [81]

While the task documenting of Adams' attitude toward Jews can be continued, it is time we paused for some evaluation of the significance of his views. First of all, it should be recognized that Adams was framing less of an indictment of individul Jews or the Jewish people, and more of a condemnation of an intellectual, moral, and economic atmosphere with which he was out of sympathy. Since Adams exploited the Jews as symbolic of his own alienation, what he had to say may be interpreted as being less disdainful of the Jew than it was of his environment. However, while it would be unwise to frame a literal interpretation of Adams' statements concerning Jews, it would be equally incorrect to state that his anti-Semitism is merely the symbol of his disaffection from society. His obsession with menacing Jews goes deeper than that: into the very nature of his personality—and it is at this point that we lose sight of it because the absence of relevant materials makes it impossible to document the process of attitude formation.

In part, Adams' anti-Semitism was merely one symtom of his acute maladjustment to society—a maladjustment symbolized by the conception of himself as a twelfth-century Norman whose misfortune it was to live in the twentieth century. At the very outset of the autobiographic *Education,* in the paragraph

80 *Ibid.,* p. 338.
81 *Ibid.,* p. 620.

following the account of his birth and ancestry, Adams declared that had he been born under the shadow of the Hebrew Temple in Jerusalem, circumcised in the Synagogue and given the name of Israel Cohen he could not have been more heavily handicapped for life in the twentieth century.[82] Later on in the volume, he admitted that had he not been brought up in the early Victorian Epoch and were it not "unfashionable by some law of Anglo-Saxon custom—some innate atrophy of mind; " he would have "cast off his old skin, and made his court to Marlborough House, in partnership with the American woman and the Jew banker. . . ."[83] Returning from Europe in 1868, after having assisted his father at the London embassy during the Civil War, Adams wrote of the sense of ostracism he felt in industrialized America. "Not a Polish Jew fresh from Warsaw or Cracow—not a furtive Yacoob or Ysaac still reeking of the Ghetto, snarling a wierd Yiddish to the officers of the customs—but had a keener instinct, an intenser energy, and a freer hand than he—American of Americans with Heaven knew how many Puritans and Patriots behind him. . . ."[84]

It is more than accidental that Adams should have thus compared himself with the Jew, whom he conceived as being everything he was not. The Jew was well-adjusted (sic!) and Adams was maladjusted; the Jew was the "economic type" of the twentieth century and Adams conceived of himself as the "imaginative type" of the twelfth; the Jew was victorious over heavy odds in the twentieth century sweepstakes for position, while Adams, with every advantage, posed as a loser. The Jew, he held, had achieved in the way of adjustment to industrialism what he, aristocrat of aristocrats, could not. "I wish I were a Jew," he growled, "which seems to me the only career suitable to the time."[85] Adams forgot that the Jew had

82 *Education*, p. 3.

83 *Ibid.*, p. 285.

84 *Ibid.*, p. 238.

85 *Letters*, II, 120.

had to adjust himself to industrialism in order to survive; he, Adams, could afford the luxuries of aloofness and criticism, for a legacy of material wealth had been bequeathed him by his ancestors in addition to all else he had obtained from them.

Adams' conception of the Middle Ages as a golden age was one that had appeared earlier in the writings of Charles Eliot Norton, who had, in turn, borrowed it from Ruskin and the pre-Raphaelites.[86] His idealization of the twelfth century omits altogether the seamier aspects—war, plague, and social conflict. He yearned after that bygone age; he felt nothing but contempt for the era in which he lived; and, being unable to recreate the world to his liking, hoped for its destruction.

In his thinking, Adams was influenced by what Miriam Beard described as "the myth of Nordic economic innocence," which conceived of our ancestors

> as swashbuckling D'Artagnans scattering louis d'or without thought of the morrow, as Richard Coeur-de-Lions (Scott makes the King disclaim knowledge of business practices), or as hairy-beary Siegfried seizing the Rhinegold in knightly fashion; that is, without offering its equivalent in goods or coupons to the mermaids. Such Gentile businessmen as intruded themselves into this fictional paradise were drawn as alien figures, unlike in their desires to the nobler mass of mankind. Indirectly all this served to increase the burden of guilt (for the growth of capitalism) laid upon the Jew, for he was supposed to have misled such gentiles as sneaked away from the Table Round to follow the stock-market quotations.[87]

Alas, the Jew in his medieval ghetto slew no dragons, paid no homage to a feudal overlord, and contributed nothing to the flowering of knighthood and the chivalric ideal. It was altogether natural to blame this quite unromantic Jew for the

86 Van Wyck Brooks, *New England: Indian Summer 1865-1915* (New York, 1940), p. 253; William Gaunt, *The Pre-Raphaelite Tragedy* (London. 1942), *passim.*

87 "Anti-Semitism—Product of Economic Myths," I. Graeber and S. H. Britt, *Jews in a Gentile World* (New York, 1942), p. 368.

capitalistic corruption of civilization which unhorsed one's Norman ancestors, stripped them of their armor, and chained them to a machine.

It is a great irony that Francis Turner Palgrave, whose influence Adams freely acknowledged, was the grandson of Meyer Cohen, an English stockbroker, springing from precisely that social matrix of which Adams was most suspicious.[88] Palgrave was the closest Adams came to knowing a Jew and it is curious that Adams, feeling as he did about Jews, seemed never to have known many in the flesh—or in the spirit either, for that matter.

Adams' anti-Semitism was, in the last analysis, of the type which was in vogue in the late nineteenth century. By that time the Jew was no longer depicted as a cringing outcast on the fringe of Christendom, but as a potent figure in the realm of finance, politics, and journalism. As a dread harbinger of socio-economic change, he stirred the apprehension of the entrenched privileged orders. It was this stereotype of the Jew against which the anti-Dreyfusards fought; it was this stereotype that Adams had in mind when he railed against the Jews. In August 1896 Adams confessed that he had " read with interest actually the extravagance of Drumont—*France Juive, Libre Parole*, and all . . . ." [89] His was far from a literal acceptance of all that the French Royalist leader and anti-Semite had written. Nevertheless, the premises of his position were not very different from those of the followers of Drumont, who sought by means of the Dreyfus case to discredit the French Republic and restore what Adams liked to describe as " traditional " France. The position of the old New England families confronted with the rising power of the factory owners

88 Harold Cater, ed., *Henry Adams and His Friends A Collection of His Unpublished Letters* (New York, 1947), p. xxxiii. This chapter was prepared in advance of the publication of the Cater volume which offers additional documentation of Adams' views.

89 *Letters*, II, 116.

must have impressed Adams as being not unlike that of the French upper classes confronted by the bourgeois republic.

With the latest chapter of the history of anti-Semitism, wherein the Jews are condemned as a race, Adams has almost no connection. He does refer to a " Norman race," but his implication is cultural and not strictly biological. He refused to define " race," but he used the term in the sense of Drumont's definition of it: as a group of people thinking alike.[90] This is not consistent with the biological meaning given to the word " race " by the Nazis. Adams' " racism," like his anti-Semitism, had become old-fashioned by the time of his death. Less than a quarter of a century after his death, the new racism and the new anti-Semitism which had been evolved in Germany made slaves or collaborationists of the French descendants of his Norman ancestors.

Perhaps that part of Adams' work which has least successfully withstood the test of time is his conception of the historical process. Adams was at his best at a kind of impression-istic writing which enabled him to produce an autobio-graphy that really is not an autobiography; a history of the Middle Ages that is less a history than an idealization. As a theorist, however, Adams made the mistake of taking seriously the second law of thermodynamics—the law that there is a universal tendency to the dissipation of mechanical energy. This principle has been demonstrated to be as invalid for the physical universe as it is for the social one to which Adams attempted to apply it—and, incidentally, it may be noted that historians have long ago given up trying to explain human activity in terms of physical laws.[91]

90 " Une race, c'est-à-dire une réunion d'individus pensants de même, un ensemble représentant un certain nombre de sentiments, de croyances, d'aspirations, d'aptitudes, de traditions . . ." La France Juive (2 vols., Paris, 1885), II, 572.

91 Roger Shumate, " The Political Philosophy of Henry Adams," American Political Science Review, XXVIII (August 1934), 609-10; James T. Adams, " Henry Adams and the New Physics," Yale Review, XIX (Winter 1930), 283-302; Roy Nichols, " The Dynamic Interpretation of History," New England Quarterly, VIII (June 1935), 163-78.

Remove from Adams' philosophy of history the basic principle of the progressive deterioration of human capacities, and the whole structure topples. If there is no immutable law fixing the peak of civilization in the Middle Ages and making all that has since transpired symptomatic of decline, then it follows that the civilization of the twentieth century is not inevitably inferior to that of the twelfth; that Adams' theory of the dominance of Norman " imaginative types " in the Middle Ages and of Jewish " economic types " in the twentieth century is more a rationalization of his pose as a failure than a valid conception of the nature of the universe and of the social process. After all, Adams' theory of the degeneration of human energies was but the antithesis of the contemporary Social Darwinist philosophy which held to the view that society, instead of running down, was progressively evolving to higher forms. Neither theory was sound; each took into consideration only such evidence as sustained it. It is significant that Adams, who represented a class declining in status and function, adopted the pessimist view, while the Social Darwinists rationalized ascendant capitalism as a peak in mankind's progress.

Adams' rationalized pessimism affected his attitude not only toward immigrant peoples but toward the entire course of American historical evolution. The social order of the United States in 1800, he characterized as " sound and healthy in every part," except for the institution of slavery. What aristocratic barriers there were to progress had been levelled by the triumph of Jeffersonianism, and ambition was given free rein. Society was at a stage of maximum mobility and few could resist the stimulant to progress which increased in strength until it reached the lowest class, " dragging and whirling them upward as in the blast of a furnace. The penniless and homeless Scotch or Irish immigrant was caught and consumed by it; for every stroke of the axe and the hoe made him a capitalist, and made gentlemen of his children." The ideal of this society was to elevate the immigrant along with the bulk of the lower classes to the status of the elite. Adams wrote understandingly of the ambition of these early immigrants, their hard labor, and of trials experienced on the frontier.[92]

After that date, American society was never so perfectly constituted. There was the Civil War, followed by industrialism, the reign of the money-changers, Grantism, and corruption in high places. What a difference between Adams' account of American society as it was in 1800 and his pictures of it as it was in the post Civil War era![93] America, it would seem, along with the rest of the world, had fallen victim to the law of the degeneration of human energies. Accordingly, Boston of the Jews and Irish was less attractive to Adams[94] than the Genessee frontier of more than half a century earlier, where numbers of immigrants had made their homes.

Along with everything else that was worthwhile, Adams thought that the Norman, too, had declined in ability; that the Norman of the late nineteenth century type could never equal the achievements of his medieval predecessors. He lamented that the Normans had lost their religion, their art, and their military spirit—that they could no longer comprehend the meaning of what they had done at Mont St. Michel. But Adams was writing the epitaph of something more than Norman achievement. He was tolling the knell of Brahmin Boston, of the political ascendancy of the Adams family, of a society in which breeding and background had had first place and Puritanism had governed. Gone was the Boston of John Adams and John Quincy Adams and in its place was the ungainly child of industrial civilization—Boston of the Irish. With this new situation, Adams refused either to compromise or to fight. Instead, withdrawing from the world, he denied all responsibility for the course the world might take. Accordingly, his anti-Semitism is not part of an aggressive philosophy that

92 *History of the United States of America*, I, 59, 159-60.

93 See his *Democracy, an American Novel* (New York, 1882).

94 *Letters*, II, 531.

would substitute a new order for one that was on the verge of collapse. Rather was it a passive commentary upon the running down of the world—part of an aloof and cynical attitude toward a civilization which, he said, was destined to be degenerate.

There is another interesting aspect of Adams' anti-Semitism. It is expressed mainly in his letters, publication of which reveal him more fully than in the case of any other historian considered in this volume. Even so, the motivation of his anti-Semitism is unclear, even as the inception of the ethnic attitudes of the other historians are products of a subtle conditioning that escapes documentation. It is possible with Henry Adams, as with the rest, to fix certain attitudes within a broader ideological framework. This, however, contributes little in the way of solving the problem of how these attitudes originate.

CHAPTER IV

EUROPEAN PEOPLES IN THE AMERICAN FOREST

SELECTION OF THE PEOPLES

THE effect of the Teutonic hypothesis upon American historical writing was to focus attention upon the European background of American institutions and to minimize the role of environmental factors in American institutional evolution. In the last two decades of the nineteenth century, the Teutonists undoubtedly dominated American historiography. However, their sway was challenged not only by those who questioned the validity of the Teutonic hypothesis and the comparative method, but by others who regarded the American environment as a dominant force in the shaping of American life.

For the tenets of their respective creeds, both the Teutonists and the environmentalists were indebted, in some measure, to the principles of Social Darwinism—although conceivably one could be either a Teutonist or an environmentalist without being a Social Darwinist. Even as the Teutonists took their texts from Tacitus and regarded the comparative method as infallible, the environmentalists read their Darwin and applied biological analogies to history. Charles Francis Adams, for example, insisted that publication of the *Origin of Species* marked a new epoch in the study of history.[1] Along with a number of other historians, Adams reinterpreted American development in terms of such concepts as natural selection and the survival of the fittest. The hardships of the voyage from Europe to America, the hazards of life in a new land, the obstacles of frontier and forest to the push westward were interpreted as selective factors which made for the development of a superior national type.

1 Merle Curti, *The Growth of American Thought* (New York, 1943), p. 569.

On the other hand, people who came after the land was settled and did not go to the frontier, or whose coming coincided
with or followed the passing of the frontier, were judged inferior
because they had not undergone the selective process.

The argument concerning the effect of the New World
environment was an old one. Certain European naturalists
had long contended that New World conditions produced
human as well as animal and vegetable types which were inferior to the European. Thomas Jefferson in his *Notes on
Virginia* had thought it worthwhile to disprove this contention. At the time of the American Civil War, the United States
Surgeon General ordered the measurement of foreign-born and
native soldiers, and interpreted the evidence, flimsy as it was,
as proving that native-born Americans were better physical
specimens than immigrant recruits. [2]

In a way Charles Darwin was but restating an old argument
in new form when he ventured the theory that " the wonderful
progress of the United States as well as the character of the
people, are the results of natural selection; for the more energetic, restless and courageous men from all parts of Europe
have emigrated during the last ten or twelve generations to
that great country and have there succeeded best." [3]

The Teutonists themselves believed that the Anglo-Saxons
who settled the American continent were a highly select group
—that centuries of historical evolution had fitted them for the

2 Merle Curti, *The Roots of American Loyalty* (New York, 1946), pp.
66, 101. B. A. Gould, *Investigations in the Military and Anthropological
Statistics of American Soldiers* (New York, 1865) ; J. H. Baxter, *Statistics,
Medical and Anthropological of the Provost-Marshal General's Bureau
during the Late War of the Rebellion* (Washington, 1875). These records,
in the opinion of Aleš Hrdlička, " While interesting, cannot be regarded as
sufficiently reliable for the present demands of anthropology. In a number of
instances . . . the results, in view of our subsequent information of these
subjects are so inaccurate as to be quite useless." " Physical Anthropology in
America," *American Anthropologist*, XVI (October-December 1914).

3 Charles Darwin, *The Descent of Man and Selection in Relation to Sex*
(New York, 1898), pp. 144-5.

task of planting Teutonic institutions in America. The Englishmen who came to the New World were better by far, it was
confidently asserted, than their ancestors in England, Germany,
or the original Aryan homeland. An additional point was made
by William B. Weeden: not only was the English stock " bred
from the purest strains of German crossed with Scandinavian
blood, " but it was from eastern England, where this mingling
was " most prevalent," that there came to this country, in the
early period of its history, the greatest number of English emi-
grants.[4]

The American environment further improved the racial type.
" The barrier of the Atlantic and the early geographical isola-
tion of the American continent made a basis of natural selection
in the first colonists coming to this country," wrote Ellen C.
Semple, American disciple of the German anthropogeogra-
pher, Friedrich Ratzel. " Only the prosperous and strong of
spirit undertook voyages in those days," she continued, " and
none but superior types survived." [5] A. P. Brigham who, like
Semple, investigated the role of geographic factors as historical
determinants, concluded: " America was first occupied by
picked men. The Old World was sifted in the unconscious
search to find men that were fit to build a new one—men with
convictions, daring endurance, and self-trusting strength." [6]

" Looking to the distant future," Darwin did not consider
that view exaggerated which said: " All other series of events—
as that which resulted in the culture of mind in Greece and that
which resulted in the empire of Rome—only appear to have
purpose and value when viewed in connection with or as sub-
sidiary to . . . the great stream of Anglo-Saxon emigration to
the west." [7] In line with Darwin's way of looking at the matter,

---

4 *Economic and Social History of New England, 1620-1789* (2 vols., New
York, 1894), I, p. 13.

5 *American History and Its Geographic Conditions* (Boston, 1903), pp.
310-11.

6 *Geographic Influences in American History* (Boston, 1903), p. 326.

7 *Op. cit.*, p. 145.

there developed a tendency among some American historians to regard the westward movement in the United States as a " process " wherein the survival value of men and institutions was tested.[8] Charles Francis Ádams viewed the pioneers of Wisconsin as select representatives of " the most thoroughly virile and withal, moral and intellectual branches of the human family," representatives who were destined to realize even more completely the racial heritage that had been manifest in New England and western New York. It was his opinion, shared by Hubert Howe Bancroft, that

> the mission of the Republic and the ideas of the founders will more especially rest in those agricultural communities of the the Northwest, where great aggregations of a civic populace are few, and the principles of natural selection have the fullest and freest play in the formation of the race. Such is Wisconsin; such Iowa; such Minnesota. In their hands and in the hands of communities like them, will rest the ark of our covenant.[9]

The factors of natural selection were said to be operative within the framework prescribed by race. Racial tendencies, asserted Brigham, were far from being ineffective before environmental influences. It was the quality inherent in his " race," rather than geographic opportunity, which enabled the Englishman in the narrow land between the sea and the Appalachian mountains to dispossess his Latin neighbors. By obeying his instincts, Brigham continued, the pioneer of Germanic stock shared in a task that began with the conquest of Britain and culminated in the growth and development of the United

---

8 F. L. Paxson, *When the West Is Gone* (New York, 1930), pp. 28, 29, 80.

9 C. F. Adams, " The Sifted Grain and the Grain Sifters," *The American Historical Review*, VI (January 1901), 199; H. H. Bancroft, *Retrospection, Political and Personal* (New York, 1915), p. 83. " Here indeed were both heredity and environment, ... eugenics and euthenics, not in opposition but working in harmony." For an account of Bancroft's mid-western background see John Caughey, *Hubert Howe Bancroft Historian of the West* (Berkeley, 1946), pp. 5-11.

States.[10] Similarly, Semple wrote of the Teutonic element in the American population constituting a superior strain, and of " the inextinguishable excellence of the Anglo-Saxon race." [11]

Nathaniel Southgate Shaler, who in 1884 made the first significant attempt at a geographic interpretation of American history,[12] wrote of the settlement of the United States as a unique achievement of the " Aryan race." Shaler believed that while the fate of a people was in large measure environmentally determined, this factor alone could not make a people great. The nation's progress was ascribed to the operation in a congenial natural environment of the inherited traditions which the early immigrants had brought from the North and West of Europe. The " Aryan race," Shaler believed, had attained its dominant qualities of stature, vigor, longevity, and intelligence in that section of Europe bordering the Baltic Sea where the winters were severe and life was a constant struggle with the cold. Because physiographic and climatic conditions in the United States paralleled those of the Baltic countries, Shaler was of the opinion that in their New World habitat the North Europeans were able to develop fully the potentialities of their racial heritage.[13] He accepted as positive proof of the emergence of a superior type in the American environment, the aforementioned report by the Surgeon General of the anthropological measurements of foreign-born and native American recruits.

With the experience of the old immigrant from northern and western Europe Shaler contrasted the type of selection

10 *Op. cit.*, p. 313.

11 " The Anglo-Saxons of the Kentucky Mountains," *The Geographic Journal*, XVII (June 1901), 329; *American History and Its Geographic Conditions*, p. 312.

12 " Physiography of North America," Justin Winsor, ed., *Narrative and Critical History of America* (8 vols., Boston, 1884-9), cited in A. M. Schlesinger, *New Viewpoints in American History* (New York, 1922), p. 45.

13 *The United States of America* (2 vols., New York, 1894), I, 2; II, 601-2; N. S. Shaler, *Kentucky, A Pioneer Commonwealth* (Boston, 1885), pp. 278, 374.

operative upon the new immigrant from southern and eastern Europe. Over a period of centuries, he maintained, the church and the army had drawn off the most capable of the peasantry in these areas into occupations which tended to make them childless, and by this selective process the growth of motives and aspirations such as had been the foundation of American democracy had been hindered. Where among the new immigrants, he asked, was the upward striving of the English middle class? Of what value to a democracy were these recent immigrants who were derived from a stock that had been drained of its ability, who were destined to be, in general, a servile class, "hardly more profitable to the best interests of the commonwealth than the cattle in the fields?" [14]

In addition to the contention that the heritage of the peoples of southern and eastern Europe was itself deficient, it was also believed that under the improved conditions of the late nineteenth century neither ocean voyage nor mountain barrier operated as a selective agent upon immigration.[15] For this reason if for no other, William Roscoe Thayer insisted that the pioneers who blazed their way into Indiana, Illinois, and the Northwest territory should not be confused with the "Irish bog-trotter [who] was as illiterate and bigoted as the Calabrian peasant or the Russian serf. . . . [and] the pitiable offscourings from the capitals of Europe who in the late nineteenth century were seeking American shores." [16]

Perhaps the foremost exponent among historians of the view that the early American was of a superior strain and that the civilization forged by him was the best the world had yet seen was Hubert Howe Bancroft, historian of the Pacific coast

---

14 Nathaniel Southgate Shaler, "European Peasants as Immigrants," *Atlantic Monthly*, LXXI (May 1893), 647-55. This argument is repeated in John Commons, *Races and Immigrants in America* (New York, 1924), pp. 10-12.

15 Brigham, *op. cit.*, p. 311.

16 William Thayer, *The Life and Letters of John Hay* (2 vols., Boston, 1915), I, 8.

area. He believed that virtually all of the world's history was teleological, culminating in the civilization of the native Californian. Bancroft was of New England stock; his parents migrated to Ohio, and he was born there. While still a young man, he moved to California. The migration from New England to Ohio, and ultimately to California, gave a kind of personal touch to Bancroft's claim that men and institutions were selected and advanced in their march westward.[17]

Bancroft belonged to that element in the California population which he described as the " old Californians " of pioneering and gold-rush days. These he considered a group apart from late-coming immigrant peoples whose ancestral stock was presumably inferior to that of the earlier settlers and who had not benefited from the selective character of the wilderness experience. In addition he conceived of his upper middle-class status, and that of " old Californians," as threatened on the one hand by the role played by immigrant labor in California politics and, on the other, by the " monopolists " and railway magnates.

Detesting the immigrant, Bancroft nevertheless recognized California's need for a cheap labor supply. He would, however, permit only those to enter who would not intermarry with and " debase " the native stock. The Europeans, because they could assimilate, were in his opinion a greater " curse " to the American commonwealth than the Asiatic and the African combined. He complained that no sooner did " the great unwashed " of Europe arrive in the United States, than they were granted the privileges of citizenship, which made them the equal of the best of the natives. Observing the progress the immigrant was making in California politics, Bancroft addressed himself to the old Americans and asked " is this your boasted republicanism, a government by the people, for the people? Rather a government by wild Irishmen, for wild Irishmen and self-serving labor leaders! "

In order to combat domination by foreigners voting at the dictation of labor leaders, Bancroft invoked a spirit of vigilant-

17 *Essays and Miscellany* (San Francisco, 1890), p. 52.

ism among native Californians urging them to suppress immigrant influences by " fire and blood." Such a " revolution," Bancroft said, was necessary to vest control of public affairs in the hands of those who would not permit foreign infusions into the ranks of the " superior race " of native Californians.[18]

From what has been said, it is apparent that the environmentalists contributed additional arguments in opposition to the coming of immigrants from southern and eastern Europe to those already advanced by the Teutonists. However, at least one point in the environmentalist arsenal of argument was challenged by John Fiske who denied that the frontier produced a superior type.

He depicted the frontier settlements as attractive more to the shiftless and undesirable than to the best elements of the seaboard population. Nor did the wilderness, in Fiske's opinion, improve those who came to it.[19]

As a rule, however, those who applied the principle of natural selection to American development asserted confidently, on the basis of *a priori* reasoning and without examination of the actual character of the frontier experience, that the wilderness brought out the best in men and in institutions. While there is no disputing the statement that the overwhelming majority of new immigrants were neither frontiersmen nor pioneers, it is after all, difficult to determine the effect of wilderness conditions upon the old immigrants and it is even more difficult to determine the effect upon the Americans of southern and eastern European origin, of not having experienced these conditions. The selective role of other factors such as the ocean voyage and the European conditions influencing migration is also more easily asserted than demonstrated. Judging from what they have written, the environmentalists, like the Teutonists, have failed to establish a basis for differentiating among immigrants to the New World.

18 *Retrospection*, pp. 24-79.

19 Fiske, *Old Virginia and Her Neighbours*, II, 316.

Francis Parkman

Neither the Teutonic hypothesis nor Social Darwinism finds expression in Francis Parkman's narrative of the American forest. Despite the attraction that the wilderness theme held for him, its influence upon men and institutions is less apparent in his writings than in the volumes of the geographic determinists. Nevertheless, his conception of how the American forest affected patterns of European civilization is germane to the present discussion, as are his attitudes toward immigrant groups in his native Boston.

Born in 1823, of a prominent New England family with established fortune, Parkman was an incorrigible romantic; he was about as much at home in commercial Boston as one of King Arthur's knights would have been.[20]

Parkman's dislike for trade and his keen longing for adventure were in keeping with an interest in Catholicism which he acquired while in his twenties. The pomp and circumstance surrounding the church ceremonial and the church's rich historic heritage were equally congenial to his spirit. The Catholic Church was intimately associated with much that appealed to him—with chivalry, with knight errantry, with feudal combat. There was still another reason for his interest in Catholicism. At the age of eighteen he had conceived the idea of writing a history of the "old French War." It was clear that no adequate account of French colonization and exploration of the North American continent could be written without preliminary groundwork in the field of "Roman Catholic ecclesiasticism in general," and Parkman's approach to Catholicism therefore became on intellectual exercise as well as a romantic excursion.[21]

In the course of a trip abroad in 1843-4, Parkman followed up this interest in Catholicism. After visiting the Benedictine

20 Mason Wade, *Francis Parkman Heroic Historian* (New York, 1942), pp. 1-7.

21 *Ibid.*, pp. 16, 99-101, 132.

monastery at Catania, he was impressed with " new ideas of the Catholic religion." " I reverenced it before," he wrote, " as the religion of generations of brave and great men—but now I honor it for itself." [22] Parkman was but twenty years old, however, when these words were written, and even at that time he was critical of both the priesthood and the doctrinal basis of Catholicism.[23] The Catholic church was, for him, mainly a means of getting " for a while out of the nineteenth century," of approaching the Middle Ages which in youth and in maturity he tended to idealize. Neither the splendor of church edifices, ceremonial richness, nor the arguments of those who sought his conversion could persuade young Parkman with regard to Catholic doctrine. [24]

In later years, Parkman's attitude toward Catholicism was as much anti-doctrinal as anti-clerical; he associated the Catholic religion with political, economic, and intellectual retrogression. At the same time, he took the early New England Puritans to task for denying religious freedom and was, for the most part, far from favorably disposed toward the Puritan theocracy.[25] His strictures against the Catholic clergy were paralleled, to an extent, by the low esteem in which he held Protestant clerics.[26] England, homeland of Anglo-Saxon Protestant civilization, Parkman greatly admired; but he was by no means an uncritical anglophile. [27]

In Boston, Parkman feared the growing political power of the Roman Catholic church and was known to have spoken apprehensively of the peaceful conquest of New England by

[22] *Ibid.*, p. 103.

[23] *Ibid.*, p. 104.

[24] *Ibid.*, pp. 131-2, 140-144; "A Convent at Rome," *Harper's New Monthly Magazine*, LXXXI (August 1890), 450.

[25] *A Half-Century of Conflict* (2 vols., Boston, 1899), I, 215; II, 98, 130.

[26] Wade, *op. cit.*, pp. 104, 197; Charles H. Farnham, *A Life of Francis Parkman* (Boston, 1907), p. 259.

[27] Wade, *op. cit.*, p. 339.

French Canadians and Irish Catholics led by priests. He made frequent and pungent comments on the fact that native Protestants had small families, and held that the decline of this element in the population constituted the gravest menace to our national institutions. [28]

Parkman's simple preference for the culture into which he was born constituted the core of whatever philosophy of history there is in his volumes on the wilderness theme. Parkman had a style of writing which unfailingly grips the reader, and he made critical use of source materials; but he was not a profound scholar. He had read little philosophy, and had scant knowledge of and even less sympathy for, the intellectual currents which were abroad in his time.[29] Consequently, tucked in here and there amidst magnificent passages of historical prose are stretches of moralizing that are unworthy of the work as a whole.

From his conviction that Anglo-Saxon Protestant civilization represented a superior form, sprang the idea, expressed in the earliest of his historical works, that the conflict between England and France in North America was basically a struggle between two opposing principles. On the one side were arrayed France, Catholicism, feudalism, and absolutism, while on the other were England, Calvinism, democracy, and freedom. In the ensuing conflict, English civilization triumphed in the New World because of its inherently superior attributes. " In the valley of the St. Lawrence, and along the coasts of the Atlantic," wrote Parkman

> adverse principles contended for the mastery. Feudalism stood arrayed against Democracy; Popery against Protestantism, the sword against the plowshare. The priest, the soldier, and the noble rules in Canada. The ignorant, light-hearted Canadian peasant knew nothing and cared nothing about popular rights and civil liberties. Born to obey, he lived in contented

28 Farnham, *op. cit.*, pp. 258, 285.

29 *Ibid.*, p. 265; Wade, *op. cit.*, p. 201.

submission, without the wish or the capacity for self-rule. Power, centered in the heart of the system, left the masses inert.[30]

The " sharpest contrast to the spiritual and temporal vassalage of Canada " Parkman discovered in Puritan New England, " where the spirit of non-conformity was sublimed to a fiery essence, and where the love of liberty and the hatred of power burned with sevenfold heat." [31] In every quality of efficiency and strength, the Canadian colonist, according to Parkman, was inferior to his English rival; but in things which please the eye and interest the imagination the Canadian excelled. He was " buoyant and gay " whereas the New Englander was " thoughtful; " he was " careless and thoughtless " and content with poverty whereas the New Englander bent" steadfast energy to his farm, or his merchandise." The Canadian, loving adventure and exploration and the fur trade, taking Indian mistresses and having children by them, was contrasted with the New Englander, " bowing reverently to the law which he himself had made; patient and laborious, and seeking for the solid comforts rather than the ornaments of life . . . ." If the New Englanders were to Parkman the " very pith and marrow of a commonwealth," by the same token Frenchmen impressed him as being a rather frothy lot who, through the zeal of priests and daring enterprise of soldiers and explorers, established forts and missions over half of America. Their achievement, Parkman asserted, was a " magnificent object to the eye, but one which the first whirlwind would prostrate in the dust." [32]

The differences between French and English settlers were, in Parkman's opinion, far from superficial. In dealing with

30 *The Conspiracy of Pontiac and the Indian War after the Conquest of Canada* (2 vols., Boston, 1899), I, 50-1.

31 *Ibid.*, 51.

32 *Ibid.*, 52-4.

the Indians, the French government was aided by "the peculiar character of its subjects,—that pliant and plastic temper which forms so marked a contrast to the stubborn spirit of the Englishman." [33] "Some races of men," Parkman believed, "seemed moulded in wax, soft and melting, at once plastic and feeble. Some races, like some metals, combine the greatest flexibility with the greatest strength." [34] The nature of the Indian Parkman described as rigid, inflexible, and unprogressive. He denied that the Indian could be assimilated to the culture of the European—"nearly every change that has been forced upon him has been a change for the worse." [35]

At the stage of western development described by Parkman, Frenchmen, Englishmen, and Indians were the largest elements of the wilderness population. Besides a great many other more realistic factors which prevented the synthesis of these people in a wilderness melting pot, it is apparent that in Parkman's opinion the racial factor was of no small significance in keeping them apart. Equally unlikely candidates for participation in a potential wilderness melting pot were the Pennsylvania Dutch—"Dutch boors" as he once called them,—whose minds had seemingly gone to sleep, [36] and the Spanish Catholics of whom he disapproved in no uncertain terms.[37] There is more than a veiled hint by Parkman that the development of the New World might have taken a different turn if the French Huguenots had not been denied a refuge in the wilderness. "Had it been granted them," he wrote, "the valleys of the west would have swarmed with a laborious and virtuous population, trained in adversity and possessing the essential qualities of self-government." Beyond the Alleghenies another France would have been created and possessed of the same rugged strength

33 *Ibid.*, pp. 81-2.

34 *Ibid.*, pp. 48-9.

35 *Ibid.*, pp. 49-216.

36 *Ibid.*, p. 97.

37 *Pioneers of France in the New World* (Boston, 1899), p. 96.

which enabled the British colonies to become great. But "as soon could the Ethiopian change his skin," concluded Parkman, "as the priest-ridden King change his fatal policy of exclusion. Canada must be bound to the papacy, even if it blasted her." [38]

"Not institutions alone," Parkman wrote in 1874, "but geographical position, climate, and many other conditions unite to form the educational influences that, acting through successive generations, shape the character of nations and communities." National character Parkman regarded as no temporary matter. The institutions of New England he dogmatically declared to be "utterly inapplicable" to the population of New France. "To each degree and each variety of public development there are corresponding institutions, best answering the public needs, and what is meat to one is poison to another." [39]

Parkman, moreover, was not content with explaining differences between French and English colonies entirely on cultural grounds, no matter how deep-seated. Were there not causes deeper than mere historical antecedents, causes which went far to determine these antecedents themselves? Parkman claimed that the

> Germanic race, and especially the Anglo-Saxon branch of it, is peculiarly masculine, and, therefore, peculiarly fitted for self-government. It submits its action habitually to the guidance of reason, and has the judicial faculty of seeing both sides of a question. The French Celt is cast in a different mould. He sees the end distinctly and reasons about it with a clearness; but his own impulses and passions continually turn him away from it. Opposition excites him; he is impatient of delay, is impelled always to extremes, and does not readily sacrifice a present inclination to an ultimate good.

38 *Count Frontenac and New France under Louis XIV* (Boston, 1899), p. 417; *Pioneers of France*, pp. 49, 442.

39 *The Old Regime in Canada* (Boston, 1922), p. 463.

He delights in abstractions and generalizations, cuts loose from unpleasing facts, and roams through an ocean of desires and theories.[40]

It was, therefore, in terms of the conflict of Old World ideals and Old World principles that Parkman interpreted the struggle for empire in America. Of these basic and far-reaching differences, he regarded the wilderness as in no sense an effective solvent.

Parkman was aware of certain of the effects of the wilderness environment on the European. For example, in the introduction to *Pontiac*, he stated that " even at an early period, clear distinctions were visible between the offshoot and the parent [English] stock." [41] Included in the same volume is an account of the effect of American conditions on warfare and a discussion of the impact on the European of contact with the Indian. While the European lost the refinements of civilization, Parkman believed that he gained in the wilderness school " a rugged independence, a self-sustaining energy, and powers of action and perception before unthought of." [42] The diary of his experiences on the Oregon trail and the book version of them contain references to modifications in the character of Americans wrought by their movement westward.[43] These, of

40 *Old Regime in Canada*, p. 465. Certain of Parkman's ideas on the subject of differences between the French and English " races " may have been influenced by a letter written him by Theodore Parker shortly after the appearance of *Pontiac* (December 22, 1851). " One thing is curious in history:—the Teutonic Race in all its 3 great divisions—the Germans, Goths, and Scandinavians—is naturally exclusive & loves to exterminate the neighboring tribes. On the other side, the Celts & Greco-Italian stock assimilate with other tribes. The history of America shows the same thing in the conduct of the English & the French toward the Indians. It would have enriched your work a little to have called attention to that fact—not generally known. It always enriches a special history to drop into it universal laws or any general rules of conduct which distinguish one nation from another." Wade, *op. cit.*, p. 312.

41 P. xiii.

42 Pp. 109-110.

43 Wade, *op. cit.*, p. 257; *The Oregon Trail* (Boston, 1899), p. 78.

course, were written early in his career; later on, years of invalidism dulled the recollection of his first-hand impressions.

The wilderness modified national character to the extent of making a " bold and hardy pioneer of the Frenchman in America." Opposing the political and ecclesiastical despotism of seventeenth century France was the spirit of liberty bordering upon license which was " in the very air of this wilderness continent." Forest and prairie, said Parkman, offered the French colonists " an unbridled liberty " which, although lawless, " gave scope to his energies, till these savage wastes became the field of his most noteworthy achievements." The wilderness influence Parkman found most apparent among voyageurs, *coureurs de bois,* and certain of his heroic figures, notably Samuel de Champlain. Parkman was willing to admit that the heritage of the Middle Ages had combined with the wilderness environment to produce unusual hardiness in the French character. He steadfastly denied, however, that the civilization of seventeenth century France was a factor in bringing this about.[44]

But in the long run, concluded Parkman, the influences of political and ecclesiastical despotism won out against the wilderness in keeping the Frenchmen servile. French progress was most apparent where church and government were strongest, and weakest in the neighborhood of the primaeval wilderness. The race of *voyageurs* grew scarce as Canadians became stable colonists and steady farmers. Under the despotism of Versailles, Parkman said, the civic virtues of the settlers withered and they became puppets of absolutism.[45]

Parkman's belief that wilderness traits were transient and tended to vanish before the heavy impact of Old World impulses, was not without influence on his ideas about the mingling of peoples. Whereas the forest in the writings of Roosevelt, Wilson, and Turner, stripped diverse European

[44] *Half-Century of Conflict,* I, 346; *Pioneers of France,* pp. xxi, 458.

[45] *Half-Century of Conflict,* I, 347-48.

peoples of their Old World characteristics and moulded them into a single distinctive type, in Parkman's history it is the European traits which prevail. What had been in Europe the character of sevententh century English Protestant or French Catholic remained, in the long run, very much the same in the New World environment, and the behavior of both peoples was in accordance with what were believed to be universal traits of the French and English " races." From Parkman's analysis one could reasonably conclude that in each of the peoples that came to explore, or settle in, the American forest, Old world characteristics were so indelibly fixed that they could not be fused in any melting pot.

Parkman was unaware of certain dynamic qualities which later historians ascribed to the wilderness. Why men should wish to establish real homes in the West was to him a mystery.[46] Parkman thought of the West not as an activating agency producing a thoroughgoing and permanent transformation in the folkways of men, but rather as a theatre—a magnificent arena for the valorous deeds of priest, soldier, and explorer. The settler horde, Parkman felt, dulled the colors and blunted the contours of the wilderness setting. He feared that the pristine beauty of the forest would be transformed by the occupants of the covered wagons into the triumphant commonplace; that commerce and gold would alter the virgin wilderness he knew and loved.

Parkman did not conceive of the wilderness as an activating agency. Nevertheless, it would seem that the forest transformed the Jesuit sufficiently for the Jesuit woodsman and explorer to gain Parkman's admiration. Parkman was both attached and repelled by the Jesuit organization which represented the epitome of Catholic absolutism. On the one hand, he was fascinated by the power, scope, discipline, and tradition of the order; on the other hand, he disliked its ultimate aim, which was to strengthen the " arm of Rome." Nevertheless, he had great admiration for those among the Jesuit priests who

46 *Oregon Trail*, p. 6.

buried themselves in deserts, facing death with the courage of heroes, and enduring torments with the constancy of martyrs. Their story is replete with marvels,—miracles of patient suffering and daring enterprise. They were the pioneers of North America.[47]

Such an attitude springs naturally from the central theme of Parkman's forest epic, the struggle of man against nature. Jesuit missionaries rose in Parkman's estimation in the degree to which their religiosity was subordinated to their pioneering spirit. The New England Brahmin himself knew the wilderness at first hand. His college vacations were spent in expeditions into the mountains of New England, expeditions which seem to have taken a great toll of his physical energy. The Oregon Trail experience gave him a certain personal acquaintance with pioneer ways, the frontier, and Indian society. In late years, Parkman often spoke and thought of these experiences,[48] and there is a sort of kinship between the author and the heroic woodsmen who stalk his pages. The feeling of comradeship that one who knows the trail feels for a kindred spirit entered into his discussion of the Jesuit missionaries. In the imagined glare of wilderness campfires, his prejudice against cassocked priests faded away, and the desire to portray the Jesuits "as they were" was born.[49]

47 *Pontiac*, I, 56; *The Jesuits in North America in the Seventeenth Century* (2 vols., Boston, 1899), II, 172-3.

48 Farnham, *op. cit.*, p. 354.

49 *Jesuits*, II, 100. "Yet, in judging the relative merits of the Romish and Protestant missionaries," Parkman would not have wanted it forgotten "that while the former contented themselves with sprinkling a few drops of water on the forehead of the proselyte, the latter sought to wean him from his barbarism and penetrate his savage heart with the truths of Christianity." However, although the Jesuits embraced the "serene and smiling falsehoods of Catholicism" with the "sincerity of martyrs and the self-devotion of saints," Parkman believed that the system itself was full of evil and that it worked harm to the converted Indians. *Ibid.*, p. 18. French imperial policy and commerce were furthered by the priests and the mission Indians, who became the instruments of French policy in the New World. *Ibid.*, pp. 131-2. Parkman said that the converted Indians were incited to use their

Parkman believed that the culture of French and Irish Catholics on the one hand and that of New England Protestants on the other blended no more successfully than the institutions of French Catholicism and English Protestantism had blended on the frontier. Not only did he find objectionable the influence of the Catholic clergy over recent immigrants but he was also distrustful of the immigrant masses themselves. He was a strong supporter of immigration restriction, and in 1878 he argued that only such a measure could save American institutions from " the muddy tide of ignorance rolled in upon us." [50] In a letter to Pierre Margry written three years earlier, he placed blame for the Boston socialist vote on the Irish immigrant.[51]

Parkman's dislike of New England's most recent immigrants is inseparable from his reactions to the industrialization of that area. In 1878 he expressed longing for the good old days when a New England village was safely governed by the votes of all its adult male inhabitants.

> But now . . . the villages have grown into a populous city, with factories and workshops, its acres of tenement houses, and thousands and ten thousands of restless workmen, foreigners for the most part, to whom liberty means license and politics plunder, to whom the public good is nothing and their own trivial interests everything, who love the country for what they can get out of it, and whose ears are opened to the promptings of every rascally agitator.

---

tomahawks against the enemies of the Church. " Their wigwams were hung with scalps, male and female, adult and infant; and these so-called missions were but nests of baptized savages, who wore the crucifix instead of the medicine bag, and were encouraged by the government for purposes of war." *Montcalm and Wolfe* (2 vols., Boston, 1922), II, 151.

However, despite Protestant carping at the religion taught the Indians by the Jesuits, Parkman found in it " the only form of Christianity likely to take root in their crude and barbarous nature." *Jesuits*, II, 418.

50 " The Failure of Universal Suffrage," *North American Review*, CCLXIII (July-August 1878), 10.

51 " Letters of Francis Parkman to Pierre Margry," *Smith College Studies in History*, VIII, nos. 3 and 4 (Northampton, 1923), December 15, 1875, p. 165.

Applied to large populations, he deemed the principle of universal suffrage a mistake.[52]

In view of all this, it is somewhat strange to find Parkman, in 1890, speaking of a " melting pot " in his native Boston and of the role of the common school in making it work. In urging the preservation of " Our Common Schools,"[53] he took the stand of moderator between two extremist viewpoints—Protestants who would deny Catholics a voice in managing the common schools and Catholics who could not be swayed from their support of the principle of parochialism in education. Parkman argued that the common schools brought together children from all walks of life and tended to weaken prejudices by mutual contact.

> The common schools are crucibles in which races, nationalities, and creeds are fused together till all alike became American. Here the Protestant and the Catholic boys and girls may learn to esteem and like each other; and the lesson may reach to their later years; teaching them that, whatever fanatics on either side may say, a *modus vivendi,* warmed by mutual good will, can always be found between the opposing communions.

Mainly, he addressed Protestants and the Catholic laity— the Catholic clergy he had no hope of converting. He told Boston's Protestants of their declining numbers and of an increase in the Catholic population. To those aggressive Protestants who wanted a showdown with the Catholics, Parkman urged postponement of the day of collision " till the race returns to its pristine vigor, and promises a good supply of recruits for the war." The wisest strategy, advised Parkman, was to avoid antagonizing Catholics lest there some day develop in New England a situation comparable to that which existed in certain

52 " The Failure of Universal Suffrage," p. 7.

53 " Our Common Schools," Citizens Public School Union (Boston, 1890).

Canadian communities where Protestants were forced by the Catholic majority to support Catholic schools.[54]

Why should Parkman expect that a blending of French and Irish Catholicism with New England Protestantism could take place in the Boston of 1890, while on the frontier he regarded French Catholic and English Protestant as inherent antagonists? Some years earlier, Parkman was sharply critical of public education for having failed to improve popular taste. Now, he believed it capable of serving as a solvent of cultural differences.[55] Nor had his anti-Catholicism been entirely a matter of anti-clericalism. Whence came this faith in the ability of the Catholic laity to resist the influence of their ecclesiastics and unite with the Protestant element in perpetuating New England's traditions?

There can be little doubt that Parkman's faith in the melting pot was not in keeping with the general trend of his thoughts. He was, of course, enough of a democrat to support the general principle of religious toleration,[56] but he liked the idea of a population which was predominatly Protestant with immigration restricted and suffrage limited to " our cultivated class, rich or not rich." [57] The current of events was, however, running counter to these ideas, and Parkman had to take account of realities. His compromise took the form of a melting pot which was to salvage the common school system of Boston from the flood of parochialism.

In the volumes of Parkman, the American forest is less of an activating agency, changing the character of men and institutions, than it was in writings of other historians of the wilderness and the frontier. The environmentalists, under the

---

54 *Ibid.*, pp. 4-6.

55 " The Tale of the Ripe Scholar," *Nation*, IX (December 23, 1869), 558-60.

56 *Pioneers of France*, p. 280.

57 " Our Best Class and the National Politics," *Boston Advertiser*, July 21, 1863 quoted in Wade, *op. cit.*, p. 363.

influence of Darwinian theory, ascribed a tremendous role to the frontier in the selection and refining of men and institutions. Parkman saw the American forest as stripping the trappings of ecclesiastical despotism and monarchy from the seventeenth century Frenchman. Once the wilderness had accomplished this divesting process, the underlying heritage of the Frenchman of the Middle Ages combined with those qualities which Parkman believed were derived from the New World environment, to produce the wilderness types which Parkman most admired: *voyageurs, coureurs de bois,* and soldiers.[58] However, he regarded the forest influence as transient and temporary. As the initial impact of the wilderness wore off, Old World culture patterns were strengthened in the New World environment. Hence, his theme is that of the separation and conflict of cultures rather than their blending.[59]

Nevertheless, his idea of what happened to Frenchmen upon first contact with the wilderness approximates the later views of Theodore Roosevelt, Woodrow Wilson, and Fredrick Jackson Turner, who contended that the wilderness seized the European, shook him loose from his cultural moorings, and paved the way for their theory of the wilderness blending of diverse peoples—of a melting pot which was the essence of American nationality. Parkman's failure to write of such a blend was here determined by the nature of his theme; by the fact that he wrote of the earliest frontier of explorer, warrior, and priest; a frontier characterized by tremendous distances and a meagre, widely-scattered population that offered few opportunities for contact between the rival settlements. He believed too, that inherent differences separated the French Catholic and the English Protestant and that the barriers of race and culture were not diminished by the wilderness.[60]

58 *Half-Century of Conflict,* II, 1-2; *Pioneers of France,* pp. xxi, 458.

59 *Half-Century of Conflict,* I, 312; II, 2-3; *Old Regime in Canada,* pp. 464-5.

60 *Ibid.,* 464-5.

THEODORE ROOSEVELT

Theodore Roosevelt conceived of his *The Winning of the West* [61] as a continuation of Parkman's narrative. In it, he described a later phase of the frontier; that of the backwoodsman and pioneer during the late colonial, revolutionary, and early national periods. His theme, unlike Parkman's, is the blending rather than the separation of peoples in the area beyond the Alleghenies. However, Roosevelt made certain to point out that the components of the blend, in the forest catalyst, were those of the average Englishman.

Roosevelt, both conscious and proud of a wide personal polygenesis,[62] objected to the terms English race and Anglo-Saxon. Reducing the average Englishman to component ancestral elements, Roosevelt believed him a mixture of Low Dutch, Celtic, Scandinavian, and Norman elements, with the Germanic strain predominant. The typical American, Roosevelt said, was much the same in make-up because apart from the basic English strain in the immigration to the United States, the greatest proportion was from Dutch and German sources, the next greatest from Ireland and the Scandinavian peninsula, while the third greatest was made up of Huguenots. Thus, " no new element of importance has been added to the blood [in America]. Additions have been made to the elemental race strains in much the same proportion as these were originally combined." [63]

---

61 *The Winning of the West, An Account of the Exploration and Settlement of Our Country from the Alleghanies to the Pacific* (2 vols., New York, 1917).

62 " Theodore Roosevelt, An Autobiography," *The Works of Theodore Roosevelt* (20 vols., New York, 1926), XX, 3-6. References are to the National Edition of Roosevelt's works.

63 *Winning of the West*, I, 17. Mr. Dooley characterized Roosevelt's election in 1904 as an "Anglo-Saxon triumph." Roosevelt replied that he (Roosevelt) had never called the United States an Anglo-Saxon country, that here in America was "a new and mixed race—a race drawing its blood from many different sources . . ." J. B. Bishop, *Theodore Roosevelt and His Times Shown in His Own Letters* (2 vols., New York, 1920), I, 346-80.

The invasion of the inner continental area, Roosevelt said, was not unlike other migrations that were part of the history of the " race." On the occasion of the invasion of Britain during the sixth century by the Germanic tribes, and on the occasion of the English colonization of the New World,[64] Roosevelt recalled that " a portion of the English race has shifted its home, in each case undergoing a marked change, due both to outside influence and to internal development; but in the main retaining, especially in the last instance, the general race characteristics." [65] Now, in the region beyond the Alleghenies, the race, " in obedience to its instincts," was repeating the process. In the backwoods, English, Germans, Huguenots, Dutch, Swedes, and Scotch-Irish were forming a new blend, which was not unlike the old.[66]

It was Roosevelt's opinion that a single generation of life in the wilderness was sufficient for the reblending process, and that when the thing was done, something more than an ethnically average Englishman had been made. He believed that the backwoodsmen in the frontier mould had become " all alike in the same shape. They resembled one another, and they differed from the rest of the world—even the world of America." Having lost all remembrance of Europe and all sympathy with things European, they were the most American of the Americans, " one in speech, thought, and character." [67] The substance of Roosevelt's conception of the frontier melting pot was the forging within one generation of a fused race of the identical strains of which the average Englishman was constituted, and the moulding by the forest environment of distinctively American characteristics.

Despite brief experience as a Dakota ranchman, Roosevelt's roots were firmly grounded in the heart of the eastern melting

64 *Winning of the West*, I, 7, 11.

65 *Ibid.*, pp. 11-18.

66 *Ibid.*, p. 81.

67 *Ibid.*, p. 89.

pot, New York City.[68] Here, in 1881, his political career began with his election to the state legislature from a city assembly district. He served in Albany for three terms; in 1886 was an unsuccessful candidate for mayor of New York City; and in 1894 was named Chairman of the Police Board of New York City. A Republican, scion of one of New York's oldest families, he was something of a political anomaly in a city whose population was composed to a considerable degree of foreign-born and second-generation Americans and whose politics were normally Democratic. If it were true that the melting pot did not function and that Old World allegiances were not weakened, then by the same token a political career for Roosevelt in New York would not have been possible.[69]

Amidst the turmoil of urban politics, Roosevelt wrote many of his historical works. Of particular interest is his *New York,* written in New York and Washington in 1890, and significant for the scrupulous care with which the author treats the ethnic elements in New York's population. If the foreign born were politically dishonest, Roosevelt is careful to point out that the political integrity of the natives was not above reproach. If foreigners participated in riotous disturbances and strikes, and agitated against property rights, Roosevelt takes care to mention the natives who joined them in such activities. He condemns hyphenated Americanism, but in the same breath attacks political nativism.[70] Although he endorses the priniciple of immigration restriction, there is no doubt in 'his mind as to the satisfactory operation of the melting pot: " in the end the German or Irishman is always Americanized." [71]

It was Roosevelt's opinion, however, that, while on the frontier the process of Americanization took but a single gen-

68 Julian Street, " Roosevelt, Citizen of New York," *Works of Roosevelt,* X, 341.

69 "Autobiography," *Works of Roosevelt,* XX, pp. 178-9, 188, 191, 192.

70 " New York," *Works of Roosevelt,* X, 518, 522, 529.

71 *Ibid.,* pp. 516, 521, 534, 538.

eration, in New York City it took at least two, and often several, successive generations. Of his foreign-born colleagues in the New York State legislature, Roosevelt found those from rural areas completely Americanized and, incidentally, sharing his own ideas concerning legislative problems; whereas German and Irish legislators from any one of the big cities retained many of their Old World peculiarities and constituted the most corrupt element in the legislature.[72] Yet it was axiomatic with him that

> the only way to teach our foreign-born fellow-citizens how to govern themselves is to give each the full rights possessed by other American citizens. . . It has been my experience moreover in the Legislature that when Hans or Paddy does turn out really well, there are very few native Americans indeed who do better.[73]

Roosevelt denounced with equal fervor Protestant and Catholic bigots, nativism, and hyphenism.[74] He opposed granting public funds to parochial schools and was outspoken against Protestants who deny school-board representation to Catholics.[75] Loyal to the American principles of individual worth, equality before the law, and the right of every individual to develop in accordance with his capacities, Roosevelt expressed almost limitless faith in the operation of the melting pot.[76] But there was to be, in the end, no compromise with immigrant culture patterns. " Above all, the immigrant must learn to talk and think and *be* United States." [77]

Yet, Roosevelt distrusted the " slumbering volcano " not only beneath New York but " under all other large cities of the

72 " Phase of State Legislation," *Works of Roosevelt*, XIII, 49.

73 *Ibid.*, p. 65.

74 *Ibid.*, p. 72.

75 " Religion and the Public Schools," *ibid.*, p. 275.

76 "Americanism," *ibid.*, XVIII, 398.

77 " True Americanism," *ibid.*, XIII, 24; "Americans of German Origin," *ibid.*, XVI, 36-8; "Americans of Irish Origin," *ibid.*, pp. 39-45.

civilized world." The danger, he felt, lay in the fact that the
rich were indifferent to justice, while the poor tried to remedy
the evils that beset them by taking as their leaders "ignorant
visionaries or criminal demagogues."[78] Because of the absence
of class or caste spirit, Roosevelt thought of country districts
as "politically very much the healthiest districts,"[79] but he was
strongly opposed to the Populist movement. He was convinced
that the nation was in danger of stumbling into anarchy and
that it could be prevented from doing so only by the intervention
of the Republican Party.[80]

As for immigration, Roosevelt considered that it made the
situation worse because it increased the numbers of the poor.
He held this to be true even as regards the early days of the
Republic, and he was still more sure that it was true as regards
what took place after, when the main source of immigration
had shifted from the North and West of Europe to the South
and East.[81] Not only—so he wrote in 1890—did the flow of
immigrants increase the ranks of the "hopelessly poor," but
the immigrants became prey of anarchistic agitators.[82] Over a
decade later, as President, he urged Congress to enact legislation excluding immigrant anarchists, and in the same message
advocated an educational test for immigrants which would
"decrease the sum of ignorance, so potent in producing . . .
anarchistic sentiment. . . ." He would call a halt to the influx
of cheap labor and so "dry up the springs of the pestilential
social conditions in our great cities, where anarchistic organizations have their greatest possibility of growth."[83] On

78 "New York," p. 531.

79 "Fellow Feeling as a Political Factor," *Works of Roosevelt*, XIII,
363-4; "Brotherhood and Heroic Virtues," *ibid.*, p. 462; "The Labor Question," *ibid.*, p. 482.

80 "The Vice-Presidency and the Campaign of 1896," *ibid.*, pp. 139-56;
"How Not To Help our Poorer Brothers," *ibid.*, pp. 157-167.

81 "New York," pp. 192, 435, 444.

82 *Ibid.*, p. 533.

83 James Richardson, ed., *Messages and Papers of the Presidents*, IX,
6649-50, December 3, 1901.

December 7, 1903 Roosevelt told Congress that the situation had eased as a result of the efforts being made to distribute immigrants in rural areas.[84]

Like Henry Cabot Lodge, Roosevelt was in favor of a policy of immigration restriction; but unlike the Senator from Massachusetts, who filled page after page of the *Congressional Record* with the most vicious sort of racism,[85] he partly favored the exclusion of " unworthy individuals " rather than the proscription of certain so-called " races ".[86] It is true that his approval of the course of immigration restriction, which he communicated privately to Lodge, was far stronger than his public statements would indicate. In the presidency he feared that political repercussions might follow a definite stand on the issue. It is also true that support of Lodge's literacy-test bill committed Roosevelt indirectly to a policy of discrimination against the new immigration from the South and East of Europe. Cleveland, Roosevelt wrote to Lodge in 1897, had, in vetoing Lodge's bill, done the greatest possible injury to the country.[87]

Nevertheless, in contrast to Lodge, Roosevelt at no time drew invidious racial distinctions between northern and western European peoples who had wrested a continent from the savage and the wilderness and the most recent immigrants from the South and East of Europe who played a meagre role in the settlement of the West. The blending of populations Roosevelt regarded as primarily a cultural phenomenon, hastened by the agency of the wilderness and retarded in an urban environment. Although at one point in *New York* Roosevelt mentioned the Scandinavians and the English as being more

84 *Works of Roosevelt*, XV, 175.

85 *Supra*, pp. 58, 60.

86 "Address before the Federal Club in New York City," *Works of Roosevelt*, XVI, 137, 138.

87 H. C. Lodge, ed., *Selections from the Correspondence of Theodore Roosevelt and Henry Cabot Lodge, 1884-1918* (2 vols., New York, 1925), I, 251, 255, 257, 260, 545; II, 226, 227, 278.

easily assimilated than other groups in the city population,[88] he erected no racial barrier to the role of any European people in the melting pot.

Nor is his faith in the melting pot entirely explainable as a political gesture. Actually, Roosevelt had a scientific basis for his belief in the successful fusion of the European immigrants with the American population.[89] In 1894, he said that " non-Aryan " peoples could be adapted to " Aryan " culture patterns.[90] Reviewing Houston Stewart Chamberlain's *Foundations of the Nineteenth Century*, he sharply disagreed with Chamberlain's view that there were distinctive Aryan and Teutonic racial types, and held, in fact, that the physical characteristics of the original Aryan language-speaking group were unknown. The ethnological composition of a state, Roosevelt asserted, had little to do with its national boundaries, and national unity was a far more significant historic force than racial unity.[91] Discussing American cultural development, Roosevelt found that American blood was " of many different race stocks, and [that] we have taken toll of the thought of many different nations." The American environment and the " new strains in our national blood " interacted, he believed, to produce a new national type which would develop either no art or literature at all or else distinctively American patterns. Roosevelt was anxious that we draw upon every " hoard of garnered wisdom," and adapt it to our own uses.[92] He repre-

88 " New York," p. 513.

89 Roosevelt claimed in a letter to Trevelyan that he had read widely in the field of anthropology. Bishop, *op. cit.*, II, 142.

90 *Works of Roosevelt*, XIII, 214. Had Roosevelt believed in racism it is more than likely that it would have found expression in his reviews of C. H. Pearson's *National Life and Character; a Forecast;* Benjamin Kidd's *Social Evolution;* and Brooks Adams', *The Law of Civilization and Decay. Works of Roosevelt*, XIII, 200-260.

91 " Biological Analogies in History," *ibid.*, XII, 40. " The Foundations of the Nineteenth Century," *ibid.*, pp. 106-112.

92 " Biological Analogies," p. 43 ; "Americanism," p. 88.

sented a mean between those Americans who blindly admired
foreign ways and those who adhered to an "unwholesome
parochial spirit in politics, literature, and art." [93]

That Roosevelt did not subscribe to the theory of racial
determinism is further apparent from his analysis of the European situation. The peoples of Europe from Russia to England,
Roosevelt maintained, were of almost the same "ancestral
culture." The differences among Slavic, German, French,
English and many other "races" he considered as infinitesimal
when compared with their likenesses.[94] He also argued that
there was lacking "real foundation in race" for the bitter
antagonism between Slavs and Germans, French and English,
which culminated in the first World War. American experience
proved that "these races not only get along well together here,
but become knit into one people, and after a few generations
their blood is mingled." [95]

Roosevelt was properly skeptical about racial theories of the
rise and decline of empires; he regarded national greatness as
being the product of such factors as "national character" and
the "homey commonplace virtues." [96] Reproduction of society's
fittest elements Roosevelt deemed essential to the maintenance
of vigorous nationhood; but in urging large families upon those
best fitted to have them his position was more eugenicist than
racist.[97] Although an ardent imperialist, he regarded American
expansion rather as a national phenomenon than as the result
of Anglo-Saxon or Teutonic strains in the population.[98] It

93 "True Americanism," *Works of Roosevelt*, XIII, 15.

94 "The Japanese in Korea," *ibid.*, XVIII, 412.

95 "How to Strive for World Peace," *ibid.*, 52.

96 "Biological Analogies," p. 43.

97 "Twisted Eugenics," *Works of Roosevelt*, XII, 202.

98 "America's Part of the World's Work," *ibid.*, XIV, 314-318; "The
Copperheads of 1900," *ibid.*, pp. 334-41, in which Roosevelt upholds the
expansion of Russia and other European nations as boding good for mankind. See also, "Free Silver, Trusts, and the Philippines," *ibid.*, pp. 346-
59; "The Expansion of the White Races," *ibid.*, XVI, 258-78. Compare

should be pointed out, however, that Roosevelt, while in general
rejecting racism, would on occasion revert to racial patterns of
thinking, and that despite knowledge of mounting evidence
against the theory of the inheritance of acquired characteristics,
he still clung to that theory.[99]

Without losing faith in the principle of the melting pot,
Roosevelt was vehement in his assaults upon hyphenated
Americans, particularly during the period of the first World
War. Though he deplored the introduction of European issues
into American politics, he himself, convinced of the justice of
the allied cause, was impatient of those whose views on the war
were different from his own or more moderate. Roosevelt's
pet target was organized Americans of foreign extraction who
were opposed to American participation in the struggle.

Since he conceived of Americanism as permitting no divided
allegiance, he denounced the German-American Alliance for
attempting to preserve German culture and further the interest
of Germany by influencing American politics.[100] The sharpness
of Roosevelt's attack during the war years may be attributed
to the gravity of the situation. The aims of the Alliance, cultural and political, were inconsistent with his view of the United
States as a composite but nevertheless united nation.[101] It is

the tone of these speeches with the aggressive Anglo-Saxonism of Albert J.
Beveridge, *Americans of To-day and To-morrow* (Philadelphia, 1908), pp.
9-10, or the Teutonism of John W. Burgess. Roosevelt was no admirer of Homer Lea, Nietzsche, or Treitschke, *Works of Roosevelt*, XVIII,
133, 156.

99 " The Origin and Evolution of Life," *ibid.*, XII, 158-9. He respected
the opinions of the French racialist, Le Bon. *Correspondence of Roosevelt
and Lodge*, I, 218.

100 Clifton Child, *The German-Americans in Politics, 1914-1917* (Madison,
1939), pp. 84-86, 88-9, 113-15, 129-30.

101 *New York Times*, March 29, 1918. Roosevelt said that the majority
of German-Americans were loyal to the United States. " But the men of
German blood who have tried to be both Germans and Americans are not
Americans at all, but traitors to America and tools and servants of Germany
against America. Organizations like the German-American Alliance have
served Germany against America. Hereafter we must see that the melting
pot really does melt. There should be but one language in this country
—the English."

probable, too, that political ambition was less of a brake than before upon Roosevelt's outspokenness.

It may be that some of Roosevelt's more glowing tributes to the melting pot should be interpreted in the light of the fact that many of his public statements were admittedly "lynx-eyed" and that he was a great maker of "weasel paragraphs." [102] His private communications to Lodge on the subject of immigration restriction and a letter to Sir Cecil Spring-Rice in which, without qualification, he lamented the "diminishing birth rate among the old native American stock, especially in the north-east" expressed sentiments which do not appear in his public utterances.[103] There can be no doubt, however, that Roosevelt was sincerely convinced that so-called racial factors were of far less importance than cultural forces in national development. Intellectual conviction, combined with an appreciation of the political advantages involved, was of sufficient strength to overcome a natural prejudice in favor of the peoples of the old frontier melting pot over those of the more recent urban mixture. However, although he was willing to recognize the United States as a country in which "the representatives of many old-world races are being fused together into a new type," he was equally insistent that "the crucible in which all the new types are melted into one was shaped from 1776 to 1789, and our nationality was definitely fixed in all its essentials by the men of Washington's day." [104]

102 H. F. Pringle, *Theodore Roosevelt* (New York, 1931), p. 504; Stuart P. Sherman, *Americans* (New York, 1922), p. 285.

103 Stephen Gwynn, ed., *The Letters and Friendships of Sir Cecil Spring-Rice* (2 vols., Boston, 1929), I, 293.

104 Speech at the unveiling of the Sheridan statue in Washington, cited in introduction to *The Jews in Nazi Germany* (New York, 1935), p. viii.

CHAPTER V
FRONTIER AND URBAN MELTING POTS

THE Social Darwinists, in interpreting the effect of the wilderness upon men and institutions, gave to American history an emphasis somewhat different from that which was provided by the Teutonists. Parkman, too, was aware of the influence of the American environment upon the settler, while Roosevelt conceived of the frontier as stripping men of their previous cultural patterns and levelling them. Taking place in the area beyond the Alleghenies, this divesting and levelling process, according to Roosevelt, was preliminary to the forging of an American type ethnically like the average Englishman. Frederick Jackson Turner was to go beyond the Social Darwinists, Parkman, and Roosevelt, in ascribing to the frontier a peculiar potency in establishing some of the major trends in American history.

The melting-pot concept, which is recurrent in the writings of Turner, was referred to by Parkman and, to a greater extent, by Roosevelt who used the term to describe the ethnic blend taking place beyond the Alleghenies. In the writings of Turner, the melting pot becomes an important institutional determinant, which it was not in the work of Parkman and Roosevelt. In Turner's view, American institutions were not of Teutonic origin; they were emergent instead from the blending of peoples on the frontier.

FREDERICK JACKSON TURNER

Turner was himself part of the Western melting pot. He was born in 1861 and grew up in the town of Portage, Wisconsin,[1] where in sight of his father's newspaper office the community sprawled. Turner remembers Portage's peoples as

1 According to the census of 1870, Portage contained about 4,000 people, almost evenly divided between native-born Americans and immigrants from northern and western Europe.

a mixture of raftsmen from the 'pineries,'—(the 'pinery road' ran by my door), of Irish (in the 'bloody first' ward), Pomeranian immigrants (we stoned each other), in old country garbs, driving their cows to their own 'Common,' of Scotch with 'Caledonia' near by; of Welsh (with 'Cambria' adjacent); with Germans some of them university-trained (the Bierhall of Carl Haertel was the town club house); of Yankees from Vermont and Maine and Conn. Chiefly, of New York-Yankees, of Southerners (a few relatively); a few negroes; many Norwegians and Swiss, some Englishmen, and one or two Italians. As the local editor and leader of his party, my father reported the community life. . . harmonized the rival tongues and interests of the various towns of the country, and helped to shepherd a very composite flock. My school fellows were from all these varied classes and nationalities, and we all 'got on together,' in this forming . . . society. . .[2]

According to his own testimony, Turner was well adjusted to this ethnic situation, and this may have had something to do with his later idealization of it.[3]

Turner did undergraduate work at the University of Wisconsin and then went East to Johns Hopkins, where, in 1883, along with Woodrow Wilson, he was a student in the seminar of Herbert Baxter Adams.[4] Some of his fellow graduate students, influenced by H. B. Adams, tended to write of the West as another "homeland" in which the Anglo-Saxon recapitulated, almost without change, the institutional life of

2 C. S. Skinner, ed., "Turner's Autobiographic Letter," *The Wisconsin Magazine of History*, XIX (September 1935), 101-2.

3 Fulmer Mood presents an interesting comparison between Turner's favorable reactions to life on the frontier and Veblen's unfavorable experience, and suggests that these early impressions were of some influence upon their later work. "The Development of Frederick Jackson Turner as a Historical Thinker," *Proceedings of the Colonial Society of Massachusetts*, XXXIV (December 1939), 285.

4 W. E. Dodd, *Woodrow Wilson and His Work* (New York, 1932), p. 20.

the " race." The " generous barbarians " of the German forests, far more than the New World environment, were credited with determining the character of American political development.[5]

Turner's doctorate showed no trace of having been influenced by the Teutonic hypothesis, although it was prepared under Adams' guidance. However, in " The Significance of History," written in 1891 after his return to Wisconsin, he avoided open conflict with the Teutonists, ascribing equal weight as institutional determinates to Teutonism and the forest environment.[6]

But if Adams and his colleagues were interested in resemblances between American and early Germanic institutions, young Turner was interested in differences. Much of what America was, he thought, could be explained in terms of its people. Immigration, Turner said in 1891, required additional historical study. Immigrants, he argued, were not just so much bone, sinew, and manual skill, so many dollars and cents—it was their deeply rooted customs and ideas that were of importance to the student. The destiny of America was tied up with the European backgrounds of its inhabitants. " The story of the peopling of America has not yet been written. We do not understand ourselves." [7]

Turner's interest in immigration was further stimulated by Reuben G. Thwaites of the Wisconsin Historical Society who, in 1889, began collecting data bearing upon the movement of peoples into the state. In this endeavour the cooperation of the

5 F. W. Blackmar, " Spanish Colonization in the Southwest," *Johns Hopkins Studies*, eighth series, 1890, p. 7; George E. Howard, *An Introduction to the Local Constitutional History of the United States* (Baltimore, 1889), p. 135; Albert Shaw, " Local Government in Illinois," pp. 10-11.

6 Turner's statement " The town and the county, the germ of our political institutions, have been traced back to old Teutonic roots " implies in the context a tacit acceptance of Adams' conviction. E. E. Edwards, ed., *The Early Writings of Frederick Jackson Turner* (Madison, 1931), p. 64. Turner's doctoral dissertation was entitled " The Character and Influence of the Indian Trade in Wisconsin," *Johns Hopkins Studies*, ninth series, 1891.

7 *Ibid.*, p. 64. See also Turner's review of Roosevelt's *The Winning of the West*, *The Dial*, X (August 1889), 71.

University of Wisconsin was enlisted and in the year 1890-1 Turner offered a seminar in the subject. Kate A. Everest, one of Turner's students, made use of the Historical Society's resources in investigating German immigration into Wisconsin.[8]

In 1892, a year before the celebrated frontier pronouncement, Turner explained American evolution as a matter of " European germs developing in an American environment." But, he added, very little had been done in the investigation of environmental forces.[9] His thesis of a year later that the frontier determined the character of American nationality was by no means a complete surrender to environmentalism. Rather was it a further development of what Turner had been saying since 1889 concerning national character: that from the varied strains of European immigration to our shores a distinctively American people was being moulded, a people which spoke the English language but was not English. The idea of a melting pot became, therefore, an adjunct of the frontier hypothesis, taking shape in his mind as one of the ways in which the frontier shaped American society.

The result of the frontier experience was, according to Turner, to create " a steady movement away from the influence of Europe." This was accomplished by the frontier environment acting upon the settler in various ways. The frontier could strip the settler of his European culture traits; build up an

8 " Thirty-Fifth Annual Report of the Executive Committee," *Proceedings of the State Historical Society of Wisconsin*, XXXVI (1889), 52-98; Kate A. Everest, " Early Lutheran Immigration in Wisconsin," *Transactions of the Wisconsin Academy of Sciences, Arts, and Letters*, VIII (1892), 288-98, Everest, " How Wisconsin Came by Its Large German Element," *Collections of the Wisconsin State Historical Society*, XII (1892), 299-334; Everest, " The Geographical Origin of German Immigration to Wisconsin," *ibid.*, XIV (1898), 341-93. From *Scribner's Statistical Atlas of the United States Showing by Graphic Methods their Present Condition . . .* (New York, 1885), Turner learned of the geographic distribution of various ethnic elements in the American population in patterns which suggested that deep-lying causes were at work to occasion these arrangements. Mood, " Development of Turner as a Historical Thinker," pp. 308-12.

9 *Early Writings of Turner*, p. 74.

entirely new pattern of reactions; and on the basis of these reactions construct a new society. At times, to be sure, European characteristics might be modified rather than obliterated; but in most instances he regarded Old World culture traits as melting away in the American environment.

" In the crucible of the frontier the immigrants were Americanized, liberated, and fused into a mixed race, English in neither nationality nor characteristics." In the vibrant American Middle West, during the thirties and forties of the nineteenth century, American society as Turner conceived it was " plastic," with native and foreign-born elements engaged in a process of mutual education " in which all gave and all received and no element remained isolated." A new national stock was in the making, a synthesis of " the old native democratic stock " with recruits from European lands who saw in America a land of opportunity, freedom, and democracy. Here the distinctive American society [differing from any and all its parts] was made, the essence of the process being the " liberation," " Americanization " and " fusion " of immigrant peoples into a " mixed race." [10]

There were occasions when Turner, in writing of the relative permanence of ethnic cultures, implied that the blending process was not an easy one. The " stocks from which people sprang," he argued in 1907, rank on a par with geographic factors in determining the nation's sectional divisions. At that time, he expected many years to elapse before " the sectional distribution of stocks, with inherited customs, institutions and ways of looking at the world, will cease to be reflected in the sectional manifestation of public opinion and in the sectional

10 Frederick Jackson Turner, *The Frontier in American History* (New York, 1920), Preface, pp. 2-4, 23, 29, 190, 206, 249-51, 264, 281-2, 350. My analysis at this point follows rather closely that of G. W. Pierson, " The Frontier and Frontiersmen of Turner's Essays," *The Pennsylvania Magazine of History and Biography*, LXIV (October 1940), 461-466. See also Pierson, " The Frontier and American Institutions A Criticism of the Turner Theory," *New England Quarterly*, XV (June 1942), 226-31.

distribution of votes in Congress." [11] But he could also write glowingly of acculturation in the Middle West, where immigrants taught the world a " lesson of national cross-fertilization instead of national enmities, the possibility of a newer and richer civilization, not by preserving unmodified or isolated the old component elements, but by breaking down the line-fences, by merging the individual life in the common product—a new product which held the promise of world brotherhood." [12] Generalizing in this manner, Turner seemed to have been carried away by devotion to a theme, considering hardly at all evidence that might lead to a less optimistic conclusion.

In 1901, Turner contributed to the *Chicago Record-Herald*,[13] a series of articles in which he traced the history of immigration from the colonial period to the late nineteenth century. Though acknowledging the role of other factors, he related the ebb and flow of the immigrant tide mainly to social and economic conditions in both Europe and the United States. The coming of immigrants, said Turner, registered " with much accuracy the changes of the social organism of the country."

Turner maintained that between 1820 and 1900 immigrants formed more than half of the country's labor supply. Without making extensive inquiry into the validity of Walker's theory that immigration merely replaced the native stock instead of swelling the total population, Turner suggested that

11 *The Significance of Sections in American History* (New York, 1932), " Is Sectionalism in America Dying Away? ", pp. 288, 312; " Geographic Sectionalism in American History," p. 195.

12 *Frontier in American History*, pp. 350-1.

13 " Studies of American Immigration," *Chicago Record-Herald*, August 28, September 4, 11, 18, 25, October 16, 1901. " German Immigration in the Colonial Period," August 28; " German Immigration into the United States," September 4; " Italian Immigration into the United States," September 11; " French and Canadian Immigration into the United States," Sept. 18; " The Stream of Immigration into the United States," September 25; " Jewish Immigration," October 16.

General Walker underestimated the growth of the Americans by immigration between the revolution and 1820, and the increase in wealth and luxury in any country tends to diminish the birth rate. It certainly is a fact that the tendency of the native Americans to withdraw from the common labor and manufacture of the country coincided in time with the advent of the immigrant, but it coincides also with the opening up, on a large scale, of the great West, whereby the native American energies found another outlet than in the common labor of factory and the railroad.[14]

Turner, far more than John Fiske, was aware that Walker had failed to take into consideration all the factors involved in population growth. Turner had earlier objected to the prediction, made by Parkman among others, that the relatively high birth rate of the French Canadians in New England would submerge the native element. These " extravagant apprehensions " were, he said, the result of failure to note the equally high infant mortality.[15]

Turning his attention to the composition by nationality of the immigration to the United States, Turner regretted that the source of immigration had moved from the North and West of Europe to the South and East. He wrote of the coming of the South Italians, Poles, Russian Jews, and Slovaks as " a loss to the social organism of the United States." Turner continued:

> The lowering of the standard of comfort, the immigrants' competition which is counteracting the upward tendency of wages, the sweatshop system, the congestion of foreigners in localities in our great cities, where they become the troops of the local boss; the increase in crime and pauperism attributable to the poorer elements in our recent immigration, and the anarchistic elements which are found among them—all

14 *Chicago Record-Herald*, September 25, *supra*, p. 39 note.

15 Fulmer Mood, ed., "An Unfamiliar Essay by Frederick J. Turner, The Rise and Fall of New France," *Minnesota History*, XVIII (December 1937), 398.

these and similar problems are presented by the transformation of our immigration.[16]

While the Germans, according to Turner, had given the state
added solidity and strength and fostered its best ideals,[17] the
contribution of South Italians " to American racial characteristics " he considered " of doubtful value judged from the ethical
point of view of the stocks that have heretofore made the
nation." [18]

Even less desirable, he thought, were the southern and
eastern European Jews, the very opposite of the frontier type
which Turner so much admired—" the world over, a city
people." The selective factors operative upon them were very
different from those which had affected the pioneer. Generations of Jews living in crowded urban quarters " produced a
race capable of living under conditions that would exterminate
men whom centuries of national selection had not adapted to
endure squalor and the unsanitary and indecent conditions of
a dangerously crowded population." This " people of excep-
tionally stunted stature and of deficient lung capacity " was
therefore able to survive better than their neighbors in the
tenements and sweatshops of New York City. In Turner's
opinion, the slight success of the Baron de Hirsch agricultural
colonies of immigrant Russian Jews indicated that " The
Jew is not ready to depart far from the city synagogue and the
market place."

Turner's description of the evils of the sweating system
was, to say the least, vivid:

> The bundles of clothes are taken home to the midst of
> squalor and disease . . . Fever germs are stitched into lin-
> ings, consumption or smallpox sewed in with the facings and
> the garments go from these tenement-house shops to the homes

16 *Chicago Record-Herald*, September 25, 1901.

17 *Ibid.*, September 4, 1901.

18 *Ibid.*, September 11, 1901.

of the well-to-do all over the country. The wonder is that, in the midst of the revolting conditions of tenement-house tailoring, contagion is not spread in a great degree. But the danger is at least sufficiently recognized to emphasize the solidarity of classes and to compel attention to the struggle for existence of this Jewish population.[19]

Another late immigrant group, the French Canadians, he blamed for destroying the homogeneity of New England through "their reluctance to lose touch with the French-Canadian language and customs, their segregation in distinct localities and their lower standard of comfort."[20] And he added: "Italians, Slovaks, Poles and other immigrants of eastern Europe, together with the Russian Jews, have struck hard blows since 1880 at the standard of comfort of the American workmen. They have made New York City a great reservoir for the pipe lines that run to the misery pools of Europe."[21] Nevertheless, Turner did not entirely despair of these later immigrant groups. If the South Italians were as he described them, he freely acknowledged that centuries of misrule had made them such. "It must always be borne in mind," Turner concluded, "that their worst traits are in part due to centuries of oppression, and that with freer and more favorable conditions in this country the nationality may reveal its strength."[22] The French Canadians, Turner was willing to admit, were, "on the whole, a law abiding, lively, cheerful, people," steadily if slowly being assimilated.[23] Under American conditions, Turner felt that the Jews, too, would improve. "A better environment, a wider distribution, would do much to relieve their misery." The circumstances under which they lived at the moment, Turner acknowledged, could do naught but breed hostility and

19 *Ibid.*, October 16, 1901.

20 *Ibid.*, September 18, 1901.

21 *Ibid.*, October 16, 1901.

22 *Ibid.*, September 11, 1901.

23 *Ibid.*, September 18, 1901.

resentment " against all government and against existing social conditions." The decline of the influence of their religious leaders would probably, he thought, aggravate this discontent; " but at present conservative tendences are manifested." [24]

What Turner wrote in the *Record-Herald* about eighteenth and nineteenth century German immigration into the United States does not support the all too facile doctrine which he expounded in " The Significance of the Frontier in American History "—the doctrine that it was the role of the wilderness to strip the immigrant of his Old World culture traits, thus bringing about the mingling and blending of peoples and the emergence of a composite American type. The Middle West was the cradle of the melting pot, the German newcomer an important element in it. Yet Turner, in dealing specifically with German immigrants in this area, ignored the melting pot frame of reference. Instead his emphasis is rather the other way, upon the conflict between Puritan and German immigrant culture traits. Not only did the German settlers provoke questions of naturalization, assimilation, and nativism, but, he observed, many of the mid-nineteenth century German immigrants

> were radicals, freethinkers and of socialistic tendency, and their utterances aroused opposition among the puritan element that was seeking the same western area. Struggles arose over beer drinking, violations of ' the American Sabbath ' and similar social questions, wherein the New England conscience and the German ideal of personal liberty were at war. Although the Know-Nothing party of this period found the main incentive in opposition to the attitude of Irish Catholics toward public schools and public policy, the German social ideals served also to recruit the party, and the Germans also furnished a Catholic element.[25]

24 *Ibid.*, October 16, 1901.

25 *Ibid.*, September 4, 1901.

Only at the end of the series of *Record-Herald* articles did Turner relate ease of assimilation to the existence of free land:

> The immigrant of the preceding period was assimilated with comparative ease, and it can hardly be doubted that valuable contributions to American character have come from this infusion of non-English stock into the American people. But the free lands that made the process of absorption easy have gone. The immigration is becoming increasingly more difficult of assimilation. Its competition with American labor under existing conditions may give increased power to the producer, but the effects upon American social well-being are dangerous in the extreme.[26]

But when the German element furnished him with the opportunity to demonstrate how, precisely, the factor of the free land facilitated assimilation, he avoided the problem. In fact, the mechanics of the melting pot were never revealed by Turner, and the entire conception is, with him, more an article of faith than a proven sociological phenomenon. Nevertheless, he frequently compared the ease of assimilation in the West with the difficulties attendant upon the process in the East, where immigrant peoples were stratified " underneath an established ruling order " and their cultures, instead of fusing, remained separate.[27] New England, concluded Turner, unlike the " newer sections of the country, was not a good mixing bowl." [28]

Although frankly preferring the old immigrants in the frontier environment to the more recent ones from southern and eastern Europe who settled in cities, Turner saw no real difference between the two groups so far as regards their motive in coming to America. The point of view which maintained that the new immigration was drawn solely by material con-

26 *Ibid.*, September 25, 1901.

27 *Frontier in American History*, " Middle Western Pioneer Democracy," pp. 350-1.

28 Frederick Jackson Turner, *The United States, 1830-50; the Nation and Its Sections* (New York, 1935), p. 55.

siderations, he declared, did not go to the heart of the problem. " The idealism and expectation of these children of the Old World, the hopes that they formed for a newer and freer life across the seas, are almost pathetic when one considers how far they are from the possibility of fruition." [29]

What prevented the fulfillment of these high aims in what Turner described as " the later days of pioneer democracy "? Turner had written even of the old immigration as swelling the ranks of cheap labor, bringing with it the problem of slums, and contributing disproportionately to the pauper and criminal classes.[30] These undesirable effects were aggravated, he maintained, in the case of the new immigration both by its own character and by the altered environment that confronted it: fuller settlement of the country, private ownership of the nation's resources, and the growth of combinations of labor and capital.[31] What happened, said Turner, was that the immigrants who took the place of the old American stock in the labor market, lowered the standard of living and increased the congestion of population. The settling of the southern and eastern European immigrants in cities caused greater antagonism between capital and labor, since the ranks of labor were recruited more and more " from nationalities who arouse no sympathy on the part of capital and little on the part of the general public." Class distinctions were accented by national prejudices, and democracy was invaded.[32]

Turner was aware of the high correlation between slum dwellings and the incidence of disease and death. So he pitied the poor of southeastern Europe who, attempting to forge a civilization in the industrial centre of Pittsburgh, had succeeded in creating " social tragedy." There Bulgar, Pole, and Italian

29 Turner, *Frontier in American History*, " Contributions of the West to American Democracy," p. 264.

30 *United States, 1830-1850*, p. 579.

31 *Frontier in American History*, pp. 243-5.

32 *Ibid.*, " Pioneer Ideals and the State University," pp. 277-8.

struggled mightily merely to earn their daily bread and eke out a brutal and degrading existence. The prevalence of such conditions alongside of the vast increase in wealth and the advancement of science caused Turner to wish, with Huxley, that if there was no hope of elevating the condition of the masses of mankind, some kindly comet would destroy the planet.[33] Yet some of the promise of American democracy was bound to filter through, he thought, to the newest immigrants, and in 1910 he was hopeful that " even in the dull brains of great masses of these unfortunates from southern and eastern Europe the idea of America as the land of freedom and opportunity to rise, the land of pioneer democratic ideals, has found lodgment." [34]

Still Turner feared that the " heady wine " of pioneer idealism might intoxicate the peoples of the new immigration to the point of revolution! [35] As early as 1891 he wrote that socialism was " brought to our shores by European immigrants "; [36] ten years later, he wrote that in periods of industrial depression, with attendant unemployment, the presence of these immigrants was " likely to offer a serious problem "; [37] and in 1924 he wrote that that section of the population which was of southern and eastern European origin was peculiarly given to interpreting America in terms of Europe and introducing Old World ideas into the United States. Mainly to the " recent aliens, who interpret America in terms of Russia," he ascribed the progress of " syndicalism " in the ranks of American labor.[38] He indicted the leaders among these new immigrants for their insistence on the preservation of the " racial group," for their

33 *Ibid.*, " The West and American Ideals," p. 300.

34 *Ibid.*, " Pioneer Ideals," p. 278.

35 *Ibid.*, p. 278.

36 " The Significance of History," *Early Writings of Turner*, p. 63.

37 *Chicago Record-Herald*, September 25, 1901.

38 *Significance of Sections in American History*, " Since the Foundation [of Clark University]," p. 224.

mockery of the melting-pot concept, and for their reference to the older stocks as " hyphenated Anglo-Americans."

Reversing his earlier attitude on the subject, Turner feared that the native stock would be eventually submerged by the higher birth rate of the new immigrants, a process which he characterized as " the peaceful conquest of the old stock by an international army of workers." [39] Their rate of reproduction, he said, served to negate a great many of the gains which otherwise would have accrued to the working class in consequence of the introduction of labor saving machinery, cheap food, " and the general improvement of their conditions." [40]

In holding the high birth rate of the recent immigrants responsible for the failure of American labor to improve its position, Turner evidently failed to distinguish between a contributory and a sufficient cause. Moreover there were occasions when he seemed to ascribe undue weight to group characteristics, particularly those of the new immigration, as determinants of such adverse features in the New World environment as slums, low wages, and the sweating system. He was sometimes tempted to make rash generalizations concerning the national type and the group contribution. He wrote, for example, that the Germans infused " into the American stock and society a conservatism and steady persistence and solidity useful in moderating the nervous energy of the native Americans "; [41] that the South Italians were " quick-witted, but supple in morals "; [42] that the Russian and Polish Jews were " alert, thrifty to disgracefulness, keen to find a way upward." " They have the traits of their race," he went on, " their ability to drive a bargain amounts to genius." [43] Such estimates

39 *Ibid.*, p. 212.

40 *Ibid.*, p. 222.

41 *Chicago Record-Herald*, September 4, 1901.

42 *Ibid.*, September 11, 1901.

43 *Ibid.*, October 16, 1901.

as these of national character are, of course, mere stereotypes rather than the result of research into the nature of the group.

At the same time, these few statements should not obscure the fact that Turner was cognizant of a number of valid approaches to the immigration problem. His writings suggest that the study of immigration to the United States should begin in Europe; that there was significant interaction between geographic and ethnic factors; that, as he suggested to Marcus L. Hansen, European peoples not only exerted an important influence upon America but that, conversely, what the peoples accomplished in America was not without effect in Europe. This, he told Hansen, one learns " by studying the reactions in Europe itself." [44] Thus the study of immigration into the United States both began and ended in Europe.

Just as both the frontier and the middle west were more effective melting pots than the eastern seaboard cities, so in Turner's opinion, America in general was a better melting pot than Europe. Without inquiring deeply into the reasons for the differences, he noted that there was in the United States no memory of national wrongs and wars; nor was there a comparable variety of language, race, and culture types. " No small portion of the American people fled to the New World to escape the European system, and the explanation of our lack of sympathy with the methods and the fundamental assumptions of continental Europe, lies in large measure in the different course which the sections of the Union ran as compared with the nations of Europe." [45] A memorandum prepared by Turner, which Wilson brought with him to Versailles in 1918, incorporated this statement: " We have given evidence that immigrants from all nations of the world can live together peacefully under a single government that does

44 C. Frederick Hansen, " Marcus Lee Hansen—Historian of Immigration," *Common Ground*, II (Summer 1942), 88.

45 *Significance of Sections*, " Sections and Nations," pp. 312, 318.

justice." [46] It was the historian's message of hope from the New World to the Old.

WOODROW WILSON

As a young man, Wilson did not need Adams' seminar to remind him of the excellences of the English tradition. Descendant of generations of Scotch-Irish and Presbyterian clergymen and proud of his extraction, Wilson had read widely in the writings of Burke, Pitt, Adam Smith, and the "master" Bagehot. The subject of his college commencement address was "Our Kinship with England." [47] A year earlier he had written in *The Princetonian* that the history of the American people was part of the history of the English people, and he deemed it "a high thought that we, as a lusty branch of a noble race, are by our national history adding lustre or stain to so bright an escutcheon." [48] The traditions of the "English race," Wilson had occasion to argue in 1880, could not be easily subverted. He had been assigned the negative in a debate on the question "Is the Roman Catholic Element in the United States a Menace to American Institutions?", and his main argument was directed not so much to disproving the statement that international Catholicism had designs on the freedom of America as to demonstrating the strength of our institutional foundations. The boundaries of Catholicism were fixed geographically and racially as they had been for centuries, Wilson said, and he added that that faith had never found firm anchorage among the "German races." In America, he insisted, self-government made papal aggression unthinkable. He cited as additional bulwarks of our freedom the old-

---

46 William D. Diamond, ed., Frederick Jackson Turner, "International Political Parties in a Durable League of Nations," *American Historical Review*, XLVII (April 1942), 549.

47 R. S. Baker, *Woodrow Wilson Life and Letters* (8 vols., New York, 1927-39), I, 96, June 18, 1879.

48 *Ibid.*, May 2, 1878. Review of Green's *Short History of the English People*.

time prejudice against Catholicism (a prejudice " peculiar to our race ") and the common school system.[49]

In *The State,* which appeared in 1889, Wilson ascribed " ancient and distinguished lineage " to the New England township, " saying that it was a spontaneous reproduction of the ancient Germanic mark " and " a direct lineal descendant from the primitive communal institutions which Caesar and Tacitus found existing in the vigor of youth among the peoples living in the ancient seats of our race." According to this interpretation, the New England Puritans invented no institutions; "they were simply letting their race habits and instincts have natural play." [50] Further comparisons by Wilson between the Teutonic mark and the New England village community were followed by the observation that " an influx of foreigners has in many places disturbed and impaired the town system." [51]

Also in *The State,* Wilson spoke of the adaptation of English institutions to the American environment. He described how each colony " borrowed what was best suited to its own situation, and originated what it could not borrow "; he told of colonies which " without losing their English character gained an American form and flavor." [52] Although he paid homage to the theory that Teutonic peoples unfailingly recapitulate the pattern of their institutions, yet he did not fail to recognize

49 Ray S. Baker and William E. Dodd, editors, *The Public Papers of Woodrow Wilson* (6 vols., New York, 1925-7), I, 60-62. Wilson made this comparison between Pitt and Disraeli. " In one respect Pitt resembled the now exalted Jew: he had an unhesitating almost boundless confidence in himself, in the wisdom of his own aims. But Beaconsfield loves and has confidence in himself alone; Pitt loved and trusted the English people as well—for he was himself an Englishman!" *Ibid.,* I, 17.

50 *The State; Elements of Historical and Practical Politics* (Boston, 1892), 526-7.

51 Wilson incorporates into his text most of the analogies which H. B. Adams drew between the German mark and the New England village. *Ibid.,* p. 528.

52 *Ibid.,* p. 450. In 1918 edition, pp. 268, 338, 342.

the existence of change in our institutional life. But it was change wrought in the manner of Englishmen in America, belonging " to the same practical political race as Englishmen in England " and demonstrating enough of the English quality of adjustment to strike out on " not a few lines of development of their own. . . . " [53]

What Wilson meant by change wrought in the English tradition he made abundantly clear in the essay entitled " The Character of Democracy in the United States." Habit, discipline, character, and political aptitude are fundamental in the maintenance of institutional stability, Wilson argued: the success of democracy is contingent upon capacity for self-government and practical aptitude for public affairs, and this capacity and this aptitude came only with training. Democracy in the United States he regarded as " a piece of developed habit " whose only stable foundation was " English character." Wilson distinguished the democracy of the " English race," " bred by slow circumstance and founded upon habit," from continental democracy, which is " bred by discontent and founded upon revolution." American democracy, child of English political development, Wilson held menaced not only by the heightened tempo of contemporary civilization but also by " the restless forces of European democratic thought and anarchic turbulence brought to us in such alarming volume by immigration. . . . " [54]

Immigrant " minds cast in every mould of race—minds inheriting every basis of environment, warped by the diverse

[53] *Ibid.*, pp. 450-60. In 1918 edition, p. 285.

[54] *Selected Literary and Political Papers and Addresses of Woodrow Wilson* (3 vols., New York, 1925-6), III, 99-103. Wilson, in 1894, was severely critical of Jefferson, identifying him with the " evil," " corrupting," philosophy of the French Revolution. He was particularly dubious of the theory which regarded liberty as a matter of abstract right rather than the fruit of political maturity and gradual historical development. Jefferson, wrote Wilson, was " not a thorough American because of the strain of French philosophy that . . . weakened all his thought." " A Calendar of Great Americans," *ibid.*, 196-7; *Public Papers*, I, 176, 177, 407, 412, 433.

histories of a score of different nations," threatened, in Wilson's view, our " Saxon habits in government."

> Were the nation homogeneous, were it composed simply of later generations of the same stock by which our institutions were planted, few adjustments of the old machinery of politics would, perhaps, be necessary to meet the exigencies of growth. But every added element of variety, particularly every added element of foreign variety, complicates even the simpler questions of politics. [55]

The ultimate danger of variety and heterogeneity in the population of the United States, Wilson felt, was national disintegration.[56]

At about the time these sentiments were expressed, Wilson became acquainted with Frederick Jackson Turner. As graduate students at Johns Hopkins they frequently discussed the role of the West in the development of the United States; they agreed that it was much neglected in conventional historical interpretation.[57] Turner's address on the " Significance of the Frontier in American History " was read to Wilson before its delivery in July 1893. Later that year it was apparent that Wilson had qualified his acceptance of the Teutonic germ theory of American development; for, in a review of Goldwin Smith's *"Views" on Our Political History,* he took the author to task for failing to recognize the role of the West in moulding the distinctive characteristics of the American people.

55 " Our own temperate blood, schooled to self-possession and to the measured conduct of self-government, is receiving a constant infusion and yearly experiencing a partial corruption of foreign blood. Our own equable habits have been crossed with the feverish humors of the restless Old World. We are unquestionably facing an ever-increasing difficulty of self-command with ever-deteriorating materials, possibly with degenerating fibre." *Selected Literary Papers,* III, 107.

56 Wilson repeated much the same ideas in an address made on April 30, 1889, entitled " Make Haste Slowly." *Ibid.,* I, 30-39.

57 Baker, *op. cit.,* II, 125.

This great continent, received European populations, European manners and faiths, European purposes, into its forests, and, finding they meant to stay, proceeded to work its will upon them. They took on a new character, and submitted to a new process of growth. Our continental life is a radically different thing from our life in the old settlements. Every element of the old life that penetrated the continent at all has been digested and has become an element of a new life. It is this transformation that constitutes our history.[58]

In " The Course of American History " (May 16, 1895) Wilson credited the frontier with having made " the great compounded nation," though he recognized that a precedent already existed since the population and institutions of the middle states of the Atlantic seaboard were themselves of a heterogeneous nature.[59] In the West, Frenchmen, Scandinavians, Celts, Dutch, Slavs, Latins, and Orientals rubbed elbows with the first stock of the settlements: English, Scots, and Scotch-Irish. Here was wrought " a mixture of peoples, a modification of mind and habit, a new round of experiment and adjustment . . . a new temper, a new spirit of adventure. . . ."[60] Wilson did not deny that the common British stock first made the country " and has always set the pace," but the persistent tide of foreign blood which came to our shores had not, he thought, received sufficient recognition from historians.[61]

What sort of recognition Wilson himself as a historian gave to immigrant peoples is apparent from his *A History of the American People*. He regarded the German and Irish immigration of the early nineteenth century as having had, on the whole, a desirable effect on national development.[62] In his

58 *Forum*, XVI (December 1893), 495-6.

59 At this time, he described the heterogeneity of the Middle Atlantic States as being most typical of American development. *Selected Literary Papers*, III, 220. This idea is incorporated into his *A History of the American People* (5 vols., New York, 1902), III, 238.

60 *Selected Literary Papers*, III, 221-222.

61 *Ibid.*, 224.

62 *History of the American People*, IV, 132-3.

opinion, the best of the tide of German and Irish immigrants settled on " the western farms and the open regions of the interior," while " its most unwholesome deposits " were left at the eastern ports. Among the latter were those " whom revolution had thrust out of the old world, men who wanted power and were apt at intrigue, restless men, many of whom were outcasts, some of whom were desperadoes "; types such as these made for uneasiness among men " born and bred to the politics and manner of America " and created a legitimate issue for Know-Nothing agitation.[63] Wilson placed a good part of the blame for the Haymarket Affair on the sort of foreigners the Know-Nothings feared, the discontented proletariat of European countries who entered our cities and preached doctrines not elsewhere tolerated. Even men of native birth were beginning to succumb to the " infection of political anarchy " introduced by the immigrants.[64]

As immigration came more and more from the South and East of Europe instead of from the North and West, Wilson found it increasingly objectionable. He noticed " an alteration in stock which students of affairs marked with uneasiness." No longer did men of the " sturdy stocks " of northern Europe or of the " Latin-Gallic stocks " of France and northern Italy constitute the main stream of " foreign blood." They were replaced by

> men of the lowest class from the south of Italy and men of the meaner sort out of Hungary and Poland, men out of the ranks where there was neither skill nor energy nor any initiative of quick intelligence; and they came in numbers which increased from year to year, as if the countries of the south of Europe were disburdening themselves of the more sordid and hapless elements of their population, the men whose standards of life and work were such as American workmen had never dreamed of hitherto.

63 *Ibid.*, pp. 162-4.

64 *Ibid.*, V, 187.

Wilson felt that the Chinese were more desirable than " most of the coarse crew that came crowding in every year at the eastern ports." That the southern and eastern Europeans were tolerated whereas the Chinese were not, Wilson explained on the grounds that the European immigrant took over the lowest place in the labor market while the Asiatics competed with the middle classes.[65]

What Wilson said about immigrant peoples in his *History* was little noticed either by immigrants or natives until he became a candidate for the presidency. Then, offense was taken by spokesmen for the groups about whom Wilson had written harshly and explanations demanded on pain of reprisal on election day. The success of Wilson's candidacy was in some degree dependent upon ability to carry the vote in urban centers, where there lived many immigrants from southern and eastern Europe.[66] Wilson replied to the protesting Agostino de Biasi, editor of the Italian review *Il Carroccio,* that in his history he was merely " deploring the coming to this country of certain lawless elements which I had supposed all thoughtful Italians themselves deplored . . . . Certainly, the Italians I have known . . . have constituted one of the most interesting and admirable elements in our American life." He salved the hurt feelings of the members of the Hungarian League with much the same language. Wilson, the master stylist, counted himself " very unfortunate if I have been so awkward in my way of expressing what I had to say as to bring injustice to a people whom I admire and respect." [67]

Between the writing of these passages in 1902 and their repudiation in 1912, Wilson's attitudes underwent still other modification. He came to realize that the twentieth-century crusade for economic reforms was in keeping with the Jeffersonian ideal of a society offering the widest opportunity for

65 *Ibid.*, pp. 212-214.

66 Dodd, *op. cit.*, pp. 109-110.

67 Baker, *op. cit.*, III, 286-7.

individual development.[68] Jefferson's conviction that the intellectual currents of the eighteenth century expressed the "thought not only of nations but of mankind," Wilson related to his own growing appreciation of the United States as a nation "linked to mankind by every tie of blood and circumstance." [69] In this period, too, Wilson acquired a new sympathy with the political aspirations of undeveloped peoples.[70] He no longer conceived of constitutional government as necessarily the exclusive possession of the English peoples. On the contrary, he conceived America's mission to be the export of the principles of such government to all the nations of the world, with the period of apprenticeship for backward nations shortened. It has been suggested that Wilson's "less strict view of the prerequisites of discipline and experience for democratic self-government" was the result of an endeavor to balance the rising power of imperialist groups in colonial areas against the new, raw forces of democracy.[71]

Along with an altered attitude toward Jeffersonian idealism and toward the politically backward peoples, Wilson came to have a changed conception of the urban melting pot. Under the banner of the New Freedom, he was fighting the battle of the people against entrenched privilege, and he was confronted with the immediate, pressing necessity of rallying the naturalized vote to the Democratic standard. Clearly this was not the time to speak of the learning of English liberty as a slow

68 "The Spirit of Jefferson," April 16, 1906, *New York Times*, April 17, 1906.

69 "What Jefferson Would Do," April 13, 1912, *Public Papers*, II, 424-5, 429.

70 "A New Latin-American Policy," Address at Mobile, October 27, 1913, *ibid.*, III, 64-69.

71 C. H. Notter, *The Origins of the Foreign Policy of Woodrow Wilson* (Baltimore, 1937), 268-270. Wilson, at about this time, began "moving away from the tradition of entrepreneur liberalism in the direction of positive governmental action as the means of eliminating economic maladjustments." William Diamond, *The Economic Thought of Woodrow Wilson* (Baltimore, 1943), p. 87.

process, a matter of gradually acquired habit, a matter of disciplining for generation after generation; clearly the period of apprenticeship in the guild of liberty had to be shortened —the melting pot worked because events prescribed that it must.

In considering Wilson's altered attitude toward the political capacities of non-English peoples, there is one thing that should be kept in mind. Not even in 1889, did Wilson claim that American democracy was biologically determined. On the contrary, he was reported as having said in 1898 that in the United States the idea of nationality had to do with " community of organization, of life, and of tradition," [72]—it was not a matter of common origin and blood. In 1891 Wilson questioned the soundness of John W. Burgess' contention that there were inherent differences in political capacity among the Slavic, Celtic, and Teutonic " races." [73] In fact, in most of his early writings the failings of the non-English peoples with regard to democracy are viewed as cultural and transient rather than racial and permanent.[74]

In 1915, Wilson asserted that with " continuity of blood " it was a comparatively simple matter to perpetuate the tradition of democratic liberty. But he hastened to add that in America it has been " generously easy " to indoctrinate those who come from lands where the concept of personal liberty neither originated nor was part of the heritage.[75] He who once feared the disintegrating ideological influence of Europe's malcontents, now welcomed the politically oppressed who were denied elsewhere the right and opportunity to agitate for what they conceived to be the natural and inalienable rights of man. Without immigration, he said, the humane ardors of American politics

---

72 Quoted in Notter, *op. cit.*, p. 104.

73 *Atlantic Monthly*, LXVII (May 1891), 694-9.

74 Notter, *op. cit.*, pp. 30, 42, 43, 46, 51.

75 " Be Not Afraid of Our Foreign-Born Citizens," October 11, 1915, *Public Papers*, III, 376.

would have cooled and men and women of native stock would not have had before them a constant reminder of early American ideals.[76]

Wilson, at this time, argued that the component elements of the melting pot had the effect of enlarging the " American consciousness," so that on " all sides it touches. elbows and touches hearts with all the nations of mankind." [77] The " fermentation of the melting pot " Wilson in 1916 characterized as the antithesis of war. War he defined as " a competition of national standards, of national traditions, and of national political systems. Europe has grappled in war, as we have grappled in peace, to see what is going to be done with these things when they come into hot contact with one another." The war, he hoped, would make cooperative international action the successor of national hatreds, and the United States which had brought peoples of the world together upon terms of liberty, cooperation and peace, was upheld as a prophetic example for mankind.

Wilson, then, conceived of the American melting pot as something bigger than America—really " as big as the world."[78] " Consciously made up, out of all the great families of mankind, we are champions of the rights of mankind." [79] Compounded of all the nations of the world, we were " the mediating Nation of the world,—able to understand them in the compound, not separately, as partisans, but unitedly. . . ." [80] In his preparedness addresses of 1916 and in arguments before the country in 1919 urging the ratification of the Covenant of

76 Veto of the First Immigration Bill, January 28, 1915, *ibid.*, III, 253.

77 *Ibid.*, III, 377.

78 " The Mecklenburg Declaration of Independence," May 20, 1916. *Ibid.*, IV, 180. See also " The Heroes of Vera Cruz," May 11, 1914, *ibid.*, III, 104-105.

79 "America Must Become Partners in the Guarantee of a Just Peace," May 30, 1916, *ibid.*, IV, 194.

80 " Call to the Associated Press," April 20, 1915, *ibid.*, III, 304.

the League of Nations, Wilson appealed for the extension of the melting pot principle to all the nations of the world.[81]

This lofty conception of the unity of the American peoples failed to take into account the fact that millions of Americans of European origin and ancestry were not indifferent to the fate of the old country.[82] Wilson's Americanism, his sense of the right and honorable, would not permit him to play the politics of the hyphen. He said as much in 1916 when he lost the normally Democratic Irish vote in addition to that of the German-American—and almost lost the election.[83] On the league issue these groups continued to harass him—the Germans sullen over the defeat of the Fatherland, the Irish distressed because he failed to take a high hand with England in demanding the independence of Ireland.[84] In addition, half a dozen or more vocal East European minorities, besides the Negro group, plagued him with their demands. America seemed to be less a melting pot than a country of " silent majorities and vociferous minorities." [85]

Wilson attempted to meet the specific demands of the minorities by preaching moral principles and a plan for the betterment of all rather than part of mankind. But the leaders of the peoples were blind, or else they would not see. Wilson defined a hyphenate as a man who carried " a dagger that he [was] ready to plunge into the vitals of the Republic " and appealed in the name of his " clients in this case . . . the children . . .

81 *Ibid.*, IV, 83, 180-182, 346; VI, 79, 82, 143.

82 Thomas A. Bailey, *Woodrow Wilson and the Lost Peace* (New York, 1944), p. 2.

83 Child, *op. cit.*, pp. 139-53.

84 Bailey, *Wilson and the Lost Peace*, pp. 204, 266. Wilson went so far as to suggest to the English government through Ambassador Page that self-government be granted Ireland to take the Irish question out of American politics. *Papers Relating to the Foreign Relations of the United States, The Lansing Papers, 1914-1920* (2 vols., Washington, 1940), II, 4-5.

85 Thomas H. Bailey, *Woodrow Wilson and the Great Betrayal* ('New York, 1945), pp. 22-7.

the next generation." He talked, too, of pledges made to those who died for a better world.[86] Alas, children and dead men had no votes and the hyphenates did. The ideals of Wilson lived on to be fought for another day—but it was Lodge rather than Wilson who seemed to understand the mood of the people at that time. Lodge could "talk Irish" to the hyphenates and denounce "perfidious Albion," Wilson could not; Lodge wept with the Italian Americans over Fiume; Wilson spoke of the principles involved in handing the city over to Yugoslavia.[87] Lodge was never the idealist about the mingling of peoples that Wilson was or pretended to be; but on the League issue specifically, upon which the peoples had most at stake, they were more willing to listen to the pandering Lodge than to the prophetic Wilson.[88]

It may be well, in summing up, to emphasize the fact that when Roosevelt, Turner, and Wilson expressed doubts concerning the successful operation of the melting pot, what they had particularly in mind was the melting pot of the city. This attitude was caused, in part, by preference for the peoples of the old immigration, the components of the early nineteenth century frontier melting pot. Unlike the frontier melting pot, which occurred earlier and was accepted as part of the process of nation making, the later mingling of peoples was looked upon more as an assimilative process whereby the peoples from southern and eastern Europe were indoctrinated in canons of Americanism established by earlier arrivals.

Roosevelt, Turner, and Wilson believed also that peoples blended best in areas where the ratio of land to population was high. The faith of these historians in land as a solvent of cultural differences did not rest entirely upon their awareness of the role played by the frontier in expanding economic oppor-

86 H. C. F. Bell, *Woodrow Wilson and the People* (New York, 1945), p. 348.

87 *Ibid.*, pp. 268, 311-12; Schriftgieser, *Lodge*, p. 327.

88 Bailey, *Wilson and the Great Betrayal*, p. 82.

tunity. Rather was the mere presence of unoccupied land accepted by them as an important aid in the process of the mingling of peoples. In the city, for the old immigration and still more for the new, assimilation was thought to be slower and, at times, not too sure.

There was an element of compulsion about the faith of Roosevelt and Wilson in the urban melting pot. Both had large political stakes in the theory that line fences separating diverse peoples were demolished by democracy. It is interesting that Turner, without personal political interest in the working of the urban melting pot, was perhaps the most pessimistic concerning its outcome.

As for the frontier melting pot, it should be noted that Turner accepted that phenomenon almost as an article of faith —he did not investigate the actual mingling process, nor were his conclusions concerning the outcome drawn with reference to what had actually occurred. Between the meagre fabric of fact presented by him on the subjects of immigration and immigrant culture and his conclusions—his faith in " Americanization," " assimilation," " composite nationality " and " new blend "—lies a jungle, unexplored by him, of complex human and environmental relationships.

In 1892, Turner seemed well aware that a vast amount of work remained to be done in this field. We really do not know America, he warned, unless we know the history of its peoples. It is unfortunate that after this date he is less historian demonstrating a process or testing an assumption and more prophet of the mingling of the American peoples.

Finally, Parkman, Roosevelt, Wilson, and even Turner have in common a feeling of optimism concerning the eventual outcome of the melting pot. No matter how dubious they may be of certain phases of the process, they have an abiding faith that the thing itself has worked.

CHAPTER VI

THE IMMIGRANT AND AMERICAN POLITICAL DEVELOPMENT

IN the eighteen eighties, the monograph was something of a novelty in American historiography, which field of study was dominated by writers who treat in a series of volumes a large period of American history. Moreover, monographs on immigration and immigrant peoples were slow in appearing even after the method in general had gained widespread acceptance. Consequently, for the treatment of the role of the immigrant in American life, one looks to the comprehensive histories of Hermann Eduard Von Holst, James Schouler, James Ford Rhodes, John Bach McMaster, Ellis Paxon Oberholtzer, and Edward Channing.

HERMANN EDUARD VON HOLST

Of all the works in which a single historian has attempted to cover in a series of volumes a sizeable period of American history, perhaps the most outdated is Hermann Eduard Von Holst's *Verfassung und Demokratie der Vereinigten Staaten von Amerika,* the first volume of which appeared in English translation in 1876.[1] Von Holst's narrative covers the period from the adoption of the Constitution to the outbreak of the Civil War. It is concerned mainly with the slavery controversy and the political and constitutional issues leading up to the war. Von Holst's discussion of immigration is incidental to the central themes about which his history revolves, and his attitude toward immigrant peoples is conditioned by their behavior in relation to these issues and by the author's own background.

In the case of Von Holst, the background factor is of exceptional interest, since he was himself an immigrant. Born

1 *The Constitutional and Political History of the United States,* translators, John J. Lalor and Alfred B. Mason (8 vols., Chicago, 1876-92).

in 1841 of German parentage in Livonia, a Baltic province of Russia, Von Holst was educated in Germany, and came to the United States in 1867, a refugee from Tsarism. He obtained a first-hand acquaintance with American democracy and, in 1872, returned to Germany to teach American history and American constitutional law at the University of Strassburg and after 1874 at Freiburg. Between 1872 and 1892, when he was appointed as head of the history department of the University of Chicago, Von Holst made only two brief visits to the United States. Five years before his death in 1904, Von Holst retired first to Italy and then to his beloved Freiburg.[2]

Although Von Holst was a German immigrant in a nation whose core, he admitted, was Anglo-American, he regarded his origin as an advantage. His history presented the German immigrant as a superior type whose coming benefited the Republic.[3] Admittedly, there was " a certain something in the character of every nation which a foreigner will never be able to completely understand, because it cannot be grasped by the judgment; it can only be felt, and in order to feel it, one's flesh and blood must be filled with the national sentiment." [4] Still, there were advantages in being a foreigner—or at least a foreigner of German origin. For example, the " intellectual and moral superiority " of the German immigrants caused them to regard the Kansas-Nebraska Bill " as an outrageous breach of faith against which German consciousness of right and German rectitude rebelled." The Irish, who were not so fortunately endowed, were, as late as 1854, still devoted to the Democratic party and " indifferent, if not ignorant, of the real issues involved in the repeal of the Missouri compromise." [5]

2 Ferdinand Schevill, "Hermann Eduard Von Holst," *Dictionary of American Biography*, IX, 177-9; Eric F. Goldman, " Hermann Eduard Von Holst: Plumed Knight of American Historiography," *Mississippi Valley Historical Review*, XXIII (March 1937), 511-32.

3 *Constitutional History*, IV, 430.

4 *Ibid.*, I, viii-ix.

5 *Ibid.*, IV, 427-8.

Von Holst further considered that his origin was an aid to him in his role as historian. It enabled him, he said, to be more objective; it prevented " his judgment from being betrayed by his feeling." Then, as if dissatisfied with this rationalization, Von Holst hastened to add that he did " feel " with the people of the United States.[6] Now, either of these positions when advanced independently is defensible but when they are advanced simultaneously, the impression is that the author protests too much. Von Holst's extravagant praise of the German immigrant and his disparagement of the immigrants from Ireland and southern and eastern Europe probably is due, in great part, to a desire to bolster up his own feeling of security.

Although Von Holst professed to " feel " with the people of the United States, whatever such feeling he may have had apparently did not extend to the democratic element, the Jeffersonians and the Jacksonians. He dismissed the Declaration of Independence as derived from the " crude theories " of Rousseau and as the American manifestation of the late eighteenth century effort to establish arbitrary premises as political truths.[7] Regarding the Anglo-Saxon as innately conservative, he characterized the American Revolution as less a defense of natural rights than an effort by conservative, rational, law-abiding Anglo-Saxons to redress specific wrongs.[8] In connection with his treatment of the Jacksonian era, he expressed the wish that the vote might be weighed in proportion to the " virtue," " respectability," and " intelligence " of the electorate. He considered it unfortunate that the ballot of the poor white of the South was counted as equal to that of the New England farmer; that in the North the ballot of the farmer, merchant, manufacturer, or tradesman was given no greater weight than that of the Irish day laborer.[9]

6 *Ibid.*, I, ix.

7 *Ibid.*, p. 32.

8 *Ibid.*, pp. 2, 34, II, 104, 107; III, 437.

9 *Ibid.*, II, 697.

From this background, the reasons for Von Holst's opposition to the Irish begin to emerge. The latter were a proletarian element and inclined to support the party of Jackson. Von Holst did not like even German immigrants who were politically thus disposed. Moreover, the Irish were assigned " politically in every other respect . . . to the lowest stage of culture "; they could easily be manipulated by demagogues into a blindly obedient political machine. The worst of it was that they were so engrossed in earning a living that they were unable to attain even " a half-way correct understanding of the nature and meaning of the slavery question." [10]

Believing history to be purposive, slavery doomed, and the victory of the national idea predetermined, Von Holst was naturally impatient with men and events that contradicted this conception of our historic destiny. The Irish, as northern members of the Democratic party, were *ipso facto* helping the cause of disunion and the cause of slavery. They were an embodied obstruction to the proper working out of what Von Holst called the Times-Spirit.[11] Von Holst opposed the Know-Nothing movement on similar grounds—that is, for its equivocation on matters of slavery and state rights. Foreignism, he said, was a false issue and in a

> modern civilized state, it is never possible lastingly and arbitrarily to supplant the cardinal problems of its political life which have their roots in actual circumstances by secondary and more or less artificial, not to say fabricated, questions.[12]

Von Holst was further opposed to the Irish because they were Catholics and " the history of the Catholic church showed how disposed and skillful the clergy were to possess themselves of political supremacy." Although the small number of Catholics in the United States during the eighteen fifties could not

10 *Ibid.*, pp. 504-5, V, 80.

11 *Ibid.*, IV, 244; I, x.

12 *Ibid.*, V, 84.

possibly have constituted a threat to the "fundamentally Protestant character which American national life had thus far borne," Von Holst envisioned a situation wherein the Catholic element, voting as a block, under hierarchal dictation might, despite its paucity of members, hold the balance between the two major political parties. After all,

> the majority of Catholics in the country stood on such a plane of culture and their antecedent circumstances had been such, that it was very natural the question should be raised, whether the Catholic clergy, if they took the matter skillfully in hand, and pursued it with persistent energy, would not succeed in misusing their power for the furtherance of their ecclesiastical purposes.

Thus far, admitted Von Holst, they have not attempted to do so "but, notwithstanding, the fears of the Know-Nothings could not be said to have no positive basis." [13]

As further proof that not all the spectres seen by the Know-Nothings were of their own manufacture, Von Holst cited expressions of "extreme Ultramontanism," gleaned from the American Catholic press. Merely a word from the hierarchy could have checked this "fanaticism," argued Von Holst.

> That they did not speak that word, was neither because they did not have the legal, ecclesiastical power to command, nor because they paid no attention to the matter, but for the reason that it semed to them the interests of the church called for no such interference on their part. The authorities of the Catholic church were industriously discreet but, to say the least, they felt no great displeasure that Ultramontanism, in its extremist form, was preached by volunteers for whose action no official responsibility rested on them. [14]

Von Holst made clear his opposition to state support for Catholic schools and in the matter of the ownership of ecclesi-

13 *Ibid.*, pp. 85-6.

14 *Ibid.*, p. 88.

astical properties insisted that the bishops had, in effect, violated a constitutional law of New York state. Von Holst thought that the federal government went too far in the direction of friendliness when it placed a naval vessel at the disposal of Cardinal Bedini, " who had come to the country to sit in judgment in a conflict between episcopal assumption and a law of the state of New York—and who, as was to be expected, decided in favor of the bishop." Having criticized the papal nuncio's mission and the federal government's " demonstrative kindness " to him, Von Holst indicated his disapproval of the " hateful proceedings " by which the Protestant populace manifested its dislike of Bedini.[15]

Though convinced that the menace of Catholicism to American institutions was no figment of the nativist imagination, Von Holst did not regard the fact that some Catholics were Ultramontanists as in any degree a justification for the Know-Nothing demand that all Catholics be disfranchised. Furthermore, he doubted whether it was, in practice, possible for that element among Know-Nothings who wished to do so to distinguish between Catholics who held Ultramontanist views and those who did not. Moreover, Von Holst at this point stated that the Know-Nothings were guilty of exactly the same sort of conspiracy that they accused Catholics of perpetrating. Know-Nothings, he said, criticized Catholics for voting at the dictation of the Roman Catholic hierarchy. But were not the Know-Nothings bound by a vow of secrecy? Were they not as loyal to the nativist hierarchy as the Catholics were to their ecclesiastical superiors? Were not the nativists contending against what they considered the evils of political Catholicism with the same weapons they accused the Catholics of using? And were not the aims and methods of the nativist cure worse than the abuses introduced by the immigrants? [16]

15 *Ibid.*, pp. 95-99.

16 *Ibid.*, pp. 102, 104, 107-11.

Despite dislike of their political behavior, Von Holst could sympathize with the position of the Irish immigrant who was forced into the Democratic party by virtue of the fact that the nativists were identified with the Whigs. The case was the same even with the German immigrant. Moreover, Von Holst was sufficiently practical to realize that, although certain aspects of nativism were " intelligible " and " excusable," yet the political ostracism of the immigrant would result in a slowing up of that flow of newcomers which was essential to American economic development. He was, too, enough of a democrat to hope that the nativist program would not prevail and that the problem of the assimilation of the immigrant would be " solved in the way in which it has been solved and is solved every day." The Catholic Church, he said, could even aid in its solution by taking the Irish in hand and mitigating the effect that their coarseness, brutality, and ignorance had upon the foundations of the healthy American democracy.[17]

Like John W. Burgess, Von Holst's belief in the supremacy of the national state was a matter of intense personal conviction. Consequently, any element of separatism and diversity which appeared to frustrate the ideal of a unified national state must inevitably arouse his opposition. This, in part, accounted for his attitude toward Catholicism and also toward immigrants of the late nineteenth century from southern and eastern Europe, whom he characterized as having

> little more in common with the people of the United States than the human shape and the most general features of human nature, thrown in solid blocks of hundreds and thousands into the country, coming with the set purpose to form and maintain distinct communities within the community, not only unable but unwilling to be assimilated politically or socially, intellectually or morally—that is a danger to make every reflecting patriot blanch.[18]

17 *Ibid.*, II, 504-5, 524-5.

18 " The Need of Universities in the United States," *Educational Review*, V (February 1893), 108; "Are We Awakened?", *Journal of Political Economy*, II (September 1894), 486, 487, 509.

He was further opposed to these newest immigrants on the ground that they were socialistically inclined. Von Holst, in the nineties, was alarmed by the restlessness of labor. Economic conservatism was an aspect of his integral nationalism, and he interpreted any threat to the existing social order as disruptive of national unity. Because of their turn of mind and their political behavior, the immigrants from the South and East of Europe were regarded by Von Holst as impeding the complete integration of the American nation.

Von Holst's history does not offer a penetrating analysis of the immigrant's role in American political life in the period covered by his narrative. However, this old-fashioned, almost archaic history, with its involved style and frequent moralizing, has this to be said for it: in dealing with the Catholic Church in American politics, it treats a subject which later historians for the most part chose to ignore. Von Holst's concern with the impact of Catholicism upon the American commonwealth was the logical outgrowth of his experience in Germany. The years of the *Kulturkampf* made a profound impression upon him and, since *The Constitutional and Political History of the United States* was "essentially a product of German historiography,"[19] Von Holst was bound to carry over into his history of the United States certain of the issues which were agitating the newly formed German Empire.[20] Students of the immigrant in American political life can afford to ignore Von Holst's impressions of German, Irish, and Southern and Eastern European immigrants as well as his crotchety prejudices; but they will find his treatment of the Catholic Church and the Know-Nothing movement of some interest.

19 Schevill, *op. cit.*, p. 178.

20 Aspects of the contemporary stereotyped conception of the Jew find expression in *The Constitutional History* in such passages as: "To be called a 'politician' is, indeed, as great an offense as to be called a 'Jew,' in certain circles." *Ibid.*, II, 78 fn; "The parliamentary Jew's traffic..." *Ibid.*, p. 447.

JAMES SCHOULER

Different in orientation from Von Holst's account was James Schouler's *History of the United States of America under the Constitution,* the first five volumes of which appeared between 1880 and 1891 (the approximate period of the publication of Von Holst's major work). Whereas Von Holst disputed the validity of the theory of the social contract and hardly approved the principles of the Declaration of Independence, Schouler vigorously affirmed these concepts. For the Federalism and Whiggism of Von Holst, Schouler substituted faith in the principles of Jeffersonianism. His is the story of the growth of American democracy from the point where the narrative of George Bancroft breaks off, and he is the inheritor of Bancroft's mantle.

On his mother's side Schouler was descended from old Massachusetts stock, but his father was a native of Scotland, who was brought to America in early life. Born in 1839, James Schouler was educated at Harvard. He was admitted to the bar in 1862; shortly thereafter he responded to Lincoln's call for volunteers. After brief war service, he resumed the practice of the law until deafness caused him to turn his attention to legal writing. He was for a number of years lecturer in the law schools of Boston University and the National University at Washington. Between 1891 and 1908, at the invitation of Herbert Baxter Adams, he lectured on American history at Johns Hopkins.[21]

Despite the character of his training, Schouler's history is less political and legalistic than Von Holst's. Freeman's idea of history as past politics impressed Schouler as "the truth" but not "the whole truth." Instead of invoking a mystical

21 There are biographical accounts of Schouler in the *Dictionary of American Biography,* XVI, 459-60; Edward Stanwood, "Memorial of James Schouler," *Massachusetts Historical Society Proceedings,* LIV (1922), 283-88; James Schouler, *Historical Briefs* (New York, 1896), pp. 196-310; L. E. Ellis, "James Schouler," *Mississippi Valley Historical Review,* XVI (September 1929).

Times-Spirit, like Von Holst, Schouler did not hesitate to make value judgments, praising what he deemed wise and good in American historical evolution and condemning what he considered reprehensible.[22]

Schouler did not utilize the comparative method of inquiry. He did, however, stress the essentially Anglo-Saxon character of the American institutional heritage and insisted that the predominance of the Anglo-Saxon " race " and " temperament " was primarily responsible for American institutional virility. Non-English elements in the colonial population, Schouler evidently believed, contributed little to " those pregnant truths " upon which the Republic was founded. " The genius of republican free government on this continent," Schouler concluded in 1897, " is Anglo-American." [23]

During Washington's second administration, wrote Schouler, peoples of the Old World were attracted to the New because of the lure of the West, the demand for labor in a new country, and the ideals of a democracy. The European immigrant, he went on, " welcomed the prospect of gaining an honest livelihood in a country where all were equals, and a man might marry and rear a family without the depressing thought that for each new mouth to be fed his scanty crust must be broken into smaller fragments." [24] In writing thus, Schouler may have been mindful of his own grandfather who came to the United States as a political refugee from Scotland.

Schouler opposed the exclusion of any who sought refuge in the United States from Old World oppressions; [25] nor did he deplore the modification which he observed in Philadelphia and New York of American tastes and habits by foreign innovations—for example, by French boarding-houses, " strange

22 *Historical Briefs*, p. 54.

23 *Ideals of the Republic* (Boston, 1908), p. 10; *Constitutional Studies, State and Federal* (New York, 1897), pp. 71, 304.

24 *History of the United States of America Under the Constitution* (7 vols., New York, 1894), I, 240.

25 *Ibid.*, pp. 351-2.

dances, strange music, and a strange language." He denounced the Federalists for their support of the Alien Acts.[26] Unlike Von Holst, who thought the legislation against aliens justifiable in the light of impending difficulties with France,[27] Schouler strongly doubted whether French machinations in this country were anything to be alarmed about. Prolonging the term of residence of an alien before he became eligible for citizenship would, in Schouler's opinion, increase the turbulence of the newcomers " in their long period of uncertain allegiance and irresponsibility." [28]

At the same time, Schouler was aware of significant differences distinguishing Anglo-Saxons from other constituents of the populaton. He thought that the " Latin blood " of the inhabitants of New Orleans hindered their assimilation; that factional strife in the middle states of the Atlantic seaboard was caused, in part, by the presence of a heterogeneous population.[29] The native citizen of " Anglo-Saxon blood," when compared with " the fickle and excitable immigrant " was

> more conservative by temperament, more respectful to superiors, more in harmony with well-ordered systems of government, less ignorant, less violent, better qualified to rise superior to early disadvantages and achieve wealth and position . . . .[30]

It was their " Saxon temperament," he said, that caused some Americans to oppose the French Revolution. Concerning the efforts of Genet to influence American opinion he wrote

> Methods of influence which Latin nations might safely employ upon one another are found ill-suited to our far less impulsive Saxon.[31]

---

26 *Ibid.*, pp. 404-5.

27 *Constitutional History*, I, 141-2.

28 *History of the United States*, I, 405-6, 410, 413.

29 *Ibid,,* II, 82, 257, 279.

30 *Ibid.*, III, 46.

31 *Ibid.*, I, 264.

Discussing the political situation in 1818, Schouler observed that a "fierce but nearly suffocated democracy, jealous and emulous of rule," was threatening to burst the chains of conservatism that restrained it.[32] To this democracy flocked the poor and downtrodden of other lands whose deep hatred of external authority popular government sought to modify

> by placing the best opportunities of wealth within their reach; by inculcating the spirit of universal brotherhood; by lowering the social barriers so as to let in the worthy and industrious; and, lest the new-comer might himself prove, hardened and intractable, by taking his children in hand, if possible, and moulding them into happy and tractable citizens.

The immigrant, Schouler felt, contributed an element of strength to the community, but shared the "spirit of envious democracy" resulting from the "inequalities of worldly goods."

> The Irish immigrants, herded together in some mean tenement, cast their votes against the landlord interest; the workman leaving home with his tin pail at sunrise recorded, if he dared, a silent protest against the mill-owners whom he served.[33]

To the part of the population which knew little of the pleasures of life; the "fierce democracy" or, in its extremist aspect, "the mob," the French Commune had owed its existence. The "fickle and excitable immigrant," fell more readily into this class than "the native citizen of Anglo-Saxon blood" because Old World oppression had so shaped habits and character that adaptation to free institutions became difficult if not hopeless; "and without hope," added Schouler, "one curses the happy." Still Schouler urged that these people be given the right to vote and protest as preliminary steps to

32 *Ibid.*, III, 44. Schouler was not in agreement with those who maintained that "the elevation of democracy in the scale of national influence, and the depression correspondingly of the superior classes" meant the downfall of the Republic. *Ibid.*, p. 45.

33 *Ibid.*, p. 45.

making good citizens of them. No lover of " fierce democracy," he insisted that " opportunity to rise dissolves individual membership in this class, and keeps jealousy from compacting mischief." [34]

Reviewing the respective attitudes of the Federalist and Republican parties toward immigrants and the lower classes, Schouler noted that the party of Jefferson was the champion of both. Schouler greatly admired Jefferson as representative of the " upper stratum in the republican politics " but he was less favorably disposed toward Jackson and his motley following.[35] Nevertheless Jacksonianism with all its abuses was, in Schouler's opinion, part of the "tendency"of the nineteenth century to extend the franchise and to place the reins of government more completely in the hands of the people.[36] Were not the " angel operatives " of the Massachusetts mill towns the " delight " of that state and the despair of cankered mill towns in the Old World?[37] Did not the " charm " of the New World republic in 1831 reside in the opportunities offered the poor and industrious of Europe and in the intelligence and freedom of the common peoples?[38] Schouler may have been apprehensive concerning some of the aberrations of democracy, but his faith in the fundamental tenets of the creed was unshaken.

At the same time, he observed that the forces of " fierce democracy " were reenforced by " unlettered and boozy foreigners, the scum of European society," Irish peasants whose " instinct " made them Roman Catholics and Jacksonian Democrats.[39] It was mainly to them that he attributed the rise of " native Americanism," a movement of protest " against foreign influence in our national affairs and religion, under the secret

34 *Ibid.*, pp. 46-7.

35 *Ibid.*, pp. 65-6.

36 *Constitutional Studies*, p. 207.

37 *History of the United States*, IV, 416.

38 *Ibid.*, p. 5.

39 *Ibid.*, p. 177.

propagation of the Vatican and Jesuit order." [40] Like Von Holst, Schouler objected to some phases of the nativist movement and found justification for others. He opposed its violent aspects; but if those who fired the Ursuline Convent were "misguided," they were also deemed to have used torch and axe "in the cause of free schools and the Protestant religion which their forefathers founded." [41]

Schouler characterized the Know-Nothing movement as "a sort of exhalation, arising from the decay of old parties and putrid natural issues . . . ." The Know-Nothings, in his opinion, cast undeserved discredit upon those German immigrants who were different from the Irish in religious profession and more "liberal" in their political leanings. Indeed, even of the Irish, Schouler, sincere democrat that he was, would not despair: despite their clannishness, proclivity toward violence, domination by priests, disproportionate contribution to crime, poverty, and misrule, they were not entirely impervious "to the cross-light of free ideas." [42]

As has been pointed out, Schouler awarded the "sacred formulas" of the Declaration of Independence a prominence denied them in the political philosophy of some of his contemporaries. The working out of these political truths, Schouler believed, was the task of the American people,[43] whose original Anglo-Saxon lineage was "dashed in destination with the blood of many other Caucasian peoples . . . ." [44] Schouler undoubtedly did not want other white settlers from the European continent to supplant "those natural leaders of America in whose veins flows the blood of a British lineage," [45] especially

40 *Ibid.*, pp. 180, 203, 206.

41 *Ibid.*, p. 177.

42 *Ibid.*, V, 304-6.

43 *Ibid.*, pp. 29-30, 220.

44 *Americans of 1776* (New York, 1906), p. 306.

45 *Ideals of the Republic*, p. 42.

since he believed that " Scandinavians, Slavonians, Teutons, Saxons and Italians, all elements in our population, differ considerably in blood and temperament." [46] However, he regarded immigration as a *fait accompli,* and believed that our heterogeneous population was likely to provide an answer to this fundamental question: " Is our doctrine of man's equal creation to be asserted for our particular race alone, or as a universal one for all races alike and for all types of mankind? " [47]

Pending the ultimate solution, Schouler suggested that the Anglo-Saxon had always maintained a balance between the will to surpass and the ideal of social equality and that the Anglo-Saxon " conscience and profound sense of justice " would result in the eventual extension of social as well as political equality to peoples like the " submissive or emotional types of continental Europe," who were less gifted.[48] Schouler called upon " authentic history " to demonstrate that among the many " races " striving for predominance, no one " race " was constantly in the lead or innately supreme. Moreover, " no conception of mankind which regards our human creation as a universal brotherhood " is consistent with the view that the maxims of the Declaration of Independence hold good only for each race separately. The true spirit of Christianity, Schouler maintained, was opposed to the notion that some races are, or should be, permanently dominant and others permanently subject.[49] Possessing the faith of a nineteenth-century liberal, Schouler believed that if there were any peoples who aspired to partake, along with the Anglo-Saxons, of the benefits of political democracy, no inherent barrier prevented them from doing so.[50]

46 *Ibid.,* p. 35.
47 *Ibid.,* p. 173.
48 *Ibid.,* pp. 263, 276.
49 *Ibid.,* p. 35.
50 *Ibid.,* p. 28.

James Ford Rhodes

Von Holst's historical bearings were taken from the star of the Times-Spirit; Schouler set up standards of right and wrong, honorable and dishonorable conduct; James Ford Rhodes was inclined to judge events "at the bar of history." Seven volumes of Rhodes' history, appearing between 1894 and 1906, covered the period 1850-77, while two volumes were devoted to the years 1877-1909. Far more than the works of Von Holst and Schouler, Rhodes' first seven volumes are acceptable to contemporary historians.[51]

Rhodes was born in Cleveland in 1848 of a prominent local family of New England origin. At twenty-two, after a very haphazard education, he went into the iron industry and for the next fifteen years his energies were devoted to a rapidly growing business. In whatever leisure time he had while thus occupied, he read extensively in various fields. Through the perusal, in 1877, of Hildreth's history, an idea he had had of writing a history of the United States was strengthened and became a resolution. Eight years later, having retired from business, he took up the task in earnest.[52]

51 Volumes I and II of the *History of the United States from the Compromise of 1850* appeared in 1893; volume III in 1895; IV in 1899; V in 1904; VI and VII in 1906. After publication of the sixth volume the title read *History of the United States from the Compromise of 1850 to the Final Restoration of Home Rule at the South in 1877*. The eighth volume, which appeared in 1919, bore the title *History of the United States from the Compromise of 1850 to the End of the Cleveland Administration 1877-1896*. The ninth volume was entitled *The McKinley and Roosevelt Administrations, 1897-1909* and appeared in 1922.

52 Graduating from the local high school in 1865 "with a thirst for history and literature," he later that year entered the University of New York as a special student. In the next three years Rhodes, in addition to attending the New York school, was a student at the University of Chicago and heard a course of lectures at the Collège de France presented by Edouard Laboulaye, from whom Von Holst had received his first idea of the United States. The books Rhodes mentioned as impressing him most during this period were Guizot's *General History of Civilization in Europe*; Buckle's *History of Civilization*; Draper's *Intellectual Development of Europe*; and

As an historian, Rhodes was influenced mainly by classical models, particularly by Thucydides and Tacitus. At the same time, he thought that historians should borrow as much as they could from the natural and social sciences and his own first volume contained numerous references to the works of Herbert Spencer, Lecky, and Buckle. His slow, careful development of most phases of the period he treats is evidence that Rhodes, like " every one who has had to trace the development of a people, the growth of an institution, or the establishment of a cause " was profoundly influenced by Darwin.[53]

Against the danger of bias in history, Rhodes erected the bulwarks of " diligence, accuracy, love of truth, impartiality," which he thought were typical of classical historiography.[54] He avowed himself " an earnest seeker after truth, trying to hold a judicial balance and to tell the story without prejudice." A philosophy of history as well as a " thesis " Rhodes steadily eschewed as likely to lead into the dark bypaths of prejudice.[55] He once expressed the opinion that bias in history writing was related to the choice of a theme, a political subject having a greater susceptibility to prejudice than a social or economic one.[56]

Did Rhodes' application of the principles of " diligence, accuracy, love of truth, impartiality "—those moral fortresses of good intent—result in an unopinionated history? Rhodes once said that complex historical problems could be treated from more than one point of view, and that it was proper for a writer of history to make his own opinions evident— it would

---

De Tocqueville's *Democracy in America*. He considered himself at this time a disciple of Buckle and admitted that he had only a second-hand knowledge of Herbert Spencer's works. M. A. De Wolfe Howe, *James Ford Rhodes American Historian* (New York, 1929), pp. 17, 20-3, 25.

53 James Ford Rhodes, *Historical Essays* (New York, 1909), pp. 4, 22.

54 *Ibid.*, p. 20.

55 Howe, *op. cit.*, pp. 149-50, 277.

56 " The Molly Maguires in the Anthracite Regions of Pennsylvania," *American Historical Review*, XV (April 1910), 547.

then be the reader's task to resolve diverse and conflicting opinions by evaluating all the evidence. By this method Rhodes himself produced a history which, to the best of the author's ability, avoided bias, but which nevertheless did not hesitate to express an opinion once, in the author's opinion, all the evidence was in.[57]

Typical of this approach was Rhodes' discussion of the treatment of the Civil War prisoners by the Union and Confederate authorities respectively: a more careful attempt to arrive at " truth " would, the reader feels sure, belong in the province of angels.[58] Of course, not all controversial subjects in Rhodes' history were given such a careful going over. Nor did he always know when a given subject contained an element of controversy; in fact, he sometimes—like the equally " unprejudiced " Von Holst—regarded his own opinion as so in conformity with the nature of things as to be unassailable.[59] All this should be borne in mind in considering his attitude toward immigrant peoples.

Rhodes' basic opinions regarding immigrants were not far different from those of Von Holst and Schouler. He was an admirer of the American middle class and what he considered to be its Anglo-Saxon aversion to violent social and political change. Native Americans, he believed, possessed " a deep conservative impulse " and were as far from anarchical as any people in the world.[60] In writing of the pre-Civil War period,

57 Howe, *op. cit.*, pp. 56, 277-8.

58 *History of the United States*, V, chap. xxix.

59 For example, his views on slavery and on the righteousness of the Union cause.

60 Howe, *op. cit.*, p. 139; *History of the United States*, III, 634. Although he wrote of the American community as "Aryan" and belonging to the " Teutonic race," Rhodes nevertheless insisted that the American, even if of English blood, was different from the Englishman. He attributed these differences partially, but not entirely, to climatic causes. *Ibid.*, pp. 16, 403; *Ibid.*, VII, 168. Rhodes at this point followed closely Nathaniel Shaler's analysis in *Nature and Man in America*, p. 265.

Rhodes preferred the German to the Irish immigrants [61] and emphasized the value of all thrifty and hard-working immigrants to an undeveloped country.[62] He also believed that the movement of peoples from Europe to America and from East to West had the effect of a " constant shifting of population, so that in America as compared with Europe, and in the Western States as compared with the Eastern, we have a constantly increasing predominance of youth, health, and ambition." [63]

Rhodes devoted less space to an account of the Know-Nothing and nativist movements than did Von Holst.[64] He merely mentioned the school and property questions and the visit of Bedini as contributing toward the " distrust of Roman Catholicism . . . a string that can be artfully played upon in an Anglo-Saxon community." [65]

According to Rhodes the Know-Nothings were quite right in asserting that the voting of ignorant foreigners had become an evil of immense proportions. " Had the remedies sought by the Know-Nothings been just and practicable," he wrote,

> and their methods above suspicion, the movement, though ill-timed, might be justified at the bar of history. But when the historian writes that a part of their indictment was true and that the organization attracted hosts of intelligent and good men, he said everything creditable that can be said of the Know-Nothing party.

Rhodes further asserted that the crusade against the Catholic church was contrary to the spirit of the constitution; that the Catholics were not sufficiently numerous to justify alarm;

61 *History*, I, 358; II, 178; VI, 393.

62 *Ibid.*, I, 355; IV, 420; V, 201, 205.

63 *Ibid.*, III, 17. Once again Rhodes accepts Shaler's theory, this time with regard to the selective factors operative in the migration process.

64 *Ibid.*, I, 50-8, 87-92. However, he did lean rather heavily on Von Holst's analysis.

65 *Ibid.*, p. 52.

that the Catholic hierarchy could only be dangerous in an age when reason was suppressed. He branded the proposed exclusion of foreigners from public office as " illogical and unjust " and the alteration or repeal of the naturalization laws as impractical. " Better means than these could be devised to correct the abuses of naturalization and fraudulent voting." [66]

Rhodes approved of the plank in the Know-Nothing platform of 1855 urging revision of the immigration laws so that felons and paupers might be excluded and the coming of honest immigrants encouraged. He was also pleased by the national convention's action in lifting the veil of secrecy from the organization. Know-Nothing leaders, according to Rhodes, realized

> that the time had come for men of sense and honor to advocate their political principles openly. From this time forward the order is better known as the American party, and it is entitled to great respect for its endeavor to work out reforms which it believed were needed. Yet the historian must aver that the Americans were not abreast of the needs of their time, for they sacrificed the greater principle to the lesser one. [67]

During the depression of 1857, Rhodes observed that the foreigners were in the vanguard of the New York City workers who demanded employment. Blame for the draft riots of July, 1863 Rhodes placed squarely on the shoulders of the foreign born, especially the Irish. He also wrote of the part taken by foreigners in the bread riots which occurred in Richmond on Holy Thursday and Good Friday of 1863.[68]

Rhodes believed that during the Civil War Jews in the North were extensively involved in contraband trading and

---

66 *Ibid.*, pp. 52-3. " Better means " were in Rhodes' opinion those suggested by Horace Greeley in the New York *Tribune*, August 16, 1854. Statistics on the growth of Catholicism in the United States, Rhodes obtained from Hambleton's *History of the Political Campaign of 1855*, a source which was also utilized by Von Holst.

67 *History*, II, 91-2.

68 *Ibid.*, IV, 321-3; V, 321, 365.

profiteering, and that at the same time Jews and foreigners in the Confederacy shared extensively in profits derived from blockade-running and trading with the enemy. He also expressed some doubt of the sincerity and integrity, though not of the ability, of Judah P. Benjamin, Secretary of State of the Confederacy, whose Hebrew parentage he noted. Benjamin, Rhodes said, " was one of the men who had lived well throughout the war." [69]

At the end of the seventh volume, Rhodes, having dealt with the restoration of home rule in the South, concluded his epic theme—the familiar story of slavery, Civil War, and reconstruction—and set out to explore American development in the late nineteenth and early twentieth centuries, when the dominant historical trends were not as readily ascertainable. Rhodes and his critics are agreed that for the proper handling of the social issues of the post Civil War period he " had a lack of basic knowledge." [70]

In approaching the issues connected with the Civil War, Rhodes showed a keen appreciation of how the principle of growth and evolution is inherent in the materials of history.[71] In the eighth volume of the history, however, the atmosphere of fierce and bloody conflict between labor and capital is projected into the narrative without the reader's being made acquainted with the developmental phases of the struggle. Earlier volumes hardly mentioned the American labor movement and suddenly its most sensational aspects are introduced. As for Rhodes' personal reaction to the wave of strikes which followed the economic crisis of 1873, the historian seems to include himself among those Americans to whom

> The action of the mob in Baltimore, Pittsburgh, Reading, Chicago and Scranton seemed to threaten the chief strongholds of society and came like a thunder-bolt out of a clear

69 *Ibid.*, III, 241 ; V, 216, 281, 285-6, 288-90, 405, 420.

70 Michael Kraus, *A History of American History* (New York, 1938), p. 367.

71 *Historical Essays*, p. 20.

sky, startling us rudely. For we had hugged the delusion that such social uprisings belonged to Europe and had no reason being in a free republic where there was plenty of room and an equal chance for all.[72]

There is a surprising lack of balance in a narrative embracing two decades of American history which devotes thirty-five pages to the Molly Maguire episode and deals only incidentally with the Knights of Labor.

Rhodes began his account of the activities of the Molly Maguires in the Pennsylvania anthracite regions with a brief description of conditions confronting the miners. Increased demand for anthracite brought about an influx of English, Welsh, Scotch, German, and at a later date Irish, into the coal fields. Of these, the Irish were the most numerous; they displaced in the poorly paid jobs the earlier immigrants, who rose to supervisory and skilled positions. Miners were paid in accordance with the weight and quality of the coal extracted, and there was constant disagreement on both points. Another source of controversy lay in the mine-bosses' opportunity to discriminate among workers by assigning some to " hard " and others to " soft " jobs.

Having presented this background of the operations of the Molly Maguires in Pennsylvania's Schuykill and Carbon Counties, Rhodes characterized the organization as a " hide-bound secret order " founded in Ireland, in which " no one but an Irish Roman Catholic was eligible for membership." The order, he said, had evolved a " deliberate system " whereby a Molly who fancied himself wronged by a mine boss would state his case before a committee which had the power to order the murder of the offending supervisor. Such meetings, " generally took place in an upper room of a hotel or saloon, and, after the serious business, came the social reunion with deep libations of whiskey." Universal suffrage played into the hands of the Mollys and, Rhodes concluded, " with the apti-

72 *History*, VIII, 46.

tude for politics which the Irish have shown in our country, they developed their order into a political power to be reckoned with."

Having named the villains and outlined their villainy, Rhodes next dealt with the elements of resistance to the Molly Maguires. Franklin B. Gowen, leading figure in the Philadelphia and Reading Coal and Iron Company, Allan Pinkerton, of the private detective agency, and James McParlan, "a native of Ireland and a Roman Catholic," emerge as heroes of the ensuing conflict.

Discussing the successful attempt of Gowen to break the miners' union, Rhodes cited Goldwin Smith to the effect that "foreigners" had carried the "instinct" of industrial strife from Europe to America. On this score, Rhodes held some nationalities more blameworthy than others. English, Welsh, and Scotch miners who, according to Rhodes, would shrink from systematic and cold-blooded murder, "will, in the intensity of conflict, burn and destroy the property of the mine owner with whom they are at war." The Irish, on the other hand, needed no such provocation. According to Rhodes, the Irishman viewed sympathetically all the outrages committed, since "true to his Irish Roman Catholic blood, he hated the capitalist and had a profound contempt for the law."

The smashing of the union provoked the Mollys still further, and there was a "recrudescence of crime," but the end of the Molly Maguire organization was in sight. "The victims," Rhodes observed, "had been Welsh, Pennsylvania-German or English, and the feeling of their blood-brothers towards the Irish Catholics was growing into a keen desire for vengeance." James McParlan had joined the Mollys and fathomed their secrets. Finally, the day came when, in the words of Rhodes, McParlan "dressed plainly in black, wearing spectacles, with an intelligent and grave countenance and gentlemanly bearing," told the judge and jury his "wonderful story." "Accurate and truthful," wrote Rhodes, "he excelled as witness as he had as detective and, when he finished his testimony, the case of the Commonwealth was won." Among others whom Rhodes credited with bringing the case to a successful conclusion was

> the Roman Catholic church which, though in a difficult situation (for the Molly Maguires were Catholic and there were many Catholic sympathizers with them outside the organization), was, as has always been the case in the United States (I believe), on the side of law and order.[73]

With the Mollys brought to justice, Rhodes took up the question of what caused them to act as they did. He thought "the racial characteristics shown in this story are worth a passing note." All the Molly Maguires, he observed, were Irish, as were McParlan and Gowen. He then went on to explain the ways of the Mollys in terms of their Old World background.

> The characteristic failings of the Celts as the ancient Romans knew them were intensified in their Irish descendants by the seven centuries of mis-government of Ireland by England. Subject to tyranny at home, the Irishman, when he came to America, too often translated liberty into license, and so ingrained was his habit of looking upon government as an enemy, that, when he became the ruler of cities and stole the public funds, he was, from his point of view, only despoiling the old adversary. With his traditional hostility toward government, it was easy for him to become a Molly Maguire, while the English, Scotch and Welsh immigrant shrank from such a society with horror.[74]

Rhodes added this final generalization concerning the Irish character.

> A peculiar feature stands out, differentiating the Molly Maguires from any criminal organization (so far as I know) or any other people of the Indo-European family. We read of

73 *Ibid.*, pp. 52-87.

74 *Ibid.*, p. 87.

strong drink and carousing, of robbery and murder but nowhere during the orgies of whiskey, of dissolute women. We read of wives and families, of marriage and giving in marriage, of childbirth but nowhere of the appearance of the harlot. The Irishman, steeped in crime, remained true to the sexual purity of his race.[75]

Turning his attention to events on the Pacific Coast during the depression of 1873-77, Rhodes favored a ban on Chinese immigration, but condemned violent attacks upon Asiatics by Irish and American " hoodlums." [76] Writing of the Chicago anarchists and the Haymarket incident, Rhodes accused German anarchists of translating liberty into license and not understanding " the saying of our fathers that there are only three generations between shirt sleeves and shirt sleeves." German anarchists, alleged Rhodes, came to the United States for the purpose of advocating theories and committing overt acts which would never have been tolerated in Germany. Rhodes complained of the slowness of judicial proceedings in the United States. German officials " would have ridiculed the many and various chances for life that our Courts and practice afforded the anarchists." [77] On the other hand, Rhodes had no objection to newcomers who accepted the *status quo* and took advantage of economic opportunities.[78]

---

75 *Ibid.*, pp. 86-7. Prostitution, Rhodes believed, was obnoxious to Irishmen and Anglo-Saxons but prevalent among the Chinese. *Ibid.*, p. 190. Cleveland's moral character, Rhodes asserted, was distasteful to the Irish, " while on the other hand the use of public position to feather one's nest was not regarded by the Irish as so grievous a sin as irregular sexual relations." *Ibid.*, p. 225.

76 *Ibid.*, pp. 184-91.

77 *Ibid.*, p. 284.

78 *Ibid.*, p. 284. At this point Rhodes quoted from J. O. Fagan, *Autobiography of an Individualist* (Boston, 1912). Rhodes wished that the German anarchists appreciated the ideas of this " immigrant and workingman " who paid homage to the " opportunity " and " democratic atmosphere " prevalent in America.

There is no unfailing correlation between an individual's status in society and the nature of his ideas. It seems likely, however, that many of the attitudes expressed in Rhodes' eighth volume arose from the circumstance of his having been himself an industrial capitalist and employer. The following characterization of striking miners may have been derived from his own experience in 1876 at the Warmington mine controlled by Rhodes and Co.[79]

A mob of coal miners is perhaps no worse in its composition than a mob of iron workmen or stevedores but its appearance is more appalling. The miners have lived in coal and breathed its atmosphere; the grime of it is in their faces and hands; and this together with their life away from the sunlight and air give them the most diabolical countenances. Their leisure hours being passed mainly in whisky-drinking, there is nothing in their recreation to make them less brutal.[80]

Rhodes was a conservative in many of his attitudes. He did not believe the political judgment of women equal to that of men,[81] and he wrote of the popular election of senators as " humbug." [82] Previously tolerant of the economic policies of Theodore Roosevelt,[83] he failed to support him in 1912, deeming it a pity that a man of Roosevelt's birth and education should appeal to the mob. Wilson's course on the Adamson Act Rhodes denounced as " a dangerous surrender to labor," and in 1916 he hoped for Hughes' election. " It had to be tested," he wrote, " whether organized labor was to rule, and perhaps now is as good a time as any to have it out at the polls." As

79 Howe, *op. cit.*, p. 42.

80 *History*, VIII, 63.

81 Howe, *op. cit.*, p. 271.

82 *Ibid.*, p. 333.

83 *Ibid.*, p. 174. Endorsing the attitude of government toward business during the Cleveland and McKinley administrations, Rhodes nevertheless found in Roosevelt's policies a source of satisfaction because needed reforms were being intelligently administered.

between the whim of an absolute monarch and the dictate of democracy he consistently preferred the latter; but considering the vast foreign immigration and the stimulus to large cities resulting from commercial and manufacturing expansion, he wished that Jefferson had not had that great faith in "The People."[84]

Rhodes was an industrial rather than a finance capitalist and he somewhat self-righteously remarked that Rockefeller had achieved success partly by steering clear of Wall Street.[85] But although opposed to the machinations of finance capitalists, Rhodes is far from being a Henry Adams determined to bring down the wrath of the gods upon their heads. On the contrary, his approach to the titans of finance is rather humble, as if the business man turned historian were overawed in the presence of Jacob H. Schiff, representative of the Warburgs.[86]

By and large, Von Holst, Schouler, and Rhodes did not attempt extensive treatments of the relationship of the immigrant to politics—" to the struggle for possession and control of the instruments of power as organized in the state."[87] Immigration was merely incidental to the central theme of their histories, which was politics itself, and their emphasis gravitated

84 *Ibid.*, pp. 179, 217, 271.

85 *Ibid.*, p. 112.

86 Rhodes tells an amusing anecdote about how on a scenic walk with Schiff he tried to sound out the banker concerning market trends and prospects. Schiff, finding the countryside interesting, professed to misunderstand Rhodes' queries. *Ibid.*, pp. 162-3.

In 1916, after having taken a severe financial loss in the stock of the Morgan dominated New York, New Haven and Hartford Railroad, Rhodes denounced the aims and judgment of financiers and his faith in democracy deepened. "We are safe," he wrote, "when we rely, as Lincoln did, on the 'plain people'." Brandeis, whom Rhodes earlier denounced as a Socialist, now rose in the historian's estimation to a stature greater than that of J. P. Morgan, Sr. "I speak feelingly," he added, "as I lost a great lot of money in New Haven from overweening confidence in J. P. M. . . . " *Ibid.*, pp. 224, 257, 268.

87 Oscar Handlin, "The Immigrant and American Politics," David F. Bowers, ed., *Foreign Influences in American Life* (Princeton, 1944), p. 84.

toward the sensational aspects of immigrant political behavior. Frequently, sensational episodes, instead of being carefully investigated were dealt with in a spirit of partisanship which was the outcome of the historian's background and conditioning. Claiming that the immigrant as a voter reacted differently from the native, Von Holst, Schouler, and Rhodes failed to interpret this distinctive response to new and complex problems in the light of the newcomer's background and experience. The political boss, the machine, the attendant corruption —all were duly noted and deplored; but the reasons for immigrant political behavior were neither explored nor understood. In fact, that behavior was sometimes ascribed simply to the operation of innate characteristics. Moreover, by concentrating on a few notorious examples, the impression was conveyed that most immigrants were radicals, whereas in point of fact, the great mass of them were as a result of forces European and American, conservatives.[88]

Although their interests were centered in politics, these historians indicated their appreciation of the immigrants' labor. They made it clear, however, that they preferred those of the newcomers who accepted the *status quo* in American social and industrial relationships. Schouler, the Jeffersonian Democrat, was perhaps more sanguine of immigrant assimilation than were Von Holst and Rhodes, but even these two historians did not regard the eventual completion of the process as out of the question.

In the light of recent reinterpretations of the nativist movement by Bean,[89] and Handlin,[90] the attitudes taken on this

[88] Marcus L. Hansen, *The Immigrant in American History* (Cambridge, 1940), pp. 85-94.

[89] William Bean, "An Aspect of Know Nothingism — The Immigrant and Slavery," *South Atlantic Quarterly*, XIII (October 1924), 319-34; "Puritan vs. Celt, 1850-60," *The New England Quarterly*, VII (March 1934), 70-89.

[90] Handlin, *Boston's Immigrants*, pp. 184-215.

subject by Von Holst, Schouler, and Rhodes are of particular significance. The present tendency to bring out the reformist aspect of the nativist movements is, in a way, a documented affirmation of the attitudes of these earlier political historians, who sympathised with nativist objection to the political behavior of the immigrants, while at the same time opposing extreme nativist remedies.

Politics, however, was but one aspect of immigrant as well as of general American experience. There were other phases of American life in which the immigrant played a greater role, and these were dealt with by historians whose emphasis was less political.

CHAPTER VII

THE IMMIGRANT AND AMERICAN SOCIETY

John Bach McMaster

WHILE Frederick Jackson Turner was writing of the need for a history concerned less with political than with social and economic themes, [1] a work of this sort was in preparation. By 1891, the first and second volumes of John Bach McMaster's *History of the People of the United States* had appeared—a pioneer endeavor towards a new type of American history. The author declared that his purpose was " to describe the dress, the occupations, the amusements, the literary canons of the times; to note the changes of manners and morals; to trace the growth of the humane spirit. . . ." McMaster's history dealt also with such subjects as mechanical inventions, agriculture, industry, the free press, education and a number of miscellaneous social phenomena including immigration. [2] Thus it was the task of a young engineer, without formal training as an historian, " sheltered by the umbrella of his ignorance " [3] from the downpour of political history emanating from Johns Hopkins, to make the first substantial contribution toward a history of the American people.

While Herbert Baxter Adams and the group surrounding him at Johns Hopkins were minutely investigating the political history of the Aryan " race " in an effort to discover the tap roots of English freedom, McMaster was thinking in terms of the relationship between geography and civilization. In contrast to Fiske's belief that republican institutions were matters of Aryan family inheritance, McMaster suggested that they

1 " Significance of History," p. 51.

2 John Bach McMaster, *A History of the People of the United States From the Revolution to the Civil War* (8 vols., New York, 1938), I, 1-2.

3 Eric Goldman, *John Bach McMaster, American Historian* (Philadelphia, 1943), pp. 15, 21.

may have been the result of the proximity of certain nations
to the sea. "The Greek," wrote McMaster, "gained his notions
of liberty from the sea from the free, joyous, unrestrained life
of the sailor or the freebooter. The dangers he met at sea
strengthened his courage. He became independent, manly, ver-
satile; liberal in his views and cosmopolitan in his feeling." [4]
Twenty years later, with his reputation as an historian
established, McMaster assailed Freeman for ascribing "un-
reasonable importance to the influence of the Teutonic element
in English history. The latter was the inevitable result of his
method of studying the past along the lines of philology, and
has carried him to extremes which taken by anybody else he
would have been quick to see." McMaster also took Freeman
to task for failing to write about how the masses of the people
lived. [5]

McMaster did not, to any great extent, modify the Anglo-
Saxonism of his predecessors and contemporaries. He considered the immigrants of the mid-nineteenth century inferior to
the early settlers, whom he described as "a highly favored
people . . . descended from the most persevering, the most
energetic, the most thrifty of races." [6] He said that the Americans accomplished their Revolution "with the sobriety, with
the dignity, with the love of law and order that has ever marked
the uprisings of the Saxon race." [7] Yet the idea of Anglo-
Saxon superiority is not thematic in McMaster's history.
Speaking at the annual banquet of the Netherlands Society in

[4] "The Influence of Geographical Position on Civilization in Egypt and
Greece," *The National Quarterly Review* (December, 1876), 48-49. For the
influence of race and geography on the character of Alexander Hamilton
see *History of the People*, I, 125-6.

[5] "Edward Augustus Freeman," Charles Warner, ed., *Library of the
World's Best Literature, Ancient and Modern* (New York, 1896-7), X,
5979-81.

[6] *History of the People*, I, 2.

[7] *Ibid.*, p. 309; Goldman, *McMaster*, p. 143.

1905,[8] McMaster, who was mainly of English ancestry with one Irish grandmother,[9] observed that a " strange jumble of nations . . . took part in founding this republic."[10] On the same occasion he extolled the " good old Dutch doctrine " of liberty of thought and freedom of speech and berated the Puritans for their persecution of Quakers and other dissenters.[11]

Because McMaster's history was concerned with a great variety of matters which the political historians either overlooked or avoided, there was bound to enter into it a somewhat broader conception of the role of the immigrant whose coming was, after all, part of the pattern of American life. He wrote of

> the daily life of a great people who, in one generation, overspread a vast continent, drew to their shores millions of foreigners, fought a civil war and paid for it, produced the most marvellous inventions and discoveries, carried on business ventures upon a gigantic scale, and made enormous fortunes the order of the day. . ."[12]

The idea of the melting pot, developed by Roosevelt, Wilson, and Turner, implied a much broader basis for American nationality than the narrow Anglo-Saxon foundations established by Freeman and Adams; but it remained for McMaster, because of the tremendous scope of his history, to place the immigrant within the main stream of American development.

The focal points of McMaster's discussion of immigration were the years 1819, 1831, 1837, and 1848—significant dates in the acceleration of the flow of European immigrants to American shores.

8 *The Netherlands Society of Philadelphia, Fourteenth Annual Banquet . . . 1905*, pp. 40-5.

9 *Dictionary of American Biography*, XII, 141.

10 *Netherlands Society Address*, pp. 40-1.

11 *Ibid.*, p. 44.

12 Substance of a speech delivered on the occasion of the " Inauguration of the New Hall of the History Society of Pennsylvania." *Pennsylvania Magazine of History and Biography*, VIII (1884), 191.

According to McMaster, immigration in 1819 and there-abouts came mainly from Great Britain and was for the most part composed of artisans, laborers, and skilled workmen. Some of these, he wrote, left the ports of debarkation for places farther West, but "a large proportion remained [in the East] and constituted an element hard to govern." [13]

The immigration of the years immediately preceding 1831 McMaster treated with considerable fulness. [14] Not only were his sources more varied than those used by Von Holst, Schouler, and Rhodes, but in keeping with the general pattern of his work he was concerned with more than merely the political aspects of the subject. For material, he relied mainly upon early immigration statistics (the inadequacies of which he appreciated); letters of immigrants; and European newspaper sources illustrative of the desire to migrate. He discussed the need of American capitalists for immigrant labor and their efforts to secure contract laborers.

" To the industrious immigrant," concluded McMaster, " even when assisted by the parish, no reasonable objection could be made. But complaint had long been current that paupers, the crippled, the lame, and the diseased were 'being dumped on our shores' . . . ." [15] For testimony as to the destitution of many of these immigrants, he referred to a contemporary English newspaper; he also quoted from the annual reports of the health officer of Baltimore.

McMaster did not modify to any great extent Von Holst's and Schouler's conception of the role of the immigrant in American politics during the first half of the nineteenth century. He wrote:

> Though the newcomers speedily became naturalized they did not by any means become Americanized. Our institutions they did not understand. Concerning our history and tradition they

13 *History of the People*, V, 124.

14 *Ibid.*, VI, 79-86.

15 *Ibid.*, p. 82.

were totally ignorant. The Declaration and the Constitution, the Fourth of July and the Twenty-second of February, Bunker Hill and Saratoga, Yorktown and New Orleans, were instruments, days, and events of which they knew nothing and for which they cared nothing. They . . . looked upon their new home as 'the land of liberty,' understanding by liberty the right to do as they pleased. In the wild scenes of turbulence, lawlessness, mob rule and riot that disgraced our country for thirty years to come, the naturalized citizen . . . was always conspicuous.[16]

Under the circumstances, McMaster thought it "but natural that a spirit of native Americanism should be abroad in the land and should find expression in angry or contemptuous criticism of the newcomers. This was, "unhappily," the attitude "of a large part of the community, and that part, in particular, least disposed to respect the law." Railroading, the rise of new industries, the growth of cities, brought native and foreign-born workers into close proximity, and this resulted in an intensification of racial and religious prejudice. "With this element, [workingmen] far more disposed in those days to act than to think, the police authorities were unable to cope." Riots and mobs had always existed, McMaster said, but by 1850 they were of frequent occurrence. Still, he considered the evil of foreign workingmen rioting "more than offset by the importance of these men to the industrial development of the country." Without the imported laborer, great works of internal improvement; railroads, turnpikes, and canals could not have been produced.

Although mindful of the contributions of the immigrant to the material progress of the nation, McMaster, in the same volume,[17] emphasized the large number of immigrants who were indigent or criminal. A disproportionate amount of space is devoted to pauper immigration and official efforts to curb it.

16 *Ibid.*, p. 84.

17 *Ibid.*, p. 85.

McMaster's sources were newspapers, official documents, and other contemporary materials. [18]

On political grounds, McMaster objected to the immigrants of the late thirties much as he had objected to those of an earlier date. Ignorant, he declared, of American political institutions, and retaining the prejudices and opinions of their native lands, the newcomers were admitted to citzenship before being Americanized. McMaster considered the Irish, who took up residence in cities, more of a problem than the German and Swiss immigrants, who went West, where labor was most needed. In the West, McMaster said, they " settled in detached associations, where they speak their own language and retain their own customs, and do not pass by easy transitions into the bosom of American society." [19]

This is an interesting contrast to Turner's view of the West as an Americanizing agency. McMaster apparently did not believe that the West stripped the immigrant of his Old World characteristics or even that it greatly modified them. In fact, in his view it was quite the other way. He presented the West as conserving Old World traits—as retarding Americanization of the sort that was taking place in urban areas.

McMaster's discussion of the immigration of 1848 [20] begins with an account of European economic conditions at that time. The story of German and Irish immigration to the New World is then told with special attention to the Old World areas tapped, the conditions of the voyage, and New World destinations. McMaster did not write of German immigrants as being indigent; in fact, he pointed out that " the German emigrant of 1846 was in no sense a poor wretch lured across the ocean by a lying prospectus." Of the six pages devoted to the 1848 migration, about one page deals with the effect of immigration upon the West. This is mainly a factual and statistical

18 *Ibid.*, pp. 421-429.

19 *Ibid.*, pp. 421-423.

20 *Ibid.*, VII, 221-7.

account of the settlement of immigrants in various western states and of their interstate migrations. [21]

With the 1850 census returns as source, McMaster presented statistics of population growth, showing among other things, both the percentage of foreign born in the total population and the extent of its concentration in urban areas. [22] Since they constituted a significant segment of the urban working class, the foreign born were bound to be affected by the hard times which followed the depression of 1857. McMaster noted that at this time in New York City and other large cities " where immigrants were numerous and where Socialism prevailed, idleness and want bred discontent." [23] While ascribing to Irish and German workers a significant role in the workingmen's agitation of the time, McMaster did not overemphasize alien nationality to the exclusion of other factors in the situation. [24] Strikes and other manifestations of labor's unrest during the decade of the fifties he put down rather to economic causes than to the cantankerousness of labor or the machinations of foreigners.

In his volume on the Civil War period, McMaster described the formation of regiments by foreign-born citizens. [25] In a discussion of draft dodging, however, McMaster had this to say about aliens:

> Everywhere this rush of aliens [to gain exemption from conscription] excited deep disgust. That men who had lived long in our country, and prospered greatly, should now refuse their help, was declared cowardly. In Cincinnati this feeling

21 *Ibid.*, pp. 226-7.

22 *Ibid.*, VIII, 68-9.

23 *Ibid.*, p. 296.

24 *Ibid.*, pp. 296-302.

25 *A History of the People of the United States during Lincoln's Administration* (New York, 1927), p. 39. This phase of Civil War recruiting McMaster observed as a youth. Eric Goldman, " Young John Bach McMaster; A Boyhood in New York City," *New York History*, XX (July 1939), 322.

ran so high that the Irish summoned their countrymen to raise
a regiment; the Germans in public meetings denounced all
aliens who, having lived five years in the country, sought
exemption. . .[26]

There is passing mention, by McMaster, of "laborers of
foreign birth" as participants in the draft riots of 1863 in New
York City.[27] An official source is quoted as stating that two-
thirds of the population of Milwaukee was of foreign birth,
opposed to the war and government, and easily aroused by
designing politicians.[28] On the other hand, McMaster noted
that advertisements placed by aliens desiring to serve as military substitutes filled the columns of the *New York Herald.*

McMaster devoted a paragraph to efforts by foreigners to
evade the draft in the Confederacy.[29] More detailed is his discussion of the charges made by members of Parliament that
Union soldiers were being recruited in Ireland. In point of
fact, said McMaster, there were other reasons for Irish immigration; hard times and poor crops in Ireland, combined with
stories of scarcity of labor, high wages, and enlistment bounties
paid in America sent thousands of young Irishmen overseas.[30]
McMaster went on to tell of efforts by the Confederacy to dis-
courage this immigration, and of the activities of Confederate
agents in Ireland.[31]

In 1894, as the nativist American Protective Association
gathered strength, there appeared in the *Forum* an article by
McMaster entitled "The Riotous Career of the Know-Nothings."[32] In this article, as in the *History of the People,*

26 *History during Lincoln's Administration,* p. 226.

27 *Ibid.,* p. 407.

28 *Ibid.,* p. 415.

29 *Ibid.,* p. 417.

30 *Ibid.,* p. 372.

31 *Ibid.,* p. 375.

32 *Forum,* XVII (July 1894), 524-36.

McMaster, while hostile to Know-Nothingism in principle, nevertheless was sympathetic toward certain aspects of nativist opposition to the foreign born. Naturalization of aliens, he said, was not the equivalent of Americanization, and he now repeated almost word for word charges levelled against the immigrant in the sixth volume of the *History*. In addition, he accused them of casting " a united vote in behalf of which ever party would buy it at the highest price." [33]

To McMaster, it was " not surprising " that the American people, who had on earlier occasions manifested their dislike of monarchy and the trappings of nobility, " should look with alarm on the rapid increase in the number of aliens strongly attached by birth, by language, and by religion to monarchial institutions . . ." To the native American, McMaster wrote, the sudden and steady flow of Catholic immigrants seemed a deliberate plot to subvert free institutions. [34]

That McMaster strongly disapproved of both the Know-Nothing movement and the A.P.A., there can be no doubt. [35] Nevertheless, he was sufficiently astute to realize that certain evils were implicit in a system of rapid mass naturalization, and particularly that a measure of conflict was inevitable from the influx of Catholics into a country whose people and traditions were mainly Protestant. [36] In general, McMaster's conception of the nativist movement was not essentially different from that of Schouler and Von Holst. McMaster, however, gave the immigrant fuller consideration than did any of these. His account was more fully documented and the sources utilized were more diversified — indeed, the political historians hardly utilized sources in their discussion of the immigrant. McMaster's account is an important step forward in the increasing recognition by historians of the immigrant's role.

33 *Ibid.*, p. 526.

34 *Ibid.*, p. 526.

35 *Ibid.*, p. 536.

36 *Ibid.*, p. 526.

ELLIS PAXSON OBERHOLTZER

Formerly a student and later a colleague of McMaster at the University of Pensylvania, Ellis Paxson Oberholtzer took up the theme of American social development at the point where McMaster's narrative broke off. There were important differences between the attitudes of the two historians toward the immigrant—differences that were the result of different social attitudes and different approaches to the subject matter of history.

In keeping with the general trend among historians from the middle Atlantic states, in choosing the subject of his major work, *History of the United States Since the Civil War,*[37] Oberholtzer evinced a traditionally nationalist viewpoint.[38] At the same time, he had written a good deal about local history and expressed strong regional and ethnic preferences.[39] Himself a Philadelphian, descendant of the ingredients of the early Pennsylvania melting pot—" German sectarians," " dissidents like the Quakers, " " belligerent Scotch-Irish and other Gaels, " and " more formal Church of England men "[40]—Oberholtzer was very conscious of belonging to the " Philadelphia Brahmin " tradition. Even his *History of the United States Since the Civil War* reflected the provincialism of an upper-class Philadelphian[41] as well as a general narrowness of social and economic outlook.[42]

---

37 (5 vols., New York, 1917-37).

38 R. H. Shryock, "Historical Traditions in Philadelphia and in the Middle Atlantic Area: An Editorial," *Pennsylvania Magazine of History and Biography,* LXVII (1943), 129; Eric Goldman, ed., *Historiography and Urbanization Essays in Honor of W. Stull Holt* (Baltimore, 1941), "Regionalism and American Historiography: A Suggestion," *passim.*

39 *The Literary History of Philadelphia* (Philadelphia, 1906), passim.

40 *Ibid.,* Introduction, xiv.

41 I, 357; II, 433; IV, 662.

42 For an account of Oberholtzer's background see " Sara Louisa Vickers Oberholtzer," *Dictionary of American Biography,* XIII, 607.

Both McMaster and Oberholtzer were conservatives, but they were conservatives in very different senses of that word of many meanings. McMaster was, on the whole, as definitely pro-Federalist and anti-Jacksonian as Oberholtzer, but he believed that by slow, orderly progress the common man in America could and should eventually acquire full political, social, and industrial rights. Shays and Robert Owen were objects of his disapproval, but his sympathy for the aims of the Dorr Rebellion was equally manifest. Moreover, McMaster credited labor unions with playing a significant role in the struggle for the rights of man. [43]

McMaster did not regard labor's demands for higher wages and fewer working hours as threats to the established social order. [44] He treated of extremist elements in strike situations, but did not overstress their role. He described the part played by foreigners in industrial disorders, but strove to achieve some sort of balance by writing of native as well as foreign demonstrators. When all was said, McMaster had faith in the abilities of the common man. [45]

To Oberholtzer, on the other hand, it was axiomatic that the comman man was incapable of solving complex social and economic problems. He considered that it was a mistake to give the vote to Negroes and recent immigrants. [46] " It was observed, too," he commented, " that these immigrants would soon have votes; they could be controlled for low and sinister ends by designing politicians. They might become, if they were not now, a menace to our republican institutions, which had been established by the Anglo-Saxon and the control of which

[43] John McMaster, *The Acquisition of Political, Social and Industrial Rights of Man in America* (Cleveland, 1903), pp. 40, 90-100, 121; *History of the People*, VII, 172.

[44] *Ibid.*, VIII, 97-111. See Allan Nevins' review of Oberholtzer's fifth volume, *American Historical Review*, XLIV (January 1939), 412-14.

[45] See especially, McMaster's " Is Sound Finance Possible Under Popular Government? ", *Forum*, XIX (April 1895), 159-68.

[46] *History of the United States*, IV, 1.

it would be well to keep in his hands." [47] Oberholtzer viewed the United States during the eighties and nineties as teetering on the verge of social revolution and he considered that the propaganda of foreign-born agitators was largely responsible.[48]

Oberholtzer also believed that the presence of the immigrant caused northerners to sympathize with southern efforts to exclude Negroes from the polls and otherwise restrict suffrage.[49] Native Americans of the North, he said, harbored the " well enough grounded " fear " that, soon or late, they would be overwhelmed at the ballot box by an ignorant rabble, even as the South had been." [50] Negroes might be disfranchised but not Slovaks, Poles, and Italians, for " they had white skins." [51]

The people of the new immigration, said Oberholtzer, lived " crowded together in ramshackle buildings in slums like beasts," ate "food that was nauseating to other men," and had " revolting and vicious habits. Being of the lower order of mankind they were repellent to those who were farther advanced in the social scale and who had higher standards of living." [52]

---

47 *Ibid.*, p. 398. Oberholtzer's own attitudes are frequently introduced into the text by the expedient, " It was observed ... "

48 *Ibid.*, pp. 10, 407, 420-1. Throughout the decade of the eighties, Oberholtzer declared, " the wrongs of the workingman due to the oppression of employers were recited and emphasized. Capital was cried down and labor was wreathed in myrtle so systematically and effectively that something like a social revolution was seen, by clear observers, to be in progress." For Oberholtzer's account of the participation of foreign elements in the social turmoil of the nineties, *ibid.*, V, 170-4, 212, 213, 216, 292. Note particularly his attitude toward Denis Kearney, Eugene Debs, John P. Altgeld, *ibid.*, pp. 273, 290, 292.

49 *Ibid.*, IV, 588.

50 *Ibid.*, V, 720.

51 *Ibid.*, p. 736.

52 *Ibid.*, p. 732. " It was said, with appearance of authority, that the children, being in our hands, could be taught our ways. But the sons were a weight greater than their parents . . . Given privileges equal to those of the oldest citizen and freed of Old World discipline, children of immigrants made shockingly large contributions to the criminal class." *Ibid.*, p. 740.

In 1932, Oberholtzer was annoyed by criticism which his work and McMaster's had undergone from the exponents of "interpretive history." He complained that the critics were too much concerned with the question of social justice. Against the "interpretive group," Oberholtzer championed the cause of "factual" history which, in his opinion, he and McMaster had written. At the same time, Oberholtzer was aware of an important difference between McMaster's history and his. McMaster, said Oberholtzer, leaned heavily "to the side of impartiality" whereas he, like Schouler, found it "not in his nature to be impartial as between right and wrong, honorable and dishonorable conduct." Value judgments such as these, Oberholtzer considered external to the realm of "interpretive history." [53]

McMaster's impartiality showed itself particularly in his treatment of immigrants. Especially in his final volume, he seems to have made it a point to present both favorable and unfavorable examples of immigrant behavior. Oberholtzer, on the other hand, having made up his mind that immigration was an evil, selected source material that went to prove this preconceived opinion . In so far as it dealt with immigration, therefore, his history became what he least wanted it to be— a "*Tendenzwerk*" in which the writer was less historian than "vendor of his own views." [54]

Edward Channing and H. L. Osgood

Edward Channing belongs to the group of dissenters from the Teutonic hypothesis to which H. L. Osgood and C. M. Andrews also belong. Of ancestry as distinguished as that of any Brahmin New Englander, Channing, while a student at Harvard, once shocked Henry Cabot Lodge by speaking of Francis Higginson, first minister of Salem, as a hypocrite.

[53] Ellis Oberholtzer, "John Bach McMaster, 1852-1932," *Pennsylvania Magazine of History and Biography*, LVII (1933), 27-9.

[54] *Ibid.*, pp. 30, 239.

" Mr. Channing," asked Lodge, " Do you know that Mr. Higginson was your ancester?"

" Yes, sir," replied Channing.

" Do you think it well to speak thus of your ancestor?" [55]

This early incident is of a piece with Channing's later reputation as an iconoclast. His *History of the United States*—the most significant endeavour by a single historian to cover a sizeable field of American history reflects his critical attitude toward ideas and institutions that had long been venerated.

A chapter devoted to " The Coming of the Foreigners " in the second volume of Channing's *History* is concerned with German, Welsh, Scotch-Irish, and Huguenot immigration into the colonies between 1700 and 1760. Published in 1907, it represents an effort to synthesize all the accounts then available bearing on colonial immigration. The chapter merits comparison with H. L. Osgood's later treatment of the same subject. (Incidentally, although Osgood's account was not published until 1923, the long interval between publication dates is misleading. Osgood died in 1918 with his four volumes on the *American Colonies in the Eighteenth Century* unpublished but substantially completed. The chapter on immigration is in the latter part of the second volume, and may have been written not many years after Channing's study appeared.) [56]

Of the two, Osgood's is the longer and more detailed treatment. This is in keeping with the fact that while Channing was writing a general history, Osgood was concentrating on the colonial period. There are, however, points of resemblance. Both historians confined themselves to the period 1700-60 and both took up the subject of naturalization. They discussed the same ethnic elements, and the proportions in which the space allotted to the subject of immigration is divided among the various immigrant peoples is about the same in the two histories.

55 Samuel Eliot Morison, " Edward Channing A Memoir," *Proceedings of the Massachusetts History Society*, LXIV (May 1931), 260.

56 Dixon Ryan Fox, *Herbert Levi Osgood, an American Scholar* (New York, 1924), pp. 103-8.

Although aware of the significance of the culture patterns of non-English peoples in colonial development and also of the survival of such patterns, Osgood did not consider them in great detail. Instead, his primary concern was "the process of immigration with special reference to the distribution of national stocks within the colonial areas, and the extension of settlement." [57] With ampler space at his disposal, Osgood was able to write of these subjects somewhat more successfully than Channing had done; but he failed to include in his history bibliographic notes critical of the sources utilized, whereas Channing had included such notes. Consequently, of the two accounts, Channing's is the more revealing if one seeks to understand the difficulties that beset both historians in this field of research.

Both Channing and Osgood devoted considerable space to the German element in the colonies and a good deal less to other ethnic groups. This was due, in part, to the availability of the *Proceedings and Addresses of the Pennsylvania-German Society,* the first volume of which appeared in 1891. [58] Although Channing evaluated these as of "uneven merit," there were at least a few good monographs upon which he and Osgood could rely. It was different with the other ethnic groups, as Channing held in little esteem the type of history served up at the congresses of the Scotch-Irish Society of America, and thought even less of the opposing claims of the "Irishman proper" as expressed by Irish-American historians. He referred to C. A. Hanna's *The Scotch-Irish or the Scot in . . . America* and to C. W. Baird's *Huguenot Emigration to America,* but they were obviously of little value to him. [59] Channing was of the opinion that the Jews, too, had published almost no significant historical material about themselves and that the publications of the American Jewish His-

57 *The American Colonies in the Eighteenth Century,* II, 486.

58 *History of the United States,* II, 421.

59 *Ibid.,* pp. 402, 403.

torical Society were "largely argumentative."[60] In fact, so little had the role of non-English peoples in American history claimed the attention of the professional historian that Channing, whose contact with primary sources was necessarily limited by the vast scope of his work, was virtually at the mercy of amateur historians and minority boosters who functioned in the various filiopietistic organizations and virtually monopolized this important field of American history.

Inadequate as were many of the accounts upon which Channing and Osgood based their treatment of immigrant peoples in the colonial period, they were superior to the sources available to Channing as his history progressed into the era of nationhood. The historians of the various ethnic groups were interested mainly in the early history of the nationality upon American soil; each sought to prove to the Anglo-Saxons, for the sake of the prestige involved, that the group in question had roots going back to the nation's beginning. The more recent history of these groups has been little written, and as Channing's narrative unfolded and immigration entered more and more into the picture, the difficulty of presenting an adequate account became greater.

Channing looked with favor upon the immigration of the early national period and presented some biographical data about Priestley, Thornton, Latrobe Hoban, L'Enfant, Clodius, and Crozet. He would not, however, have wanted it forgotten while acknowledging indebtedness "to those who came to our aid from outside" that it was the "grandeur of the imagination of Washington and Jefferson and other Americans that made possible the construction of such great works as the City of Washington, the Erie Canal, and the Portage Railway system." [61] Channing evidently believed that an

---

60 *Ibid.*, p. 453; V, 219. He thought, however, that Ezekiel and Lichtenstein's *History of the Jews of Richmond*, "gives promise of better things."

61 *Ibid.*, pp. 291-3.

American nationality was in the making as early as 1763 by which time, he observed, the early English stock had lost many of the characteristics associated with Anglo-Saxons.[62]

Channing considered the radical element in the early immigration partial justification for enactment of the alien and sedition legislation. Moreover, his discussion of the issues arising out of immigration in 1798 reflected to some extent his attitude toward immigrants of a later date. He wrote,

> In America they condemned whatever magistrate they found in power without fear of guillotine, axe, Bastille, or Tower. These outpourings have been looked upon as harmless, if only they had been left unnoticed; but it is impossible to take this view at the present day when one is constantly witnessing the effects produced upon public opinion by speeches, by letters, and by public appeals of all kinds and varieties. It was inevitable that in 1798, some one should ask by what right a lot of foreigners came over here and malignantly reproached those whom the voters had placed in high station? If those foreigners did not like the men and things that appealed to the majority of American voters, let them keep away, or if they had come over, let them get out.[63]

Many of the aspects of early nineteenth-century immigration with which Channing was concerned, McMaster had already dealt with. He described some of the causes of European emigration; presented an account of the conditions of the voyage; utilized census data in discussing the distribution of immigrant settlement; and noted some of the more obvious effects of the immigrant influx into the large cities. More than McMaster, however, Channing made the immigrant community the focus of his discussion of early and mid-nineteenth century immigration. This was definitely a step forward in the historiography of immigration, but Channing was unable to realize fully the potentialities of this basically sound approach because

62 *Ibid.*, III, 13.

63 *Ibid.*, IV, 220.

his efforts at describing the group settlements were hampered by the dearth of preliminary work in the field. Even when attempting a mere factual outline of the immigration of the prenational period, Channing had complained of the inadequacy of the available sources. As his history advanced, and the character of immigrant communities became the object of his study, his task became still more difficult.[64]

For information about immigrant settlements in the early nineteenth century, Channing was compelled to turn to histories of states, counties, cities, and towns. These were extremely uneven in quality, and only occasionally yielded the kind of material the historian was seeking. [65] Channing voiced the entirely justified complaint that he was forced to rely upon " isolated treatments " of what was a general movement. Turning from local histories to accounts of the various nationalities, he was again dissatisfied with the materials with which he was compelled to work. Not only were they devoid of " literary treatment " but there was almost complete absence of "correlation." So long as this situation existed, the various peoples who composed the American population could not, in Channing's opinion, hope to receive from historians the recognition they sought. [66]

Channing's account of Swedish settlement was confined almost entirely to the Bishop Hill colony because of the author's reliance upon Mikkelsen's convenient monograph.[67] German settlement in Texas received considerable attention in his work because it had been previously investigated. [68] His account of English, Scotch, and Welsh settlements based on sources varying from T. S. Allen's *Directory of the City of*

64 *Ibid.*, II, 422.

65 *Ibid.*, V, 475-7.

66 *Ibid.*, p. 495.

67 " Michael A. Mikkelsen, " The Bishop Hill Colony," *Johns Hopkins University Studies*, tenth series, no. 1.

68 *History of the United States*, V, 472-4.

Mineral Point for the Year 1859 to the manuscripts of the British Temperance Society [69] is less detailed, but he is almost the only historian to give the subject of immigration from the British Isles any attention at all. [70]

Concerning the Irish community, Channing complained that although " several books have been published relating more or less to the Irish immigration to America . . . none of them is satisfactory for this period." [71] Channing differed little from Von Holst, Schouler, and McMaster in what he had to say about the Irish. For example: " their strong racial and religious feelings kept them for fifty years or so in the same places and positions that they were in the first ten years of their coming "; that they " everywhere have secured political position and power "; that " unlike the English, the Germans, and the Swedes; the Irish came as individuals and families; there was no occasion for them to form themselves into colonies and communities, because their race and religion bound them together indissolubly." [72]

Despite his far-sighted realization of the importance of the immigrant community, Channing was unaware of the subtler implications of immigrant impact; of the sociological processes involved in intergroup contact. He was particularly hostile toward immigrants who he regarded as importing alien ideologies, bringing " to their new homes the social prejudices and theories of their old places of habitation," [73] as " would-be remodellers of the American social organization." [74] Some of them, it seemed, were redeemed by the American environment: " foreigners, who had been in the country for several years,

69 *Ibid.*, p. 476.

70 McMaster had dealt with some of the social consequences of early nineteenth century English immigration.

71 *History of the United States*, V, 495.

72 *Ibid.*, p. 479.

73 *Ibid.*, p. 71.

74 *Ibid.*, p. 106.

did not take kindly to . . . experiments in socialism and communism." [75]

In addition, Channing was wont to endow separate nationalities with distinctive character. German settlers, he observed, came from a " martial race and when the time of war required their services in defense of freedom and right, they have always been freely given. In later days, also, the descendants of these Germans have won renown in politics and business." [76] He referred to the " typical dourness " of the Scot; [77] the " industrious, intelligent, and upright " Huguenot " race" ;[78] the martial character of the German " race." [79] He observed that " from time to time a longing for variety has come over sections of the German race," and that this trait was responsible, more than the devastations of the French, for the Palatine migration of the eighteenth century. [80] The Irish, in Channing's opinion, " had no technical skill to speak of or special mental aptitudes, but they had strength of body and the will to work." [81]

Turning to the subject of nativism, Channing again complained of being handicapped by the absence of a " modern scientific work treating the nativist movement of 1840 to 1860 as a whole." His account centered about the fortunes of the Know-Nothings in the states of Massachusetts and New York, where preliminary studies had been made. [82] Channing was of the opinion that the main source of trouble between Roman Catholics and other American citizens " was in the clannishness of the Irish Roman Catholics. They lived apart by

75 *Ibid.*, p. 111.

76 *Ibid.*, II, 411.

77 *Ibid.*, p. 401.

78 *Ibid.*, p. 403.

79 *Ibid.*, p. 404.

80 *Ibid.*, p. 404.

81 *Ibid.*, V, 479.

82 *Ibid.*, VI, 147.

themselves and acted on the advice of their priests. . . ."
Channing was opposed to the Catholic attitude toward the
public school system; he agreed with Von Holst that the papal
envoy, Bedini, committed an impropriety in endeavoring to
settle in his official capacity a property dispute that might well
have been determined by the normal methods of civil procedure. [83]

At the beginning of volume six—*The War for Southern
Independence*— Channing, in iconoclastic vein, denied the
claim that the population of the South was of "cavalier" and
"gentle" descent. "There were," he said, "so many white
persons of German, French, and Irish extraction and of recent
arrival within the states of the South that the white population
was by no means 'homogeneous' and in many ways was not
at all 'gentle'." [84]

Of all the other historians considered in this volume, there
is none whose treatment of immigrant peoples is as satisfactory
as Channing's. Channing was willing to recognize that, since
the immigrant did not immediately become assimilated to the
culture patterns of the American people, since he retained for
a time certain of his Old World traits, the historian should
be concerned with these traits because they, too, were part of
American history. This understanding attitude was particularly manifest in the account, however sketchy and limited, of
immigrant communal settlement following 1840. At least in
conception, that account surpassed anything of the kind that
had thus far been attempted. And indeed, although Channing's
treatment is not without limitations, the limitations are due
less to failure to comprehend the implications of the problem
than to the nature of the sources upon which the discussion
was necessarily based. The difficulties that confronted
Channing can be understood only after some consideration of the histories of ethnic groups upon which he was
compelled to rely.

83 *Ibid.*, p. 131.

84 *Ibid.*, p. 9.

CHAPTER VIII

TOWARD A CORRECTIVE VIEWPOINT

To a limited extent a corrective viewpoint in the treatment of the immigrant in American history was in the making during the half century covered by this volume. The period 1875-1925 marked the advent of the monographic and scientific techniques in historiography; of the economic interpretation; of the frontier hypothesis, and of increased emphasis upon intellectual history. As the half century drew to a close, historians were more and more apt to extend the frontiers of their discipline into the domain of the other social sciences, so that there came into existence a "sociological school of historians."[1] Historians of immigration who wrote after 1925 did benefit from the general advance that had taken place in methods of writing history. Moreover, particularly in the volumes of McMaster, Turner, and Channing there is evidence that to some extent these historians were precursors of a newer approach to the immigrant in American history.

In general, the historians considered in this volume did not formulate theses about immigration and its effects upon the American commonwealth and did not think too deeply about the broader implications of the presence of the immigrant. Consequently, we have had to deal less with theses about immigration than with the attitudes of historians toward immigrants. Summarizing these, we find that the historian generally took for granted the superiority of the old stock; was suspicious of the immigrant as a social and religious innovator; welcomed him as an economic asset; extended some sympathy to the better intentions of the nativists; and hoped that the immigrant would conform to the Anglo-Saxon institutional pattern. There are, of course, deviations from this pattern by individual historians—but it appears to be the norm of the historians' opinions of the immigrant. It is also significant

[1] Carl Becker, "Some Aspects of the Influence of Social Problems and Ideas upon the Study and Writing of History," *The American Journal of Sociology*, XVIII (March 1913), 641 ff.

that, regardless of the conception of the subject matter of history, whether the historian adheres to the frontier hypothesis, whether he stresses political or social history, the attitudinal core remains the same.

This more or less basic attitude pattern originates in the derivation of American historians from middle- or upper-class, Protestant and old-stock American backgrounds. Yet, while the social matrix is important in attitude formation, it is not an invariable determinant of historians' opinions. Class, religious, and ethnic forces may have been major factors influencing the attitudes of historians toward immigrants, but they were certainly not the only forces at play. Channing and Lodge were of very similar background and their writings reflect the general attitudes of historians regarding the immigrant. Yet, it cannot be denied that there are also important differences in what they had to say, not only about the immigrant but also about their own ancestors. These differences are motivated not only by the socio-economic background, but by the distinctive pattern of individual reactions to the milieu. Since in any broad sociological grouping the conditioning of no two of its members is the same, there is inevitably a variety of individual reactions to specific issues. This accounts for what differences there are in attitudes toward immigrants expressed by historians of the same social background.

The historians' basic conception of the immigrant reflected, in some degree, their feeling that the newcomer somehow constituted a threat to what they hold dear, ideologically and materially, in the society in which they lived. It is this basic insecurity that motivated many of their hostile attitudes. However, even more insecure than the historians with generations of American historians behind them were those of recent immigrant ancestry, whose histories of the groups from which they themselves were derived, we are about to consider. Their particular pattern of insecurity manifested itself in extreme forms of ancestor veneration (filiopietism) and in hostility toward other ethnic elements in the population. Because their insecurity was greater, the jingoism of the historians of recent immigrant ancestry far exceeded the chauvinism of historians derived from the older American stock.

FILIOPIETISM

Channing would have had much easier sailing in the section of his history devoted to immigration if the historians of the various immigrant groups had reached a level of sophistication regarding their ancestry comparable to that attained by certain historians who were descendant from the old New England stock. As early as 1883, filiopietism in the historiography of New England, exemplified by Palfrey's *History of New England,* was under attack by Charles Francis Adams, son of the father with a like name, to whom Palfrey dedicated his fourth volume. Adams' son, however, challenged much of what Palfrey held dear in expressing the opinion that the early times in New England were not pleasant times in which to live, and that "the earlier generations were not pleasant generations to live with." With a backward glance at Palfrey, Adams warned that "in the treatment of doubtful historical points there are few things which need to be more carefully guarded against than patriotism or filial piety." [2]

Now, the work of Charles Francis Adams did not end filiopietism in the histories written by the descendants of the Pilgrims. The retreat from ancester worship, however, gained in strength and eventually became the dominant interpretation. Such a tendency was not at all manifest in the histories written about non-English groups in the American population. While Charles Francis Adams and Edward Channing were typical of a growing number of New England historians who adopted a critical attitude toward their ancestors, historians belonging to the non-English ethnic groups, as we shall see, endeavoured as best they could to add cubits to their ancestors' stature—

2 *Three Episodes of Massachusetts History,* II, 561, 802.

frequently omitting what was worthwhile in their ancestors' achievement.

Between 1875 and 1925, a rather large historical literature about immigrant peoples was produced. [3] Nevertheless, there were few really significant historical studies even of limited aspects of the subject. The field of immigration was, in fact, one that seldom attracted the professional historian. Mainly it was the province of the amateur; of the filiopietist whose stamping ground was the historical society of his particular ethnic group, and who received the plaudits of a limited and special ethnic audience. Although the filiopietists did much to open up this important field of research, their prejudices were often detrimental, in the end, to the historiography of the very groups they wrote about. They were apt to claim too much in the name of the group, to deal at too great length with the outstanding individual as representative of the group and to regard the group as an independent entity—unmindful both of its marginal position [4] and of its relationships with the community at large.

In writing about a particular ethnic group, the filiopietist was inspired by what the professional historian would consider extraneous motives. He generally felt obliged to demonstrate that the particular group, by reason of its achievement, was entitled to stand alongside the Anglo-Saxons in the soil of American nationality. This was, in part, a reaction to the group having been ignored or in some way slighted by professional historians; but, however one may account for it, filiopietism, with its effort to obtain " just recognition "

3 A good deal of it derived from historical societies organized along ethnic lines. Among these were the Huguenot Society of America organized in 1886; the Scotch-Irish Society of America organized in 1889; the American Irish Historical Society organized in 1898; the American Jewish Historical Society organized in 1892; the Pennsylvania-German Society organized in 1891.

4 Everett Stonequist, *The Marginal Man* (New York, 1937).

for group accomplishment,[5] was a form of ethnic jingoism. In this connection, it is ironic that the English, who have " contributed " most to American life, have been investigated least. Marcus L. Hansen observed truly:

> There is no English-American historical society, no separate history of the English stock. Discussions of English influence in America are invariably confined to the colonial period and to the legal, economic and social institutions they planted. Such studies ignore the steady inflow of Englishmen that continued all through the nineteenth century.[6]

Who were the Huguenots who signed the Declaration of Independence, the Scotch-Irish who fought and bled in the Revolutionary War, the Germans who pioneered in western settlement, the Irish who gave their all in the War of 1812, the Jews who stood by Lincoln? Tremendous industry went into the discovery of a number of lesser folk heroes who shared with the Anglo-Saxon giants the major trials of the Republic. Inevitably, the tendency was to claim too much. John Fiske could justifiably comment:

> In reading the memoirs and proceedings of Huguenot societies, Holland societies, Jewish societies, Scotch-Irish societies, etc., one is sometimes inclined to ask whether the people about whom we are reading ... ever left anything for other people to do ... Amid so many claims that of England to further recognition as the mother country of the United States seems for the moment overridden.[7]

While he was not willing to credit the New England Puritans with all the virtues that had been ascribed to them, Chan-

5 George Flom, *A History of Norwegian Immigration to the United States from the Earliest Beginning down to the Year 1848* (Iowa City, 1909), pp. 16-17; H. J. Ford, *The Scotch-Irish in America* (Princeton, 1915), pp. 525, 539; R. B. Anderson, *The First Chapter of Norwegian Immigration (1821-40) Its Causes and Results* (Madison, 1896), p. 31.

6 Marcus L. Hansen, *The Immigrant in American History* (Cambridge, 1940), p. 148.

7 *Dutch and Quaker Colonies*, I, 27-8.

ning was equally intolerant of the exaggerated claims of various other nationalties to what they considered their " due place in history." Such claims, he said, were based in part upon the dubious theory that the outstanding individual belonged to a particular group. Channing argued:

> Is the place of a man's birth the determining factor? Is any man born in Ireland an Irishman? Was the Duke of Wellington an Irishman? The case of James Logan, Penn's agent, is to the point: he was born at Lurgan in the northern part of Ireland while his parents were temporarily residing there; they had come from Scotland and passed the remainder of their days in England, while he lived and laboured in America for more than half a century,—was he a Scot, an Irishman, a Scotch-Irishman, or an American? The American nation is composed of so many elements that one man may be descended from half a dozen stocks and as many religions. Shall an historical society belonging to each one of these races and religions claim the distinguished personage for its own?...[8]

In illustration of this last point, Channing constructed the following hypothetical ancestral tree:

Scottish	Irish	French	Spanish	Hebrew	German	Dutch	English
(Presbyterian)	(Roman Catholic)	(Huguenot)	(Roman Catholic)	(Jewish)	(Lutheran)	(Reformed)	(Church of England)
great grandfather	great grandmother	great grandfather	great grandmother	great grandfather	great grandmother	great grandfather	great grandmother
grandfather		grandmother		grandfather		grandmother	
father				mother			
distinguished personage							

8 *History of the United States*, II, 421-2.

No attempt will be made to deal with all the histories written by the filiopietists; those here discussed are for the most part typical. It is well to state at the outset that in the ensuing discussion the constructive aspects of this phase of American historiography may have been slighted; that these accounts offer much important information concerning peoples of non-English origin which is not elsewhere available. Our present aim, however, is to demonstrate the filiopietist's conception of the group in its relation to the general course of American history.

Much as conceptions of the immigrant by professional historians tend to conform to a pattern, so do accounts of the various ethnic groups by their historians have certain features in common. The immigrant was endowed by the filiopietists with a distinctive national character, that character itself being regarded as a " contribution " to American greatness. In the opinion of one of their number, history should be re-written along " racial or ethnic " lines so that it might perform " its proper function of tracing the causes which form the national character and decide national destiny.[9] " In accordance with this tendency, A. O. Fonkalsrud wrote of the " psychic Scandinavian type " as compounded of

> virility, pride in feats of endurance ... deep-seated loyalty, devoted steadfastness in conjugal relationships; also possessing fervent religious tendencies, love of the supernatural, affection for poetry, strong sex consciousness and all-powerful love of adventure and glorious independence.[10]

Some of the filiopietists professed to detect the operation of selective factors in the moulding of national character. L. J. Fosdick recalled how

9 Julius Goebel, "The Place of the German Element in American History," *Annual Report of the American Historical Association* (Washington, 1909), p. 186; Ford, *op. cit.*, p. 525.

10 A. O. Fonkalsrud, *Scandinavians as a Social Force in America* (New York, 1913), p. 1, 8.

for two hundred years France had been like a vast furnace; the fires of persecution had been refining and testing until only the pure gold was left.... Free America, Protestant America, owes a vast debt to the Protestants of France.[11]

And George Cohen argued that among the Jews persecution brought about selection and "those that survived did so by virtue of certain superior faculties of mind."[12] Albert Faust did not resort to the use of selective factors as an explanation of German greatness, but he was none the less convinced that there was a German character marked by "honesty, industry, deep religious spirit, and many other minor yet noble traits." The German, according to Faust, gave to the nation the physical and mental qualities of vigor, sturdiness and vitality, and the moral qualities of genuineness, virility, and aspiration.[13]

Having endowed various nationalities with inherent characteristics, argument began as to the relative importance of the ethnic groups. At this point, the grosser forms of chauvinism, jingoism, and prejudice entered into the historiography of peoples of non-English derivation. Georg von Skal and Frederick Schrader were convinced that the history of the United States proved that the Germans did more for its development than all other nationalities combined.[14] Another account of German achievement in the United States denied that the West was won for civilization

11 L. J. Fosdick, *The French Blood in America* (New York, 1906), p. 16.

12 George Cohen, *The Jews in the Making of America* (Boston, 1924), p. 243.

13 Albert Faust, *The German Element in the United States with Special Reference to Its Political, Moral, Social, and Educational Influence* (New York, 1909), II, 475. For an account of the "national character" of the Scotch-Irish, see Ford, *op. cit.*, p. 539.

14 Georg von Skal, *History of German Immigration in the United States and Successful German-Americans and Their Descendants* (New York, 1908), p. 41; Frederick Schrader, *The Story of New Netherland, the Dutch in America* (New York, 1909), p. 179.

by the Anglo-Celts and the enervated Europeans who detested agriculture, held law and order in low esteem, and lived like Indians on wild game whose hides they bartered for whiskey. The honor belongs preeminently to the German farmer. . . who clung with feelings entirely different from those of the Anglo-Celts to the soil which he had with his own hands wrested from the wilderness.[15]

Faust took issue with Theodore Roosevelt who, he insisted, over-emphasized the role of the Scotch-Irish in western settlement at the expense of the German immigrants. [16]

On the other hand, Charles A. Hanna was certain that the Scotch-Irish were second to none in the importance of their contribution to American civilization, in which contention he was supported by H. J. Ford. [17] Douglas Campbell endorsed in part the claims put forth by the historians of the Scotch-Irish, but he was mainly insistent upon the primacy of the Dutch. [18] This view was sustained by a somewhat less extreme partisan, Irving Elting, who took it upon himself to demonstrate that American institutions were derived from a Dutch source. [19] Again, Ramus B. Anderson gave his readers to understand that no ethnic group could boast of having made a contribution greater than that of the Norwegians. [20]

Another aim of the filiopietist was to show that the ethnic minority to which he belonged was closely related to the dominant group. Fonkalsrud established common ground between Scandinavians and Anglo-Saxons as fellow-members of the

15 *The German Element in the United States* (*A Condensation of Julius Goebel's Das Deutschtum in den Vereinigten Staaten von Nord-Amerika* (Philadelphia, 1909), pp. 12-15.

16 Faust, *op. cit.*, I, 361.

17 *The Scotch-Irish*, chap. vii; Ford, *op. cit.*, p. 524.

18 Douglas Campbell, *The Puritan in Holland, England and America* (2 vols., New York, 1892), I, Introduction, pp. i ii, 11-18.

19 " Dutch Village Communities on the Hudson River," *passim*.

20 Anderson, *op. cit.*, pp. 1-36.

"great Teutonic branch of the Aryan race," a factor which was supposed to have facilitated the Americanization of the Scandinavian immigrant. [21] K. C. Babcock, too, believed that the Scandinavian, being a "Nordic," was material suited to Americanization. [22] Finally, W. E. Griffis found the Dutch and the Germans perfectly adapted to life in the American republic because, he maintained, the republic was "less the fruit of English than of Teutonic civilization." [23]

Not only racial, but religious ties were exploited for the purpose of establishing a connection with the dominant Anglo-Saxon element. [24] Huguenot historians were apt to stress the tie of religion that bound the Huguenots to the Puritans rather than the tie of nationality that bound them to the Catholic French of Canada, the Mississippi Valley, and New England.[25] It was much the same with the Scotch-Irish and the Jews: each of these peoples had its historians who claimed for the group a religious heritage in common with the Puritan.

A significant aspect of the historiography of non-English peoples is the tendency to revive Old World religious and racial antagonisms. Dinsmore attempted to justify the hatred of the Scotch-Irish for Roman Catholicism. He asked

> Had not Rome robbed, tortured and burnt their forefathers?
> .... If they were intolerant, it was because they learned the lesson from those who had done their utmost to burn them.

21 Fonkalsrud, *op. cit.*, pp. 1, 8.

22 *The Scandinavian Element in the United States* (Urbana, Illinois, 1914), p. 10. Babcock, however, cannot be dismissed as a filio-pietist.

23 W. E. Griffis, *The Story of New Netherland; the Dutch in America* (Boston, 1909), p. 275.

24 Fosdick, *op. cit.*, p. 16; J. W. Dinsmore, *The Scotch-Irish in America* (Chicago, 1896), p. 17; Straus, *The Origin of Republican Form of Government*, pp. 70-88.

25 Fosdick, *op. cit.*, p. 16; Elizabeth Avery, *The Influence of French Immigration on the Political History of the United States* (Redfield, South Dakota, 189?), p. 67.

How can we expect one to tolerate the man who is trying to assassinate him? It is too much to ask of one who is in a death grapple with a burglar that he shall treat him gently; that he shall wear the smirk of a dancing master? [26]

Henry Martyn Baird insisted that French Huguenots had not merely a purer creed but a higher standard of morals than the Catholic community in which they lived.[27] Proud of traits allegedly shared with Huguenot and Puritan, Scotch-Irish historians were at the same time insistent that the blood of Irish Protestant and Catholic never mingled except, as Dinsmore said, on the battlefield when the two peoples were locked in mortal combat.[28] Hanna denied that intermarriage took place between the Scotch and the Irish, maintaining that:

> These Scottish people in Ireland today exhibit all the distinctive racial characteristics of their Scottish forefathers; and have none of the peculiar qualities attributed to the offspring of mixed marriages between Irish Protestants and Roman Catholics.[29]

The Irish replied in kind, labelling their Scotch-Irish, Huguenot, and Puritan antagonists " priest-ridden . . . hard and fast bigots." Scotch-Irish historians were denounced as " humbugs " whose practice was to select " any or all Irishmen who have attained eminence in public life, lump them together and label the lump 'Scotch-Irish.' " Anglo-Saxon historians, from

26 Dinsmore, *op. cit.*, p. 13.

27 H. M. Baird, " Some Traits of Huguenot Character," *Proceedings of the Huguenot Society of America*, I (1883-4), 11. Baird was author of a number of books on the Huguenots among them being: *History of the Rise of the Huguenots of France* (2 vols., New York, 1879) ; *The Huguenots and Henry of Navarre* (2 vols., New York, 1886) ; *The Huguenots and the Revocation of the Edict of Nantes* (2 vols., New York, 1895). Henry Martyn Baird is not to be confused with Charles Washington Baird whose *History of the Huguenot Emigration to America* (2 vols., New York, 1885), is more critical in tone.

28 Dinsmore, *op. cit.*, p. 14.

29 Hanna, *op. cit.*, I, 161.

Bancroft on, were accused of perpetrating a large-scale conspiracy to suppress and ridicule everything Irish in American history. [30]

Although much of the prejudice against immigrant groups in American historiography was due to the fact that great masses of them were industrial workers living in large cities, this aspect of the matter was ignored by the filiopietists, who in their eagerness to clasp Revolutionary martyrs, Civil War heroes, and sturdy pioneers to their respective bosoms, had no time for interest in the common people. Moreover, immigrant radicals and labor leaders found few sympathizers or defenders in the ranks of the filiopietists. Olof N. Nelson said that " the moderation and self-restraint inherent in the cold blood of the North " made the Scandinavian " constitutionally inclined to trust in slow and orderly methods [in government] rather than swift and violent ones." [31] Fonkalsrud stressed the political independence of the Scandinavians and discussed their contributions to the Populist and Progressive movements; but, he made it clear that " they are, as a people, Republican," despite a tendency to shift allegiance " from party to party, thus exhibiting the same characteristic that is seen in their 'vandrelyst' and Viking nature centuries ago." [32] Peter Wiernik, historian of the Jews in America, defined Americanization as " the abandonment of extreme views on all subjects." The Russian-Jewish mind he found " much inclined to theorizing";

30 Edward Condon, *The Irish Race in America* (New York, 1887), pp. 23, 26; *Journal of the American Irish Historical Society*, I, 7, 8, 86, 88; II, 53. See also the review by J. F. Jameson of Michael J. O'Brien, *A Hidden Phase of American History: Ireland's Part in America's Struggle for Liberty* (New York, 1920), in *American Historical Review*, XXVI (July 1921), 797.

31 Olof N. Nelson, *History of the Scandinavians and Successful Scandinavians in the United States* (Minneapolis, 1900), p. 39. T. C. Blegen presented a more realistic interpretation of Scandinavian political behavior in a paper entitled " The Scandinavian Element and Agrarian Discontent," *American Historical Review*, XXVII (April 1922), 417-8.

32 Fonkalsrud, *op. cit.*, p. 71.

but, he said, " radicalism was a passing phase in the development of the Russian-Jewish immigrants "; the naturalized immigrant, " even when he remained a manual worker, was soon voting for one of the two great American parties." [33]

There can be no doubt but that the filiopietists, with their stress upon the group contribution, give a somewhat broader view of the immigrant's role than that offered by the major American historians. On the other hand, none of the latter ventured to write of the English element in the American population in a manner quite as laudatory as, for example, that in which Faust wrote of the German strain or Ford of the Scotch-Irish. It may be argued that it was because the filiopietists were forced to be on the defensive that they were over-zealous in demonstrating the worth of the group. But to this it might be countered that peoples of non-English origin are far from being " suppressed nationalities " in the United States, and that therefore the jingoism of their historians appears rather uncalled for.

A scholar recently protested that despite the care with which each of the filiopietists reckoned up the contribution made by his own ethnic group, they all had a way of omitting the things we should most like to know. They rarely concerned themselves, for example, with such questions as these:

> What was life like in the German agricultural village? In what kind of homes did the Swiss peasants live? What was the character of the peasant art of the Rhine Palatinate? What were the cultural influences of Ulster? Whence came the octagonal churches of Long Island and northern New Jersey? What have been the inheritances in religion, edu-

33 Peter Wiernik, *History of the Jews in America from the Period of the Discovery of the New World to the Present Time* (New York, 1912), pp. 273, 301. Faust's treatment of the Haymarket affair and early German participation in the Socialist movement is relatively sympathetic. II, 194-200. On the other hand, M. Haiman's *Polish Pioneers of Virginia and Kentucky, with Notes on Genealogy of the Sadowski Family*, praises the early Polish immigrants for their endurance in the face of oppression. (Chicago, 1937), p. 49.

cation, art, government, of the vast number of Swedes, or
Russians, or Italians who for decades poured through Ellis
Island to become bone of our bone, flesh of our flesh? [34]

In their anxiety to impress the reader with what has been
achieved in this country by members of the group, they devoted too much space to lists of statesmen, soldiers, poets,
novelists, and educators; and too little to an account of the
everyday life of the group in the town, the village, or the
city ward, where, as Hansen said, "the leaven in the lump
can be detected." [35] The filiopietists, for the most part, failed to
realize that immigrant and native cultures were dynamic and
changing as a consequence of their interaction, and they therefore missed the core of the problem. It was highly unrealistic
of them to conceive of a " contribution " as being made by an
ethnic group, particularly after the latter had been in America
for many generations and had been assimilated to the dominant culture pattern. Moreover, the individual making the
" contribution " might not be truly representative of the group
culture. He might, in fact, have achieved success in so far as
he cast off the group culture and became assimilated. [36] Ethnic
cultures in America are not so much separate entities as aspects
of a larger whole; and they should be regarded by historians
as such. [37]

Throughout the half century of American history writing
that we have been considering, there was an increasing trend
toward " scientific " historiography that is, toward "restrained

34 Thomas Jefferson Wertenbaker, *The Founding of American Civilization. The Middle Colonies* (New York, 1938), p. 12.

35 *The Immigrant in American History*, p. 206.

36 J. S. Roucek and others, " Summary of the Discussion," pp. 86-9; " Cultural Groups in the United States," by Caroline F. Ware, pp. 62-73, and "Approaches to the Study of Nationality Groups in the United States," by
Maurice R. Davie and others, pp. 74-86, in Caroline F. Ware, ed., *The
Cultural Approach to History* (New York, 1940).

37 Samuel Koenig, " Second- and Third-Generation Americans," pp. 471-
86; Maurice R. Davie, " Our Vanishing Minorities," pp. 540-51; in F. J.
Brown and J. S. Roucek, ed., *One America* (New York, 1945).

expression, caution in statement, and a broader consideration of the social and economic background." [38] There can be no doubt that filiopietism ran counter to that trend. Yet a good deal of sound scholarship entered into some of these volumes, particularly with regard to fact-finding, and filiopietism, it should be remembered, was but an aspect of a larger contribution. Also, these early efforts in the history of non-English peoples should be viewed in their proper perspective as pioneer achievements. T. C. Blegen took this approach to the problem when he acknowledged the "pioneering work" of Anderson and Flom in the field of Norwegian immigration. [39]

It should be kept in mind that almost all the history written about immigrant groups was the result of these writers' untutored efforts. Moreover, in the historical societies organized along lines of nationality there was at least the stimulus of interest—interest which, if intelligently directed, was sure to result in constructive achievement. That such organizations need not forever indulge in the grosser forms of ancestor worship is apparent from the assistance which the Norwegian American Historical Society has recently given to that outstanding scholar T. C. Blegen, and from the fact that that Society is planning an exhaustive research into the history of the Norwegian element in the United States. [40]

Largely because of the efforts of the filiopietists, A. M. Schlesinger in 1922 could point to a "valuable and growing literature dealing historically with separate racial elements in the United States." [41] Although the readers of these histories

38 Kraus, *op. cit.*, p. 291.

39 *Norwegian Immigration to America, 1825-1860* (Northfield, Minnesota, 1931), preface, p. x.

40 T. C. Blegen, "A Review and a Challenge," *The Norwegian American Historical Association* (Northfield, 1938).

41 "The Influence of Immigration on American History," in *New Viewpoints in American History* (New York, 1922), pp. 1-22. The "Bibliographic Note" includes a number of books mentioned earlier in this chapter by Anderson, Faust, Flom, Ford, Hanna, Nelson, pp. 21-2.

were cautioned by Schlesinger against "the temptation of the author to give undue importance to the nationality with which he is dealing," it is clear from Schlesinger's account that histories of specific nationalities, precisely because of the efforts of the filiopietists, were more numerous than the historical literature devoted to the general subject of immigration into the United States. Indeed, Schlesinger pointed out that despite the vast literature on immigration in the form of books, magazine articles, government reports, and the interest in immigration "as a social problem," the historian had neglected this important approach to American history. Schlesinger mentioned a number of general surveys of the field of immigration—but only two by historians: those by S. P. Orth and Max Farrand. [42] The former is a rather inconsequential and frequently biased account, [43] while Farrand's articles in the *New Republic* [44] are no more than a rapid survey. Not only could Schlesinger point to no comprehensive study by an historian of the field of immigration, but even today this task remains to be done. There has not yet appeared "the man with the magic touch, who by a process known only to the master" could produce a "masterpiece of historical synthesis" embracing the entire field of immigration into the United States. [45]

BEYOND 1925

If the subject of how the theme of immigration is treated in American historical writing were carried beyond 1925, the pattern of such an account would be considerably different from that of the present volume. Emphasis would be less upon the attitudes of general historians toward European immigrants

42 *Ibid.*, p. 21.

43 *Our Foreigners* (New Haven, 1920). See his comments upon Jewish immigration, p. 179.

44 "Immigration in the Light of History," *New Republic*, IX (December 2, 9, 16, 23, 1916).

45 G. M. Stephenson, "When America Was the Land of Canaan," *Minnesota History*, X (September 1929), 237.

and more upon the intensive work done in the field by those who have specialized in it. This is due to the changed character of historical writing in the past two decades. After Channing, the study of American history became more specialized (a trend that had been long in the making), and the writing of many-volumed panoramic accounts of our national development became increasingly infrequent. Almost all aspects of American history have been refined and subjected to intensive research, and immigration is no exception.

It should be said in passing that the arguments of the filiopietists, concerning the superiority of one group or another had very little to do with bringing obout the progress that has been made since about 1925 in the historiography of immigrant groups. The best of the contemporary writing on immigration is in the earlier monographic tradition of Kate Everest, K. C. Babcock, and M. A. Mikkelsen; it develops more fully points of view set forth earlier by McMaster, Turner, and Channing; it is the product of the general advance in historical writing by historians who have greatly increased the scope of their narratives by levying upon the contributions of their colleagues in the fields of geography, anthropology, ethnography, economics, psychology, and particularly, sociology. [46]

It should be noted, too, that although in the past two decades the output of group historical societies has been comparatively small, chauvinism in the writing of ethnic history is by no means extinct. Its most recent manifestation—before an audience broader than the filiopietists ever reached—is the work of Louis Adamic, who, in his *A Nation of Nations* repeats the stock arguments of the ethnic jingoists. Like them, he approaches his theme in a spirit of indignation over the way in which American historians generally have ignored the role of the non-Anglo Saxons. In this mood, he goes back to the nine-

46 Becker, *op. cit.*, passim; Kraus, *op. cit.*, p. 319.

teenth century to kick the old dead bones of John Fiske and Henry Cabot Lodge for sins of omission and commission. Then, with fervent insistence upon the multinational origin of the American people—a thesis no one today seriously challenges —he recapitulates the glories of forgotten ethnic heroes. He also devotes page after page to such revelations as that " one of Edward R. Stettinius' grandfathers was a Reilly " and that " George Washington was kin to a branch of the McCarthy family." [47]

There might have been an excuse for such labored jingoism if Adamic had been writing in the 1880's or the 1890's, but there is no excuse for it now; for the contemporary American historians treat the immigrant rather fairly. Adamic's performance points up by contrast the progress that has recently been made in immigrant and ethnic historiography—a progress which is the result not only of the rise of a few trained scholars who have specialized in immigration and ethnic problems, but also of the general advance in the techniques of writing American history.

After 1925, there emerged a few trained historians who adopted immigration as a field of major interest. In the course of the past two decades, these scholars have rescued immigrant and ethnic history from the filiopietists, and have produced several interesting monographic accounts of special phases of the subject. Mainly as a result of their efforts, there has come about in recent years at least the beginnings of an historiography of immigration.

Outstanding among these scholars was Marcus L. Hansen, who, in a masterly essay entitled " The History of American Immigration as a Field for Research," [49] suggested a great number of problems having to do with immigration and its place within the framework of our national development. So wide was Hansen's grasp of the subject that his essay is im-

47 (New York, 1945), pp. 315, 341.

49 *American Historical Review*, XXXII (1926-7), 500-18.

portant not only as a guide to research, but also as an outline for a survey of the entire field.

Despite Hansen's efforts, very few of his research suggestions have been adopted. Historians still tend to avoid the field of immigration. This is partly due to the fact that most research in immigrant and ethnic history presupposes acquaintance with another language, but other factors also may enter in. The ill-repute which the filiopietists lent this field of inquiry may cause the trained historian to steer clear of it. And it may be that historians of ethnic descent have followed in the pattern of the great majority of the non-Anglo-Saxons in our population who have been ready to turn their backs upon their ancestral cultures and inheritances.

Another reason why Hansen failed to attract a host of followers is that he did not try to do with immigration the sort of thing that Turner had tried to do with the frontier concept: he did not try to establish immigration as a key to the understanding of America. Hansen's essay did not contain the sort of extravagant statement that is to be found in Turner's argument, and for this reason it was less discussed and therefore attracted less attention among scholars. The opposition which might have been expected to develop between the environmentalist frontier hypothesis and Hansen's concern with the immigrant's role, simply did not materialize because Hansen was less interested in offering an interpretation of history than he was in opening up a field of historical research.

However, in 1938, when Hansen had occasion to deal directly with the frontier hypothesis, he took issue with it, insisting that the relative roles of environmental, and European, and Eastern influences in shaping the character of the Middle West be evaluated before any conclusion was reached as to the effect of the frontier upon men and institutions.[50] Further criticism of the hypothesis was expressed by Blegen:

---

[50] "Remarks" on the discussion of the Turner thesis, Dixon Ryan Fox, ed., *Sources of Culture in the Middle West* (New York, 1934), pp. 108-11.

Turner's hypothesis, invaluable as it was in focusing attention upon some mainsprings of our national life, nevertheless did not wholly explain the great diversity in the customs and attitudes and in the material and spiritual culture of the peoples living within the boundaries of the United States. As scholars sought to understand the social development of the American people, a new emphasis gradually made itself felt—an emphasis that took into account the varied backgrounds of the racial elements that lend color and richness to the epic of America.[51]

Although both Hansen and Blegen criticized the frontier hypothesis, both recognized that Turner had made a contribution to the historiography of immigration. Hansen acknowledged Turner's influence upon his work,[52] and Blegen stated that Turner was fully conscious of the importance of immigration as a factor in our national evolution.[53] Turner's status as the outstanding figure in the earlier period of the historiography of immigration, is due not so much to his having advanced the frontier hypothesis as to the breadth of his view of the true nature of history, and to his willingness to consider all aspects of the social process. His contention that to know America one must know the peoples who made it is, after all, the key to the problem. Of Turner, more than of any other historian, it may be said that it is a pity he did not attempt a history of immigration.

Other approaches to American history, apart from the frontier hypothesis, were developed in the period 1875-1925 and made their influence felt upon the historiography of immigration in the years following. The conception of the " transit of civilization," which Edward Eggleston promulgated in 1901,[54] but barely developed, found expression in the volumes

---

51 "A Review and a Challenge," pp. 6-7.

52 Hansen, " Marcus Lee Hansen—Historian of Immigration," p. 88.

53 *The American Transition*, p. 592.

54 William P. Randel, *Edward Eggleston* (New York, 1946), pp. 226-8.

of Marcus L. Hansen, Theodore C. Blegen, Thomas Jefferson Wertenbaker, and George M. Stephenson. These writers begin the story of immigration in Europe and then seek to discover how immigrant culture and thought patterns were modified in the American environment; it is much the same sort of thing that Eggleston attempted to do with the early New England settlers. Interest in the transit and modification of the folk cultures of immigrant and ethnic groups was really part of a larger trend, initiated mainly by McMaster and apparent also in the work of Lodge and Eggleston,—a trend toward giving history the task of describing how, in various times and places, the mass of the common people have lived.

The importance of intellectual history, which emerged as the period covered by this volume drew to a close,[55] was a trend which carried over into the years following 1925 and was manifest in such studies as G. M. Stephenson's *The Religious Aspects of Swedish Immigration*[56] and Howard M. Jones' *America and French Culture, 1750-1848.*[57] Statistical analysis reveals that it is in the fields of literature, fine arts, religious leadership, science, and learning that the immigrant has achieved greatest distinction.[58] We may expect, therefore, that increased emphasis upon intellectual history will tend to reveal more and more of the immigrant's role in our national life. Nevertheless, the writers of our cultural history have not erected the organization of their volumes upon the contribution of the ethnic group. This is, on the whole, a rather wise decision because ethnic cultures have not, as a rule, endured in the American environment and there are other cultural determinants more fundamental. It should be noted, however, that there is greater recognition of the immigrant's role, *per se,*

55 Kraus, *op. cit.*, p. 318.

56 (Minneapolis, 1932).

57 (Chapel Hill, 1927).

58 Dumas Malone, " The Intellectual Melting Pot," *The Atlantic Presents We Americans* (Boston, 1939), p. 81.

in Merle Curti's recent *The Growth of American Thought*[59] than in Vernon L. Parrington's earlier treament.[60]

The importance of economic factors, which Charles A. Beard impressed upon the historical profession in 1913,[61] was to an increased extent recognized by historians following 1925. Moreover, emphasis upon the economic determinant would seemingly lessen the tendency to ascribe major changes in American life to innate immigrant characteristics. Writing from this point of view, John Bates Clark had this to say of the assimilability of the " new immigrants":

> Americanizing goes on effectively when the economic conditions of this country itself are such as to ensure it. Conditions take precedence over racial qualities because the change in prevailing conditions is far different than the changes of race. There is far more likeness between different branches of the European family than there is between the economic conditions into which immigrants came in the third quarter of the last century, and those into which they come today. Then they could have farms for the asking, while now most of them must go into mills, mines, shops, and railroad plants or become employees or tenants of farms owned by others. In such places the americanizing goes on under difficulties and the marshalling of many of the immigrants in the army of trade unionism, on the one hand, or that of socialism on the other, becomes natural and inevitable.[62]

It is possible that had Rhodes written of the Irish or Oberholtzer of the new immigrants with some conception of economic realities, their accounts would have been considerably more fair than they were. Yet Beard presented the immigrants

59 (New York, 1943), 491 ff.

60 V. L. Parrington, *Main Currents in American Thought; An Interpretation of American Literature from the Beginnings to 1920* (3 vols., New York, 1927-30).

61 *An Economic Interpretation of the Constitution of the United States* (New York, 1913). Beard assails the Teutonic hypothesis, *ibid.*, pp. 2-3.

62 John R. Commons and Associates, *A Documentary History of American Industrial Society* (10 vols., Cleveland, 1910), I, 52.

in an unfavorable light despite his conception of the strength of economic forces as historical determinants. [63] John R. Commons, who was well aware of the importance of economic factors, nevertheless wrote that " race differences are established in the very blood and physical constitution. They are most difficult to eradicate, and they yield only to the slow processes of centuries." [64]

Thus, while awareness of economic factors may furnish additional insight into the histories of immigrant groups, it is by no means the key to the problem. In fact, no single approach is the key, whereas almost any recognized approach will prove revealing, if it is intelligently used. That the political historians, Von Holst, Schouler, and Rhodes, treated immigration unsatisfactorily does not mean that the political approach to that subject is necessarily fruitless; it merely means that these historians failed to realize its possibilities. Mere choice of a social or intellectual theme is no guarantee of satisfactory use of that theme; witness Oberholtzer's discussion of immigration and S. G. Fisher's appraisal of the immigrant's influence upon American culture.

Although in the historical investigation of immigration it matters less what approach is chosen than how wisely the approach is made, that view of history which is broadly sociological seems to be, on the whole, the most rewarding: it is such a view that Oscar Handlin takes in his study of an immigrant community, *Boston's Immigrants, 1790-1865*. In this work, which ingeniously combines the techniques of historian and sociologist, Handlin states, as did Hansen before him, that " the character of the environment—the community in its broadest sense—is particularly important in the study of the contact of dissimilar cultures. It is the field where unfam-

---

63 C. A. Beard and C. W. Bagley, *The History of the American People* (New York, 1930), pp. 523, 529; C. A. Beard and Mary R. Beard, *The American Spirit A Study of the Idea of Civilization in the United States* (New York, 1942), p. 549.

64 Commons, *Races and Immigrants in America*, pp. 2, 3, 8, 70-1.

iliar groups meet, discover each other, and join in a hard relationship that results in either acculturation or conflict. . . ." Handlin's aim was to analyze what Durkheim described as the " internal constitution of the social *milieu* " an aim which brought him to the frontier of his function as an historian. [65] This is the inevitable position of a specialist in immigrant and ethnic history who, to comprehend group reactions, must possess an understanding of related fields.

On the whole, the study of immigration permits the historian to exercise his function in its broad rather than its narrow, fact-finding sense. Since the historian of immigration is also historian of the peoples, his domain embraces the field of the social sciences. To the extent that the historian of immigration makes himself master of latest developments in the other social sciences, his function becomes more difficult and also more valuable. The historian of immigration is in a strategic position with reference to these new developments. Because of the nature of the materials with which he deals, he has a particularly good opportunity to contribute to the advancement of his profession.

[65] *Op. cit.*, Foreword, vii-viii.

LIST OF REFERENCES

I. Writings by Historians

Adams, C. F., "The Genesis of the Massachusetts Town and the Origin of Town-Meeting Government," Proceedings of the Massachusetts Historical Society, second series, VII (January 1892), 174-211. Comments of A. C. Goodell, Jr., *ibid.*, 211-14. Comments of Mellen Chamberlain, *ibid.*, 214-42. Comments of Edward Channing, *ibid.*, 242-63.

——, *Massachusetts; Its Historians and Its History. An Object Lesson*, Boston, 1894.

——, "The Sifted Grain and the Grain Sifters," *American Historical Review*, VI (January 1901).

——, *Three Episodes of Massachusetts History*, 2 vols., Boston, 1892.

Adams, Henry, *The Degradation of the Democratic Dogma*, New York, 1920.

——, *Democracy, an American Novel*, New York, 1882.

——, *The Education of Henry Adams, An Autobiography*, Boston, 1918.

——, ed., *Essays on Anglo-Saxon Law*, Boston, 1876.

——, *Historical Essays*, New York, 1891.

——, *History of the United States of America*, 9 vols., New York, 1891.

——, *Mont-Saint-Michel and Chartres*, Boston, 1905.

Adams, H. B., *Bluntschli's Life Work*, Baltimore, 1884.

——, "The Church and Popular Education," *Johns Hopkins Studies*, eighteenth series, 1900, nos. VIII-IX.

——, Editorial introduction to J. H. Johnson, Jr., "Rudimentary Society Among Boys," *Johns Hopkins Studies*, second series, 1884, no. XI.

——, "The Germanic Origin of New England Towns. With Notes on Co-operation in University Work," *Johns Hopkins Studies*, first series, 1883, no. II.

——, *History of the Thomas Adams and Thomas Hastings Families of Amherst Massachusetts*, Amherst, 1880.

——, "Leopold Von Ranke," *American Academy of Arts and Sciences*, XXXII, pt. 2.

——, "Methods of Historical Study," *Johns Hopkins Studies*, second series, 1884, nos. I and II.

——, "Norman Constables in America," *Johns Hopkins Studies*, first series, 1883, no. VIII.

——, "Notes on the Literature of Charities," *Johns Hopkins Studies*, fifth series, 1887, no. VIII.

——, "Saxon Tithing-Men in America," *Johns Hopkins Studies*, first series, 1883, no. IV.

——, *The Study of History in American Colleges and Universities*, Washington, 1887.

——, "Village Communities of Cape Ann and Salem," *Johns Hopkins Studies*, first series, 1883, nos. IX and X.

——, "Work Among Workingmen in Baltimore," Notes supplementary to the *Johns Hopkins Studies*, sixth series, 1889.

Adams, J. T., *History of the Town of Southampton (East of Canoe Place)*, Bridgehampton, Long Island, 1918.

Allen, W. F., "A Survival of Land Community in New England," *The Nation*, January 10, 1878.

Anderson, R. B., *The First Chapter of Norwegian Immigration (1821-40) Its Causes and Results*, Madison, 1896.

Andrews, C. M., *The Old English Manor A Study in English Economic History*, Baltimore, 1892, *Johns Hopkins Studies*, extra vol. XII.

——, "The River Towns of Connecticut A Study of Wethersfield, Hartford, and Windsor," *Johns Hopkins Studies*, seventh series, nos. VII-VIII-IX.

——, "The Theory of the Village Community," *Papers of the American Historical Association*, V (New York, 1891).

Avery, E. H., *The Influence of French Immigration on the Political History of the United States*, Redfield, South Dakota, 189?.

Babcock, K. C., *The Scandinavian Element in the United States*, Urbana, 1914.

Baird, C. W., *History of the Huguenot Emigration to America*, 2 vols., New York, 1885.

Baker, R. S. and Dodd, W. E., eds., *The Public Papers of Woodrow Wilson*, 6 vols., New York, 1925-7.

Bancroft, H. H., *Essays and Miscellany*, San Francisco, 1890.

——, *Retrospection, Political and Personal*, New York, 1912.

Beard, Charles A., *An Economic Interpretation of the Constitution of the United States*, New York, 1913.

Beard, C. A. and Bagley, C. W., *The History of the American People*, New York, 1930.

Beard, C. A. and Beard, Mary R., *The American Spirit A Study of the Idea of Civilization in the United States*, New York, 1942.

Beveridge, A. J., *Americans of To-day and To-morrow*, Philadelphia, 1908.

Blackmar, F. W., "Spanish Colonization in the Southwest," *Johns Hopkins Studies*, eighth series, 1889, no. IV.

Blegen, T. C., *The American Transition*, Northfield, Minnesota, 1940.

——, "The Scandinavian Element and Agrarian Discontent," summary account in *American Historical Review*, XXVII (April 1922).

——, *Norwegian Immigration to America, 1825-1860*, Northfield, Minnesota, 1931.

——, "A Review and a Challenge," *The Norwegian American Historical Association*, Northfield, Minnesota, 1938.

Brigham, A. P., *Geographic Influences in American History*, Boston, 1903.

Burgess, John W., *America's Relations to the Great War*, Chicago, 1916.

——, "The German Emperor," letter in the *New York Times*, October 17, 1914.

——, "Germany, Great Britain and the United States," *Political Science Quarterly*, XIX (March 1904).

——, *Germany and the United States: An Address Delivered before the Germanistic Society of America, Jan. 24, 1908*, New York, 1909.

——, "The Ideal of the American Commonwealth," *Political Science Quarterly*, X (September 1895).

——, Letter in the *Springfield Republican*, August 17, 1914.

——, "The Methods of Historical Study and Research in Columbia University," in G. S. Hall, ed., *Methods of Teaching History*, Boston, 1883.

——, *Political Science and Comparative Constitutional Law*, 2 vols., Boston, 1902.

——, "Political Science and History," *Annual Report of the American Historical Association*, I (1896).

——, *Reminiscences of an American Scholar, The Beginnings of Columbia University*, New York, 1934.

Campbell, Douglas, *The Puritan in Holland, England and America*, 2 vols., New York, 1892.

Cater, Harold, ed., *Henry Adams and His Friends A Collection of His Unpublished Letters*, New York, 1947.

Channing, Edward, "Town and Country Government in the English Colonies of North America," *Johns Hopkins Studies*, second series, 1884, no. X.

——, *A History of the United States*, 6 vols., New York, 1925.

Condon, Edward O'Meagher, *The Irish Race in America*, New York, 1887.

Diamond, William, ed., Frederick Jackson Turner, "International Parties in a Durable League of Nations," *American Historical Review*, XLVII (April 1942).

Dinsmore, J. W., *The Scotch-Irish in America*, Chicago, 1906.

Dole, S. B., "Letters of Sanford B. Dole and John W. Burgess," *Pacific Historical Review*, V (1936).

Dunning, W. A., *Truth in History and Other Essays*, New York, 1937.

Edwards, E. E., ed., *The Early Writings of Frederick Jackson Turner*, Madison, 1938.

Eggleston, Edward, *The Transit of Civilization from England to America in the Seventeenth Century*, New York, 1901.

Elting, Irving, "Dutch Village Communities on the Hudson River," *Johns Hopkins Studies*, fourth series, 1886, no. I.

Everest, Kate, "Early Lutheran Immigration in Wisconsin," *Transactions, Wisconsin Academy of Sciences, Arts and Letters*, VIII (Madison, 1892).

——, "The Geographical Origin of German Immigration into Wisconsin," *Collections, Wisconsin State Historical Society*, XII (Madison, 1898).

——, "How Wisconsin came by Its Large German Element," *Collections, Wisconsin State Historical Society*, XII (Madison, 1892).

Farrand, Max, "Immigration in the Light of History," *New Republic*, IX.

Faust, A. B., *The German Element in the United States with Special Reference to Its Political, Moral, Social, and Educational Influence*, 2 vols. in one, New York, 1927.

Fisher, Sydney G., "Alien Degradation of American Character," *Forum*, XIV (January 1893).

——, *The Evolution of the Constitution of the United States*, Philadelphia, 1897.

——, "Has Immigration Increased Population?", *Popular Science Monthly*, XLVIII (December 1895).

Fisk, E. F., ed., *The Letters of John Fiske*, New York, 1940.

Fiske, John, *American Political Ideas Viewed from the Standpoint of Universal History*, New York. 1911.

——, *The Beginnings of New England; or, The Puritan Theocracy in Its Relations to Civil and Religious Liberty*, Boston, 1899.

——, *A Century of Science and Other Essays*, Boston, 1899.

——, *The Critical Period of American History, 1783-1789*, New York, 1916.

——, *The Dutch and Quaker Colonies in America*, 2 vols., Boston, 1900.

——, *Essays, Historical and Literary*, 2 vols., New York, 1902.

——, *Excursions of an Evolutionist*, Boston, 1885.

——, *It Must Be Done Again The Case for a World Federal Union*, New York, 1940.

——, *Old Virginia and Her Neighbours*, 2 vols., Boston, 1897.

——, *The Unseen World and Other Essays*, Boston, 1876.

Flom, G. T., *A History of Norwegian Immigration to the United States from the Earliest Beginning down to the Year 1848*, Iowa City, 1909.

Fonkalsrud, A. O., *Scandinavians as a Social Force in America*, New York, 1913.

Ford, H. J., *The Scotch-Irish in America*, Princeton, 1915.

Ford, W. C., ed., *Letters of Henry Adams, 1858-1918*, 2 vols., Boston, 1930-8.

Fosdick, L. J., *The French Blood in America*, New York, 1906.

Freeman, E. A., *Comparative Politics*, New York, 1873.

——, "An Introduction to American Institutional History," *Johns Hopkins Studies*, first series, 1883, no. 1.

——, *Some Impressions of the United States*, New York, 1883.

Goebel, Julius, "The Place of the German Element in American History," *Annual Report of the American Historical Association*, Washington, 1909.

——, *The German Element in the United States (A Condensation of Julius Goebel's Das Deutschtum in den Vereinigten Staaten von Nord-Amerika*, Philadelphia, 1909.

Goldman, E. F., ed., "Young John Bach McMaster: A Boyhood in New York City," *New York History*, XX (July 1939).

Griffis, W. E., *The Story of New Netherland, The Dutch in America*, Boston, 1909.

Haiman, Mieczyslaw, *Polish Pioneers of Virginia and Kentucky, with Notes on Genealogy of the Sadowski Family*, Chicago, 1937.

Hanna, C. A., *The Scotch-Irish; or, the Scot in North Britain, North Ireland and North America*, 2 vols., New York, 1902.

Hansen, M. L., *The Immigrant in American History*, Cambridge, 1940.

Hart, A. B., *Introduction to the Study of Federal Government*, Boston, 1891.

——, "Methods of Teaching History," G. S. Hall, ed., *Methods of Teaching History*, Boston, 1902.

Hay, John, "The Pioneers of Ohio," *The Magazine of History*, extra vol., no. 10 (1924).

Von Holst, H. E., "Are We Awakened?", *Journal of Political Economy*, II (September 1894).

——, *The Constitutional and Political History of the United States*, translators, John J. Lalor and Alfred B. Mason, 8 vols., Chicago, 1876-92.

——, "The Need of Universities in the United States," *Educational Review*, V (February 1893).

Holt, W. S., ed., *Historical Scholarship in the United States, 1876-1901: As Revealed in the Correspondence of Herbert B. Adams*, Baltimore, 1938.

Hosmer, J. K., *The Last Leaf; Observations, During Seventy-Five Years of Men and Events in America and Europe*, New York, 1912.

——, "Samuel Adams, The Man of the Town Meeting," *Johns Hopkins Studies*, second series, 1884, no. IV.

——, *Outcome of the Civil War 1863-1865*, New York, 1907.

——, *Samuel Adams*, New York, 1885.

——, *A Short History of Anglo-Saxon Freedom. The Polity of the English-Speaking Race. Outlined in Its Inception, Development, Diffusion and Present Condition*, New York, 1890.

——, *The Story of the Jews Ancient, Mediaeval, and Modern*, New York, 1893.

Howard, G. E., *An Introduction to the Local Constitutional History of the United States, Johns Hopkins Studies*, Baltimore, 1889, extra vol. IV.

Johnston, Alexander, *Connecticut: A Study of Commonwealth-Democracy*, New York, 1891.

——, "The Genesis of A New England State," *Johns Hopkins Studies*, first series, 1889, no. XI.

Jones, H. M., *America and French Culture, 1750-1848*, Chapel Hill, 1927.

Kuhns, L. O., *The German and Swiss Settlements of Colonial Pennsylvania: a Study of the So-called Pennsylvania Dutch*, New York, 1901.

Larned, J. N., ed., *The Literature of American History*, Boston, 1902.

Lodge, H. C., *Certain Accepted Heroes and Other Essays in Literature and Politics*, New York, 1897.

——, *Early Memories*, New York, 1913.

——, "The Distribution of Ability in United States," *The Century Magazine*, XLII (September 1891).

——, *The Democracy of the Constitution and Other Addresses and Essays*, New York, 1915.

——, *A Fighting Frigate and Other Essays and Addresses*, New York, 1907.

——, *A Frontier Town and Other Essays*, New York, 1906.

——, *Historical and Political Essays*, Boston, 1892.

——, *Speech on the Subject of Immigration . . .* before the Boston City Club, March 20, 1918, Senate Doc. No. 423, 60th Congress, 1st Session.

——, *Immigration*, Speech of Hon. Henry Cabot Lodge of Massachusetts in the House of Representatives, Washington, 1891.

——, *Boston*, New York, 1891.

——, *The Restriction of Immigration*, Speech of Hon. Henry Cabot Lodge of Massachusetts in the Senate of the United States, March 6, 1896.

——, *A Short History of the English Colonies in America*, New York, 1881.

——, *Life and Letters of George Cabot*, Boston, 1887.

——, *Early Memories*, New York, 1913.

——, "Our Blundering Foreign Policy," *Forum*, XIX (March, 1895).

——, "Lynch Law and Unrestricted Immigration," *North American Review*, CDII (May 1891).

——, *Selections from the Correspondence of Theodore Roosevelt and Henry Cabot Lodge, 1884-1918*, 2 vols., New York, 1925.

Lonergan, T. S., *The Irish Chapter in American History*, paper read at the annual meeting of the American Irish Historical Society, January 12, 1912.

McMaster, J. B., *The Acquisition of Political, Social and Industrial Rights of Man in America*, Cleveland, 1903.

——, *Address before the Netherlands Society of Philadelphia*, The Netherlands Society of Philadelphia, Fourteenth Annual Banquet . . . 1905.

——, *A History of the People of the United States From the Revolution to the Civil War*, 8 vols., New York, 1938.

——, *A History of the People of the United States during Lincoln's Administration*, New York, 1927.

——, "Edward Augustus Freeman," Charles D. Warner, ed., *Library of the World's Best Literature, Ancient and Modern*, 30 vols., New York, 1896-7.

——, Substance of a speech delivered on the occasion of the "Inauguration of the New Hall of the Historical Society of Pennsylvania," *Pennsylvania Magazine of History and Biography*, VIII (1884).

——, "The Influence of Geographical Position on Civilization in Egypt and Greece," *The National Quarterly Review*, LXVII (December 1876).

——, "Is Sound Finance Possible Under Popular Government?", *Forum* XIX (April 1895).

——, "The Riotous Career of the Know-Nothings," *Forum*, XVII (July 1894).

Maine, Henry, *Dissertations on Early Law and Custom*, New York, 1883.

——, *Village Communities in the East and West*, London, 1871.

von Maurer, G. L., *Einleitung zur Geschichte der Mark-, Hof-, Dorf- und Stadt Verfassung und der offentlichen Gewalt*, Munchen, 1854.

Mikkelsen, M. A., "The Bishop Hill Colony," *Johns Hopkins Studies*, tenth series, no. I.

Mood, Fulmer, ed., "An Unfamiliar Essay by Frederick Jackson Turner, The Rise and Fall of New France," *Minnesota History*, XVIII (1937).

Nelson, Olof N., *History of the Scandinavians and Successful Scandinavians in the United States*, Minneapolis, 1900.

Oberholtzer, E. P., *A History of the United States Since the Civil War*, 5 vols., New York, 1917-1937.

——, *The Literary History of Philadelphia*, Philadelphia, 1906.

——, *Philadelphia A History of the City and Its People A Record of 225 Years*, 4 vols., Philadelphia, 1912.

O'Brien, M. J., *A Hidden Phase of American History: Ireland's Part in America's Struggle for Liberty*, New York, 1920.

——, *Irish Firsts in American History*, Speech delivered . . . under the auspices of the Illinois chapter of the American Irish Historical Society, April 28, 1917.

Orth, S. P., *Our Foreigners, a Chronicle of Americans in the Making*, New Haven, 1920.

Osgood, H. L., *The American Colonies in the Eighteenth Century*, 4 vols., New York, 1924.

——, " Scientific Anarchism," *Political Science Quarterly*, IV (March 1889).

Parkman, Francis, *The Conspiracy of Pontiac and the Indian War after the Conquest of Canada*, 2 vols., Boston, 1899.

——, "A Convent at Rome," *Harper's New Monthly Magazine*, LXXXI (August 1890).

——, *Count Frontenac and New France under Louis XIV*, Boston, 1899.

——, " The Failure of Universal Suffrage," *North American Review*, CXXVII (July-August 1878).

——, *A Half-Century of Conflict*, 2 vols., Boston, 1899.

——, *The Jesuits in North America in the Seventeenth Century*, 2 vols., Boston, 1899.

——, " Letters of Francis Parkman to Pierre Margry," *Smith College Studies in History*, VIII, nos. 3 and 4, Northampton, 1923.

——, *Montcalm and Wolfe*, 2 vols., Boston, 1898.

——, *The Old Regime in Canada*, Boston, 1899.

——, *The Oregon Trail*, Boston, 1899.

——, " Our Best Class and the National Politics," *Boston Advertiser*, July 21, 1863.

——, " Our Common Schools," Citizens Public School Union, Boston, 1890.

——, *Pioneers of France in the New World*, Boston, 1899.

——, " The Tale of the Ripe Scholar," *Nation*, IX (December 23, 1869).

Parrington, V. L., *Main Currents in American Thought; An Interpretation of American Literature from the Beginnings to 1920*, 3 vols., New York, 1927-30.

Paxson, F. L., *When the West Is Gone, New York*, 1930.

Rhodes, J. F., *Historical Essays*, New York, 1909.

——, *History of the United States from the Compromise of 1850*, 9 vols., New York, 1893-1922.

——, " The Molly Maguires in the Anthracite Regions of Pennsylvania," *American Historical Review*, XV (April 1910).

Randel, W. P., *Edward Eggleston*, New York, 1946.

Roosevelt, Theodore, Speech before the Maine Republican State Convention, *New York Times*, March 29, 1918.

——, *The Winning of the West, An Account of the Exploration and Settlement of our Country from the Alleghanies to the Pacific*, 2 vols., New York, 1917.

——, *The Works of Theodore Roosevelt*, National Edition, 20 vols., New York, 1926.

Schlesinger, A. M., *New Viewpoints in American History*, New York, 1922.

Schouler, James, *Americans of 1776*, New York, 1906.

——, *Constitutional Studies, State and Federal*, New York, 1897.

——, *Historical Briefs*, New York, 1896.

——, *History of the United States of America Under the Constitution*, 7 vols., New York, 1884-1913.

——, *Ideals of the Republic*, Boston, 1908.

Schrader, Frederick, *The Story of New Netherland, the Dutch in America*, New York, 1909.

Semple, E. C., *American History and Its Geographic Conditions*, Boston, 1903.

——, "The Anglo-Saxons of the Kentucky Mountains," *The Geographic Journal*, XVII (June 1901).

Shaler, N. S., "European Peasants as Immigrants," *Atlantic Monthly*, LXXI (May 1893).

——, ed., *The United States of America*, 2 vols., New York, 1894.

——, *Kentucky, A Pioneer Commonwealth*, Boston, 1885.

——, *Nature and Man in America*, New York, 1906.

Shaw, Albert, "Local Government in Illinois," *Johns Hopkins Studies*, first series, 1883, no. III.

——, *Political Problems of American Development*, New York, 1907.

Skinner, C. S., ed., "Turner's Autobiographic Letter," *The Wisconsin Magazine of History*, XIX (September 1935).

Stephenson, G. M., "When America Was the Land of Canaan," *Minnesota History*, X (September 1929).

——, *The Religious Aspects of Swedish Immigration*, Minneapolis, 1932.

Straus, O. S., *The Origin of Republican Form of Government in the United States of America*, New York, 1885.

Thayer, W. R., *The Life and Letters of John Hay*, 2 vols., Boston, 1915.

Thwaites, R. G., "Thirty-Fifth Annual Report of the Executive Committee," *Proceedings of the State Historical Society of Wisconsin*, XXXVI (1889).

Turner, F. J., *The Frontier in American History*, New York, 1920.

——, "The Character and Influence of the Indian Trade in Wisconsin," *Johns Hopkins Studies*, ninth series, 1891.

——, *The Significance of Sections in American History*, New York, 1932.

——, "Studies of American Immigration," *Chicago Record-Herald*, August 28, September 4, 11, 18, 25, October 16, 1901. "German Immigration in the Colonial Period," August 28; "German Immigration into the

United States," September 4; "Italian Immigration into the United States," September 11; "French and Canadian Immigration into the United States," September 18; "The Stream of Immigration into the United States," September 25; "Jewish Immigration," October 16.

——, *The United States, 1830-50; the Nation and Its Sections*, New York, 1935.

——, Review of Theodore Roosevelt's, *The Winning of the West, The Dial*, X (August 1889).

Tyler, M. C., *The Literary History of the American Revolution, 1763-1783*, 2 vols., New York, 1897.

Vickers, R. H., *History of Bohemia*, Chicago, 1894.

Vinogradoff, Paul, *Villainage in England; Essays in English Mediaeval History*, Oxford, 1892.

Wade, Mason, ed., *The Journals of Francis Parkman* (2 vols., New York, 1947).

Weeden, William, *Economic and Social History of New England, 1620-1789*, 2 vols., New York, 1894.

Wertenbaker, T. J., *The Founding of American Civilization, The Middle Colonies*, New York, 1938.

——, *Patrician and Plebian in Virginia or the Origin and Development of the Social Classes of the Old Dominion*, Charlottesville, Virginia, 1910.

White, A. D., "Historical Instruction in the Course of History and Political Science at Cornell University," Hall, ed., *Methods of Teaching History*.

Wiernik, Peter, *History of the Jews in America. From the Period of the Discovery of the New World to the Present Time*, New York, 1912.

Wilson, J. G. and Fiske, John, *Appletons' Cyclopaedia of American Biography*, 7 vols., New York, 1887-1900.

Wilson, Woodrow, *A History of the American People*, 5 vols., New York, 1902.

——, "Our Kinship with England," *The Princetonian*, June 18, 1879.

——, *Selected Literary and Political Papers and Addresses of Woodrow Wilson*, 3 vols., New York, 1925-6.

——, *The State; Elements of Historical and Practical Politics*, Boston, 1892.

——, "The Spirit of Jefferson," *New York Times*, April 17, 1906.

Winsor, Justin, ed., *Narrative and Critical History of America*, 8 vols., Boston, 1884-9.

II. Writing about Historians

Adams, J. T., "Henry Adams and the New Physics," *Yale Review*, XIX (Winter 1930).

Bailey, T. A., *Woodrow Wilson and the Great Betrayal*, New York, 1945.

——, *Woodrow Wilson and the Lost Peace*, New York, 1944.

Baker, R. S., *Woodrow Wilson: Life and Letters*, 8 vols., New York, 1927-39.

Becker, Carl, "Some Aspects of the Influence of Social Problems and Ideas upon the Study and Writing of History," *The American Journal of Sociology*, XVIII (March 1913).

Bell, H. C. F., *Woodrow Wilson and the People*, New York, 1945.

Bishop, J. B., *Theodore Roosevelt and His Times Shown in His Own Letters*, 2 vols., New York, 1920.

Caughey, John, *Hubert Howe Bancroft Historian of the West*, Berkeley, 1946.

Clark, J. S., *The Life and Letters of John Fiske*, 2 vols., New York, 1917.

Diamond, William, *The Economic Thought of Woodrow Wilson*, Baltimore, 1943.

Dodd, William E., *Woodrow Wilson and His Work*, New York, 1932.

Ellis, L. E., "James Schouler," *Mississippi Valley Historical Review*, XVI (September 1929).

Falnes, Oscar, "New England Interest in Scandinavian Culture and the Norsemen," *New England Quarterly*, X (June 1937).

Farnham, C. H., *A Life of Francis Parkman*, Boston, 1922.

Fox, D. R., ed., *Sources of Culture in the Middle West*, New York, 1934.

——, *Herbert Levi Osgood, an American Scholar*, New York, 1924.

Goldman, E. F., "Hermann Eduard Von Holst: Plumed Knight of American Historiography," *Mississippi Valley Historical Review*, XXIII (March 1937).

——, ed., *Historiography and Urbanization Essays in Honor of W. Stull Holt*, Baltimore, 1941.

——, *John Bach McMaster, American Historian*, Philadelphia, 1943.

Gooch, G. P., *History and Historians in the Nineteenth Century*, New York, 1935.

Hansen, C. F., "Marcus Lee Hansen—Historian of Immigration," *Common Ground*, II (Summer 1942).

Holdsworth, W. S., *The Historians of Anglo-American Law*, New York, 1928.

Holt, W. Stull, "The Idea of Scientific History in America, *Journal of the History of Ideas*, I (June 1940).

Howe, M. A. DeWolfe, *James Ford Rhodes, American Historian*, New York, 1929.

Jameson, J. F., review of M. J. O'Brien, *A Hidden Phase of American History: Ireland's Part in America's Struggle for Liberty*, *American Historical Review*, XXVI (July 1921).

Johnson, Allen and Malone, Dumas, eds., *Dictionary of American Biography*, 20 vols., New York, 1928.

Kraus, Michael, *A History of American History*, New York, 1938.

Latane, J. H., "James Schouler," *Dictionary of American Biography*, XVI, 459-60.

Lingelbach, A. L., "Sara Louisa Vickers Oberholtzer," *Dictionary of American Biography*, XIII, 607.

Mood, Fulmer, "The Development of Frederick Jackson Turner as a Historical Thinker," *Proceedings of the Colonial Society of Massachusetts*, XXXIV (December 1939).

Morrison, S. E., "Edward Channing A Memoir," *Proceedings of the Massachusetts Historical Society*, LXIV (May 1931).

Nevins, Allan, review of Oberholtzer's *A History of the United States Since the Civil War*, vol. V, *American Historical Review*, XLIV (January 1939).

Nichols, R. F., "The Dynamic Interpretation of History," *New England Quarterly*, VIII (June 1935).

Notter, C. Harley, *The Origins of the Foreign Policy of Woodrow Wilson*, Baltimore, 1937.

Oberholtzer, E. P., "John Bach McMaster, 1852-1932," *Pennsylvania Magazine of History and Biography*, LVII (1933).

Paxson, F. L., "A Generation of the Frontier Hypothesis, 1893-1932," *Pacific Historical Review*, II (March 1933).

Pierson, G. W., "The Frontier and American Institutions A Criticism of the Turner Theory," *New England Quarterly*, XV (June 1942).

——, "The Frontier and Frontiersmen of Turner's Essays," *The Pennsylvania Magazine of History and Biography*, LXIV (October 1940).

Pringle, H. F., *Theodore Roosevelt, A Biography*, New York, 1931.

Schafer, Joseph, "Francis Parkman, 1823-1923," *Wisconsin Magazine of History*, VII (March 1924).

Schevill, Ferdinand, "Hermann Eduard Von Holst," *Dictionary of American Biography*, IX.

Schriftgiesser, Karl, *The Gentleman from Massachusetts, Henry Cabot Lodge*, New York, 1944.

Shryock, R. H., "Historical Traditions in Philadelphia and in the Middle Atlantic Area: An Editorial," *Pennsylvania Magazine of History and Biography*, LXVII (1943).

——, "The Pennsylvania Germans as Seen by the Historian," Ralph Wood, ed., *The Pennsylvania Germans*, Princeton, 1942.

Shumate, R. V., "The Political Philosophy of Henry Adams," *American Political Science Review*, XXVIII (August 1934).

Smith, Joseph, "American History as it is Falsified," *Journal of the American Irish Historical Society*, I (1898).

Social Science Research Council, *Theory and Practice in Historical Study: A Report of the Committee on Historiography*, New York, 1945, Bulletin no. 54.

Stanwood, Edward, "Memorial of James Schouler," *Massachusetts Historical Society Proceedings*, LIV (1922).

Thompson, J. W., *A History of Historical Writing*, 2 vols., New York, 1942.

Wade, Mason, *Francis Parkman Heroic Historian*, New York, 1942.

Ware, C. F., ed., *The Cultural Approach to History*, New York, 1940.

III. GENERAL REFERENCES

Adamic, Louis, *A Nation of Nations*, New York, 1945.

Bagehot, Walter, *Physics and Politics*, New York, 1876.

Beard, Miriam, "Anti-Semitism—Product of Economic Myths," I. Graeber and S. H. Britt, *Jews in a Gentile World*, New York, 1942.

——, *The Atlantic Presents: We Americans*, Boston, 1939.

Bowers, D. F., ed., *Foreign Influences in American Life*, Princeton, 1944.

Brooks, Van Wyck, *New England: Indian Summer 1865-1915*, New York, 1940.

Child, C. J., *The German-Americans in Politics, 1914-1917*, Madison, 1939.

Cohen, M. R., *Reason and Nature, An Essay on the Meaning of Scientific Method*, New York, 1932.

Commons, J. R. and Associates, *A Documentary History of American Industrial Society*, 10 vols., Cleveland, 1910.

——, *Races and Immigrants in America*, New York, 1924.

Curti, Merle, *The Growth of American Thought*, New York, 1943.

——, *The Roots of American Loyalty*, New York, 1946.

Darwin, Charles, *The Descent of Man and Selection in Relation to Sex*, 2 vols., New York, 1898.

Delbrück, B., *Introduction to the Study of Language; A Critical Survey of the History and Methods of Comparative Philology of the Indo-European Languages*, Leipzig, 1882.

Dewey, D. R., ed., *Discussions in Economics and Statistics by Francis A. Walker*, 2 vols., New York, 1899.

Drumont, E. A., *La France Juive*, 2 vols., Paris, 1885.

Gaunt, William, *The Pre-Raphaelite Tragedy*, London, 1942.

Gould, B. A., *The Military and Anthropological Statistics of the Rebellion*, New York, 1865.

——, *Statistics, Medical and Anthropological of the Provost-Marshal General's Bureau* (1875).

Gwynn, Stephen, ed., *The Letters and Friendships of Sir Cecil Spring-Rice*, 2 vols., Boston, 1929.

Handlin, Oscar, *Boston's Immigrants, 1790-1865* (Cambridge, 1941).

Hewes, Fletcher and Gannett, Henry, eds., *Scribner's Statistical Atlas of the United States Showing by Graphic Methods Their Present Condition and Their Political, Social and Industrial Development*, New York, 1885.

Hofstadter, Richard, *Social Darwinism in American Thought, 1860-1915*, New York, 1943.

Hrdlička, Aleš, "Physical Anthropology and its Aims," *The Anatomical Record*, II (August 1908).

——, "Physical Anthropology in America," *American Anthropologist*, XVI (October-December 1914).

Koenig, Samuel, "Second-and-Third-Generation Americans," in F. J. Brown and J. S. Roucek, eds., *One America*, New York, 1945.

MacIver, R. M., *Social Causation*, Boston, 1942.

Malone, Dumas, "The Intellectual Melting Pot," *The Atlantic Presents We Americans*, Boston, 1939.

Peake, H. J., "Village Community," *Encyclopedia of the Social Sciences*, 8 vols., New York, 1937, VIII, 253-9.

Reuter, B. A., *Anglo-American Relations during the Spanish-American War*, New York, 1924.

Sly, J. F., *Town Government in Massachusetts (1620-1930)*, Cambridge, 1930.

Stegner, Wallace, "Who Persecutes Boston?", *Atlantic Monthly*, CLXXIV (July 1944).

Stonequist, E. V., *The Marginal Man*, New York, 1937.

Thoron, Ward, ed., *The Letters of Mrs. Henry Adams, 1865-1883*, Boston, 1936.

U. S. Department of State, *Papers Relating to the Foreign Relations of the United States, The Lansing Papers, 1914-1920*, 2 vols., Washington, 1940.

Wappäus, J. E., *Allgemeine Bevölkerungsstatistik*, 2 vols., Leipzig, 1859-61.

INDEX